Voices of the Civil War

Voices of the Civil War · Atlanta

By the Editors of Time-Life Books, Alexandria, Virginia

Contents

THE FIELD AT ATLANTA

Three successive battles raged in the rolling terrain around Atlanta during July 1864. The artist's rendering shows the beleaguered city ringed by 12 miles of defensive earthworks.

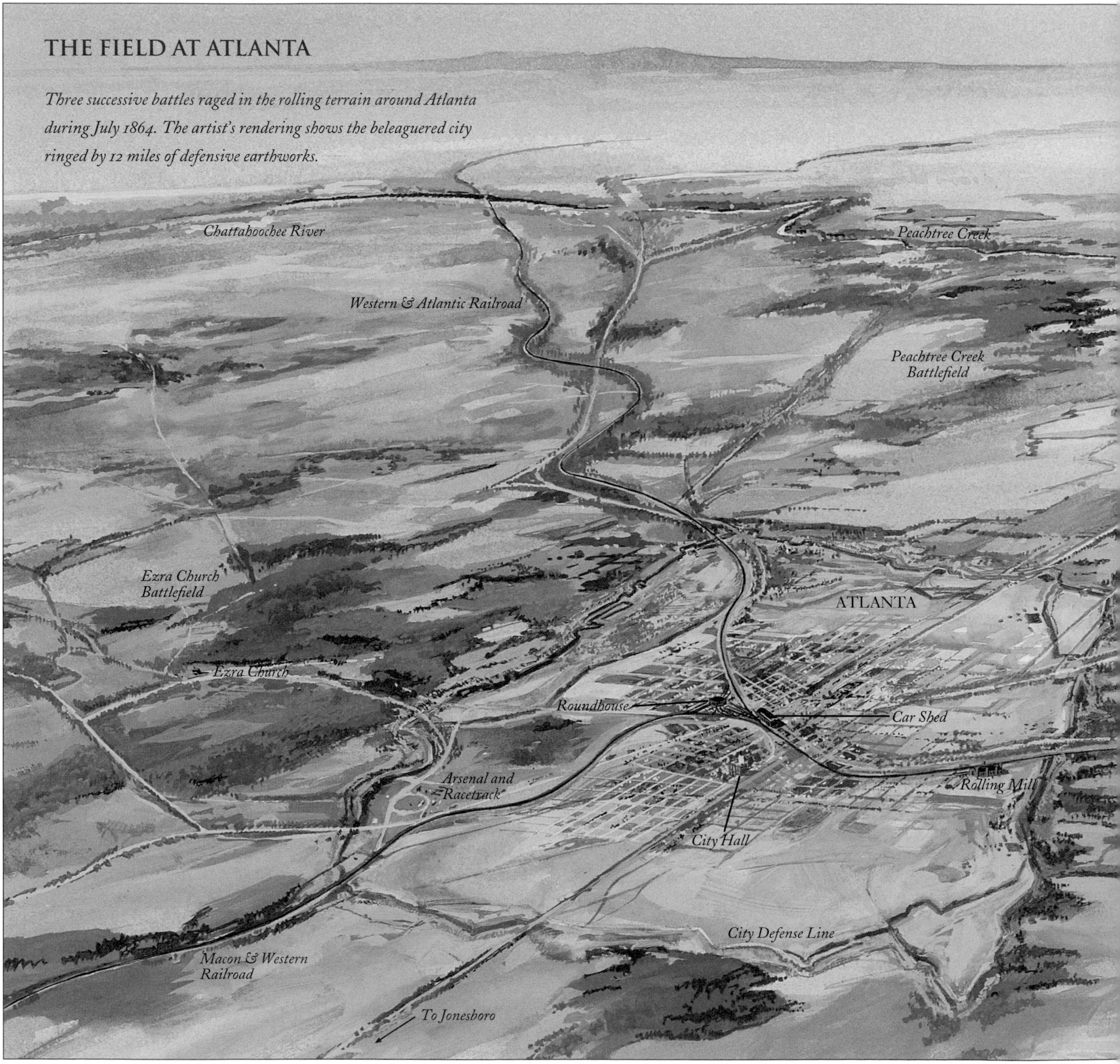

Chattahoochee River

Peachtree Creek

Western & Atlantic Railroad

Peachtree Creek Battlefield

Ezra Church Battlefield

Ezra Church

ATLANTA

Roundhouse

Car Shed

Arsenal and Racetrack

Rolling Mill

City Hall

City Defense Line

Macon & Western Railroad

To Jonesboro

N

DECATUR

Georgia Railroad

Atlanta
Battlefield

Bald Hill

Quest for the Gate City

Christmas of 1863 was only a week away, but the Confederate soldiers of the Army of Tennessee saw little cause to celebrate the holiday. With the army firmly settled into winter quarters near Dalton, Georgia, the Southern troops knew there would be slight chance of fighting before the spring. But the respite from active campaigning brought little comfort to the gray-clad warriors. They huddled about their campfires, exhausted and dispirited, their dream of an independent Southern Confederacy an ephemeral and distant hope.

"The morale of the army was gone," wrote Sam R. Watkins, a 24-year-old private serving in Company H of the 1st Tennessee Infantry. Everywhere he looked, Watkins saw evidence of the dismal aftermath of defeat; the fearless, battle-tested units were now "in rags and tatters, hungry and heart-broken, the morale of the men gone, their pride a thing of the past." To Watkins it seemed as if the entire Army of Tennessee was pervaded with "a feeling of mistrust."

The weary soldiers encamped at Dalton were made all the more despondent by the realization that a scant three months earlier they had achieved their greatest victory of the war. On September 19 and 20, just south of the Tennessee border along the banks of a creek called the Chickamauga, the Army of Tennessee had smashed its way through Major General William S. Rosecrans' Federal army and driven the beaten Yankees back to their heavily fortified base at Chattanooga. For two months Chattanooga had been held in a virtual stranglehold. But in late November a new Federal commander, Major General Ulysses S. Grant, had turned the tables on the besieging Southern forces, routing them from their seemingly impregnable stronghold on Lookout Mountain and Missionary Ridge.

Most of the Confederate fighting men saw the disaster at Chattanooga as the result of neither Grant's leadership nor any want of valor on their part. The blame, they felt, rested squarely on the shoulders of their commanding officer, General Braxton Bragg.

At 46 Bragg was a veteran of a quarter century of service in the Regular Army and had

One of the vital links along Sherman's supply line during his drive on Atlanta, this railroad bridge (opposite) boasts blockhouses and a permanent garrison to defend the span against the constant threat of Rebel cavalry.

won plaudits for his gallant performance in the Mexican War. But he possessed a dour and quirky personality, was a notoriously strict disciplinarian, and did little, as Sam Watkins put it, to "cultivate the love and respect of his troops." When the Army of Tennessee collapsed in the face of Grant's assault at Chattanooga, Bragg was unable to rally his troops, who merely hooted and jeered as they passed. "Bragg looked so scared," Watkins recalled, "he looked so hacked and whipped and mortified and chagrined at defeat." Denied the fruits of their victory at Chickamauga, the Army of Tennessee had lost all confidence in their commander. "Bully for Bragg," one Rebel exclaimed sarcastically, "he's hell on retreat."

Within days of the debacle at Chattanooga Bragg tendered his resignation, and Confederate president Jefferson Davis saw no alternative but to accept. Bragg was transferred to Richmond, where he soon assumed a position as military adviser to Davis and his cabinet. With Lieutenant General William J. Hardee exercising temporary command of the Army of Tennessee, Davis pondered his choice of a replacement for Bragg.

Hardee was a respected theorist and tactician—he had revised the U.S. Army's drill manual before the outbreak of war—but preferred corps command to the greater responsibilities of army leadership. Two division commanders, Major Generals Benjamin Franklin Cheatham and Patrick R. Cleburne, were highly esteemed for their prowess in combat, but both were junior to Hardee and lacked the necessary experience of corps command. Reluctantly, President Davis decided to tender the position to the commander of the Army of Mississippi, General Joseph E. Johnston.

In the course of two and a half years of war, the relationship between Davis and Johnston had soured to one of mutual distrust that bordered, at times, on enmity. Johnston was a distinguished veteran of the war with Mexico and had attained the rank of brigadier general in the Regular Army before resigning to cast his lot with the Confederacy. As senior field commander in Virginia, he had won the first great engagement of the war at First Manassas. But the general's decision to move his force to the environs of Richmond in March 1862, and his subsequent reluctance to bring Union general George B. McClellan's army to battle in the Peninsula campaign, caused Davis to regard Johnston as an overcautious, even timid commander.

On May 31, 1862, Johnston was severely wounded at the Battle of Seven Pines, and General Robert E. Lee assumed command of the Confederate forces defending Richmond. Following a lengthy convalescence, Johnston was placed in command of the Department of the West, a post befitting his rank as one of the Confederacy's senior officers. But his penchant for second-guessing Davis and the Confederate cabinet, and his controversial performance in the Vicksburg campaign of 1863, contributed to the fall of that strategically vital Mississippi River fortress.

For all his faults Johnston possessed one great strength—the ability to inspirit and motivate his soldiers. It was a rare gift, and one the dapper 57-year-old West Pointer possessed in abundance. If anyone could reinvigorate the waning morale of the Army of Tennessee, Davis believed, Johnston was the man. "Your presence, it is hoped, will do much to inspire hope and reestablish confidence," Confederate secretary of war James A. Seddon wrote Johnston on December 18,

1863; "as soon as the condition of your forces allow it is hoped you will be able to resume the offensive."

When Johnston arrived at Dalton on December 27, he found the Army of Tennessee in no condition to resume the offensive anytime soon. Sickness and desertion had reduced available strength to fewer than 40,000 men. Food and ammunition were in short supply, many of the cavalry horses had died, and most of the artillery horses were too weak to pull the heavy guns. "More than half the infantry are without bayonets," Johnston reported to Davis, "and the want of shoes is painful to see." Until he could bring his army up to strength, resupply them, and restore morale, the initiative would of necessity rest with the numerically superior Federal forces at Chattanooga, 30 miles to the north. "The more I consider the subject, the less it appears practicable to assume the offensive," Johnston informed the Confederate president; "this army is not in condition for the field."

Despite his gloomy strategic prognosis, Johnston set about bettering the condition of his soldiers with a will. Sam Watkins was impressed by Johnston's bearing, calling him "the very picture of a general." When Johnston reviewed Watkins' unit, the private noted the new commander's "restless black eye, that seemed to read your very inmost thoughts." Johnston strolled through the camps, chatting with individual soldiers and listening to their complaints. More and better rations were issued, and it became clear to the men in the ranks that Old Joe was, as one soldier put it, a "feeding general." In a move guaranteed to boost morale, Johnston began to grant furloughs so that men who had not seen their families in months, or even years, could travel to their distant homes.

Benevolent as he was, Johnston was also a professional soldier and a disciplinarian. He instituted a rigid schedule of mandatory drills, dress parades, and target practice. Mock battles and even large snowball fights were held to get the troops in fighting trim. As spring approached it was clear that, thanks to Johnston, the Army of Tennessee had undergone a remarkable transformation. "He was loved, respected, admired; yea, almost worshipped by the troops," Watkins declared; "I do not believe there was a soldier in his army but would gladly have died for him."

Johnston's soldiers would need all the devotion they could muster, for while the Confederate commander was equipping and reorganizing, his Federal opponents were preparing to take the offensive on an unprecedented scale. The coordinated strategy that had eluded President Abraham Lincoln and his senior officers for two and a half bloody years was finally coming to fruition under the guidance of the Union's preeminent military leaders, Major Generals Ulysses S. Grant and William T. Sherman.

Grant's remarkable victories at Vicksburg and Chattanooga had turned the tide of war in the western theater and brought the quiet and unpretentious officer wide renown. Despite rumors of heavy drinking, in Grant's persistence, single-mindedness, and ability to see the big picture Lincoln had found the promise of ultimate victory.

In late February Lincoln promoted Grant to the rank of lieutenant general and summoned him to Washington as general in chief of all the Union armies. Supremely confident of Grant's judgment, the president gave him enormous latitude in strategic planning. Both men knew that if the South was to be vanquished, the spring campaign would have to be waged aggressively, and on two fronts.

As general in chief, Grant decided to take personal charge of the Federal forces in the eastern theater, where Robert E. Lee's dauntless Army of Northern Virginia remained the South's most potent field command. At Grant's recommendation the commander of the Union Army of the Tennessee, General Sherman, would assume leadership of Grant's previous command, the Military Division of the Mississippi, and thus oversee operations in the western theater. The two would launch simultaneous offensives at the beginning of May. The plan was simple: As Sherman later wrote of Grant, "He was to go for Lee and I was to go for Joe Johnston."

In the course of the war Grant and Sherman had forged a remarkable bond of friendship and mutual trust, though the two were quite dissimilar personalities. At 44, the lean and grizzled Sherman was four years older than his friend Grant. While Grant's fame had steadily grown, Sherman's military career had seen its share of ups and downs, with some critics going so far as to question Sherman's sanity. But Grant remained steadfastly loyal to his comrade in arms. "He stood by me when I was crazy," Sherman once said, "and I stood by him when he was drunk."

Brigadier General Jacob D. Cox, who would serve under Sherman in the coming campaign, described his commander's "nervous and restless temperament, with a tendency to irritability," but noted that in battle Sherman's "eccentricities" disappeared. "His mind was never so clear, his confidence never so strong, his spirit never so inspiring, and his temper never so amiable as in the crisis of some fierce struggle," Cox wrote. Intellectually acute, and genuinely popular with the fighting men, Sherman was the type of sol-

dier Grant needed to take on Joe Johnston's forces and push the western armies forward to Atlanta—the vital Confederate transportation hub and supply depot that was dubbed the Gate City of the Deep South.

With a wartime population in excess of 20,000—second only to the Confederate capital, Richmond—Atlanta had grown in less than two decades from a ramshackle crossroads to a thriving boomtown. It was a manufacturing and financial center whose four railroad lines were crucial arteries of supply to Southern forces in Alabama, eastern Georgia, the Carolinas, and Virginia.

The exigencies of war had flooded Atlanta with troops, civilian auxiliaries, and thousands of slaves who labored to construct the city's formidable earthen fortifications. There were dozens of mills and factories, an arsenal, and scores of hospitals that treated the wounded from the battlefields in Tennessee. If Sherman could take Atlanta, his forces would be poised to strike a fatal blow to the Southern heartland.

Although active campaigning would not begin in earnest until spring, Sherman had tested his Southern opponents in February when he led a three-week-long foray from Vicksburg to Meridian, Mississippi. Effectively outmaneuvering the Confederate Army of Mississippi, Sherman had demonstrated his willingness to bring war home to the civilian population. Demolishing railroad lines, laying waste to mills and farms, and confiscating supplies as he went, he gave a taste of even greater destruction to come. When one woman protested the pillaging of her property, Sherman defined his grimly realistic philosophy. "War is cruelty," he told the woman; "there is no use trying to reform it, the crueller it is, the sooner it will be over."

Following the Meridian raid, and his assumption of supreme command in the west, Sherman began to concentrate and reorganize the disparate elements of his Military Division of the Mississippi at Chattanooga—the launching point for his drive against Johnston and Atlanta. Sherman was pleased to see that many regiments whose three-year terms of enlistment had recently expired were re-enlisting en masse, thanks to the payment of a generous bounty and the granting of month-long "veteran furloughs." But even if he would not lack for soldiers, an army of 100,000 men would have to be sustained on the march. "The great question of the campaign was one of supplies," Sherman later wrote, and the stockpiles in Chattanooga's warehouses were dwindling. General Cox recalled that "fully one-third of the command had lost and worn out some material portion of their clothing," and that "whole brigades had been without soap for two months."

With an energy comparable to that of his opponent, Johnston, Sherman began amassing the food and ammunition his troops required to live in the field. Railroad locomotives and boxcars were confiscated by military authorities, the rations that had been issued to pro-Union Tennesseans were diverted to the army, and a group of experienced quartermasters set to work organizing and dispensing the matériel in Chattanooga. Once the campaign got under way, even if the lines of supply broke down, Sherman was prepared to live off the land. "Georgia has a million of inhabitants," he informed Grant. "If they can live, we should not starve."

In formulating his strategy for the Atlanta campaign, Sherman would draw upon the combined efforts of three Federal armies. The largest of these was the Army of the

Cumberland, 73,000 strong, commanded by Major General George H. Thomas, whose heroic rearguard action during Rosecrans' defeat the previous September had earned the stocky, 46-year-old Virginian the sobriquet Rock of Chickamauga.

Thomas' IV and XIV Corps had recently been reinforced by the addition of the newly created XX Corps, the largest in Sherman's force. The XX Corps was an amalgam of Federal units transferred from the eastern theater and commanded by Major General Joseph Hooker, whose defeat by Lee the previous summer had seen him removed from command of the Army of the Potomac.

Both Grant and Sherman were appreciative of Thomas' determination but tended to regard the stalwart army commander as slow to take the initiative. And the presence of the politically scheming and ambitious Hooker was something both men would have preferred to do without. Conversely, in Major General James B. McPherson, leader of the 24,500 troops of the Army of the Tennessee, Grant and Sherman saw a kindred spirit and worthy protégé. At 35, McPherson was an affable and universally popular West Pointer who seemed to hold great potential as Sherman's successor in command of the hard-fighting westerners composing the XV, XVI, and XVII Corps. McPherson and his men held the confidence of his commander and would be called upon to execute some of the trickiest maneuvers of the coming offensive.

The final element of Sherman's force, Major General John M. Schofield's Army of the Ohio, was the smallest and least experienced. Though a titular army commander, the 32-year-old Schofield had only one complete corps, the XXIII. Having helped to fend off General James Longstreet's foray

against Knoxville, Tennessee, the previous winter, Schofield was called upon to join the great spring offensive.

The 254 guns composing Sherman's available artillery lent his force considerable firepower. In addition, four separate divisions of cavalry would work in conjunction with the seven infantry corps, although the lack of a centralized command for the mounted arm would work to Sherman's disadvantage in the weeks and months to come. But Sherman was pleased with his massive strike force. "I think I have the best army in the country," he wrote his wife, Ellen, "and if I can't take Atlanta and stir up Georgia considerably I am mistaken."

While Sherman was massing his forces near Ringgold, a mere 12 miles northwest of Dalton, General Johnston continued to prepare his outnumbered army for the inevitable Federal juggernaut. With some 54,000 troops, 144 guns, and only 2,400 of 8,500 cavalrymen with horses, Johnston was facing odds of more than 2 to 1. The general urged Jefferson Davis to bolster his command with Lieutenant General Leonidas Polk's 20,000-strong Army of Mississippi. This the Confederate president was reluctant to do, fearing another Yankee incursion from Vicksburg into eastern Mississippi and Alabama. Time and again Davis and his secretary of war tried to prod Johnston into committing his army to an offensive that would strike into Tennessee before the Yankees were ready to move. And each time Johnston demurred, even raising doubts as to his army's ability to successfully defend its base of operations at Dalton. "The position of Dalton had little to recommend it as a defensive one," Johnston later wrote. "It had neither strength nor strategic advantage. It neither covered its own communications nor threatened those of the enemy."

Despite his reservations, Johnston was loath to abandon his position at Dalton. Sticking to his defensive strategy, he would wait for the Federals to make the first move. "I can see no other mode of taking the offensive here than to beat the enemy when he advances," Johnston informed his president, "and then move forward." Hoping to prevent any more excuses on Johnston's part, Davis reluctantly ordered Polk's Army of Mississippi to the field of operations in Georgia.

On March 2, 1864, Lieutenant General John Bell Hood arrived at Dalton and assumed command of the division formerly commanded by Major General Thomas C. Hindman. Johnston welcomed the presence of one of the most intrepid fighters in Lee's Army of Northern Virginia, and Hood greeted his new commander warmly.

At 32, the tall, blond-bearded Kentuckian had led the famed Texas Brigade through the Seven Days' Battles of the Peninsula campaign and had commanded a division at Second Manassas and Antietam. Although his left arm had been permanently crippled by a Yankee shell at Gettysburg, Hood was back in the saddle two months later, only to suffer an even more severe wound at Chickamauga—one that cost him his right leg. Although in constant pain and unable to mount his horse without assistance, Hood seemed the very embodiment of Southern fortitude, and just the type of man Johnston wanted to lead a division in the coming struggle.

But Hood cherished a well-concealed contempt for the commander of the Army of Tennessee. He was what Johnston most decidedly was not—an intimate of Jefferson Davis. And even as Johnston continued to protest the wisdom of launching an offensive against Sherman, Hood was reinforcing Davis'

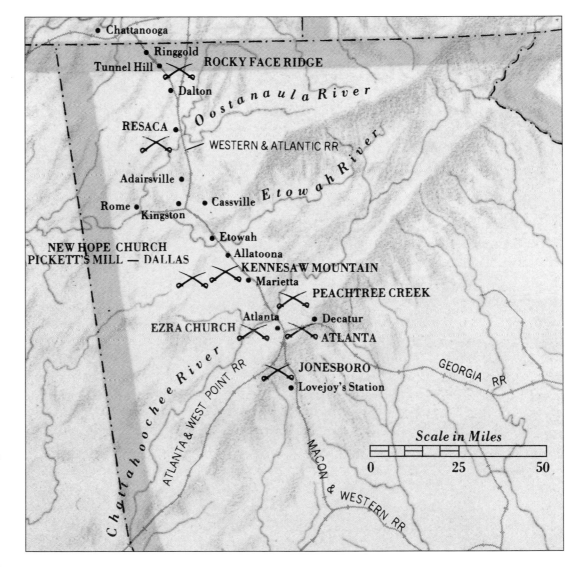

Between Ringgold and Atlanta lay some of the most daunting terrain faced by any army during the war. The rugged landscape provided Confederate defenders with ideal ground to conduct a fighting retreat.

own views in a series of letters written without the knowledge of his superior. "We should march to the front as soon as possible," Hood wrote on March 7, "so as not to allow the enemy to concentrate and advance upon us."

On May 4, 1864, Grant's forces began their great offensive against Lee's Army of Northern Virginia. The following day the two armies locked in battle amid the tangled undergrowth known as the Wilderness. Sherman had hoped to get his own offensive under way on May 5, but McPherson's column was delayed in its march toward Ringgold, and Sherman was compelled to postpone the launch date to May 7. Sherman had considered and then scrapped two plans of operation in favor of a strategy that would avoid a costly head-on assault against Johnston's defenses at Dalton. In an approach that would characterize much of the campaign to come, Sherman hoped to bypass the Confederate strongpoint and pry the enemy loose with a sweeping maneuver against the vulnerable Rebel flank and rear.

Stolid George Thomas had suggested the strategy that Sherman now adopted. While Schofield's and McPherson's armies made a feint against Johnston's main line at Tunnel Hill and Buzzard's Roost, Thomas' Army of the Cumberland would march south, beyond the western flank of Rocky Face Ridge. Thirteen miles south of Dalton, Thomas would turn east and pass through Snake Creek Gap, then sever the line of the Western & Atlantic Railroad at Resaca.

If Johnston was slow to react to the threat, the maneuver would effectively surround the Rebel army. Simultaneous assaults by all the Federal forces would destroy the Army of Tennessee and leave an open road all the way to Atlanta.

Although Sherman embraced Thomas' proposal, he made a crucial change in assignments. Perhaps because he doubted Thomas' ability to move his army quickly, Sherman gave the job of flanking Johnston at Snake Creek Gap to General McPherson. Thomas would work in conjunction with Schofield to pin Johnston at Dalton, while the Army of the Tennessee marched south to Snake Creek Gap and Resaca.

By the evening of May 6, Sherman's legions were finally ready. "The army was at its fighting weight," one Illinois lieutenant wrote, "ready and willing to give and take hard knocks." In the grueling campaign for Atlanta, there would be hard knocks aplenty.

CHRONOLOGY

May 1864	*Sherman begins march on Atlanta (May 7)*
	Opening Federal attacks: Rocky Face Ridge (May 8–12)
	Confederate withdrawal: Dalton to Resaca (May 12–13)
	Battle of Resaca (May 13–15)
	Confederate withdrawal: Resaca to Cassville (May 15–18)
	Affair at Cassville (May 19)
	Confederate withdrawal: Cassville to Allatoona (May 20–21)
	Sherman flanks Allatoona (May 23–25)
	Battles of New Hope Church, Pickett's Mill, and Dallas (May 25–28)
June	*Duel along the Mountain Lines (June 11–27)*
	Battle of Kolb's Farm (June 22)
	Battle of Kennesaw Mountain (June 27)
July	*Sherman flanks the Mountain Lines (June 27–July 3)*
	Engagements along the Smyrna Line (July 4)
	First Federals cross the Chattahoochee River (July 8)
	Confederates fall back across the river to Atlanta defenses (July 9–10)
	Federals cross the river in strength (July 16–18)
	Johnston replaced by Hood (July 17)
	Battle of Peachtree Creek (July 20)
	First shells fall on Atlanta (July 20)
	Battle of Atlanta (July 22)
	Battle of Ezra Church (July 28)
August	*Sherman moves south (August 25–30)*
	Battle of Jonesboro (August 31–September 1)
September	*Hood evacuates Atlanta (September 1)*
	Federals enter the city (September 2)
	Sherman expels Atlanta's residents (September 12–21)

ORDER OF BATTLE

ARMY OF TENNESSEE (Confederate)

Johnston   70,000 men

Hardee's Corps

Cheatham's Division	Cleburne's Division	Walker's Division	Bate's Division
Maney's Brigade	*L. E. Polk's Brigade*	*J. Jackson's Brigade*	*Lewis' Brigade*
Carter's Brigade	*Lowrey's Brigade*	*Gist's Brigade*	*Tyler's Brigade*
Strahl's Brigade	*Govan's Brigade*	*Stevens' Brigade*	*Finley's Brigade*
Vaughan's Brigade	*Granbury's Brigade*	*Mercer's Brigade*	

Hood's Corps

Hindman's Division	Stevenson's Division	Stewart's Division
Deas' Brigade	*Brown's Brigade*	*Stovall's Brigade*
Manigault's Brigade	*Cumming's Brigade*	*Clayton's Brigade*
Tucker's Brigade	*A. Reynolds' Brigade*	*Baker's Brigade*
Walthall's Brigade	*Pettus' Brigade*	*Gibson's Brigade*

Polk's Corps

Loring's Division	French's Division	Walthall's Division
Featherston's Brigade	*Ector's Brigade*	*Quarles' Brigade*
Adams' Brigade	*Cockrell's Brigade*	*D. H. Reynolds' Brigade*
Scott's Brigade	*Sears' Brigade*	*Cantey's Brigade*

Cavalry Corps Wheeler

Martin's Division	Kelly's Division	Hume's Division	W. Jackson's Division
Allen's Brigade	*Anderson's Brigade*	*Ashby's Brigade*	*Armstrong's Brigade*
Iverson's Brigade	*Dibrell's Brigade*	*Harrison's Brigade*	*Ross' Brigade*
	Hannon's Brigade		*Ferguson's Brigade*
	Williams' Brigade		

MILITARY DIVISION OF THE MISSISSIPPI (Federal)

Sherman   113,000 men

ARMY OF THE CUMBERLAND Thomas

IV Corps Howard

1st Division Stanley	2d Division Newton	3d Division T. Wood
Cruft's Brigade	*F. Sherman's Brigade*	*Willich's Brigade*
Whitaker's Brigade	*Wagner's Brigade*	*Hazen's Brigade*
Grose's Brigade	*Harker's Brigade*	*Beatty's Brigade*

XX Corps Hooker

1st Division A. Williams	2d Division Geary	3d Division Butterfield
Knipe's Brigade	*Candy's Brigade*	*Ward's Brigade*
Ruger's Brigade	*Ruschbeck's Brigade*	*Coburn's Brigade*
Robinson's Brigade	*Ireland's Brigade*	*J. Wood's Brigade*

XIV Corps Palmer

1st Division Johnson	2d Division Davis	3d Division Baird
Carlin's Brigade	*Morgan's Brigade*	*Turchin's Brigade*
King's Brigade	*Mitchell's Brigade*	*Van Derveer's Brigade*
Scribner's Brigade	*D. McCook's Brigade*	*Este's Brigade*

Cavalry Corps Elliot

1st Division E. McCook	2d Division K. Garrard	3d Division Kilpatrick
Dorr's Brigade	*Minty's Brigade*	*Klein's Brigade*
La Grange's Brigade	*Long's Brigade*	*C. Smith's Brigade*
	Wilder's Brigade	*Murray's Brigade*

ARMY OF THE TENNESSEE McPherson

XV Corps Logan

1st Division Osterhaus	2d Division M. Smith	4th Division Harrow
Woods' Brigade	*G. Smith's Brigade*	*R. Williams' Brigade*
Williamson's Brigade	*Lightburn's Brigade*	*Walcutt's Brigade*
Wangelin's Brigade		*Oliver's Brigade*

XVI Corps Dodge

2d Division Sweeny	4th Division Veatch
Rice's Brigade	*Fuller's Brigade*
Burke's Brigade	*Sprague's Brigade*
Bane's Brigade	*Grower's Brigade*

XVII Corps Blair

3d Division Leggett	4th Division Gresham
Force's Brigade	*Sanderson's Brigade*
Scott's Brigade	*Rogers' Brigade*
Malloy's Brigade	*Hall's Brigade*

ARMY OF THE OHIO Schofield

XXIII Corps

1st Division Hovey	2d Division Judah	3d Division Cox	Cavalry Division Stoneman
Barter's Brigade	*McLean's Brigade*	*Reilly's Brigade*	*I. Garrard's Brigade*
McQuiston's Brigade	*Hascall's Brigade*	*Manson's Brigade*	*Biddle's Brigade*
	Strickland's Brigade	*Byrd's Brigade*	*Capron's Brigade*
		Crittenden's Brigade	*Holeman's Brigade*

"All that has gone before is mere skirmishing. The war now begins."

MAJOR GENERAL WILLIAM T. SHERMAN
COMMANDER, MILITARY DIVISION OF THE MISSISSIPPI

Sherman regularly wrote long letters to his wife, Ellen. This passage, underscoring the magnitude of the coming campaign and the continuing resolve of the enemy, was penned on March 12, 1864, six days before Sherman officially assumed command of the armies that would march on Atlanta.

I would rather occupy my present relation to the military world than any other command and therefore must serve out this campaign which is to be the test. All that has gone before is mere skirmishing. The war now begins, and with heavy well-disciplined masses the issue must be settled in hard fought battles. I think we can whip them in Alabama and it may be Georgia. . . . No amount of poverty or adversity seems to shake their faith: niggers gone, wealth and luxury gone, money worthless, starvation in view within a period of two or three years, and causes enough to make the bravest tremble. Yet I see no signs of let up—some few deserters, plenty tired of war, but the masses determined to fight it out.

PRIVATE SAM R. WATKINS
1ST TENNESSEE (C.S.) INFANTRY, MANEY'S BRIGADE

Like most of his fellow soldiers, young Watkins had developed a healthy contempt for the dour Braxton Bragg, the commander they blamed for their defeat at Chattanooga. But Watkins and his mates soon discovered a leader worthy of high praise in Bragg's replacement, Joseph Johnston.

*B*ut now, allow me to introduce you to old Joe. Fancy, if you please, a man about fifty years old, rather small of stature, but firmly and compactly built, an open and honest countenance, and a keen but restless black eye, that seemed to read your very inmost thoughts. In his dress he was a perfect dandy. He ever wore the very finest clothes that could be obtained, carrying out in every point the dress and paraphernalia of the soldier, as adopted by the war department at Richmond, never omitting anything, even to the trappings of his horse, bridle and saddle. His hat was decorated with a star and feather, his coat with every star and embellishment, and he wore a bright new sash, big gauntlets, and silver spurs. He was the very picture of a general.

But he found the army depleted by battles; and worse, yea, much worse, by desertion. The men were deserting by tens and hundreds, and I might say by thousands. The morale of the army was gone. The spirit of the soldiers was crushed, their hope gone. The future was dark and gloomy. They would not answer at roll call. Discipline had gone. A feeling of mistrust pervaded the whole army.

A train load of provisions came into Dalton. The soldiers stopped it before it rolled into the station, burst open every car, and carried off all the bacon, meal and flour that was on board. Wild riot was the order of the day; everything was confusion, worse confounded. When the news came, like pouring oil upon the troubled waters, that General Joe E. Johnston, of Virginia, had taken command of the Army of Tennessee, men returned to their companies, order was restored, and "Richard was himself again." General Johnston issued a universal amnesty to all soldiers absent without leave. Instead of a scrimp pattern of one day's rations, he ordered two days' rations to be issued, being extra for one day. He ordered tobacco and whisky to be issued twice a week. He ordered sugar and coffee and flour to be issued instead of meal. He ordered old bacon and ham to be issued instead of blue beef. He ordered new tents and marquees. He ordered his soldiers new suits of clothes, shoes and hats. In fact, there had been a revolution, sure enough. He allowed us what General Bragg had never allowed mortal man—a furlough. He gave furloughs to one-third of his army at a time, until the whole had been furloughed. A new era had dawned; a new epoch had been dated. He passed through the ranks of the common soldiers, shaking hands with every one he met. He restored the soldier's pride; he brought the manhood back to the private's bosom; he changed the order of roll-call, standing guard, drill, and such nonsense as that. The revolution was complete. He was loved, respected, admired; yea, almost worshipped by his troops. I do not believe there was a soldier in his army but would gladly have died for him. With him everything was his soldiers, and the newspapers, criticising him at the time, said, "He would feed his soldiers if the country starved."

. . . Old Joe had greater military insight than any general of the South, not excepting even Lee. He was the born soldier; seemed born to command. When his army moved it moved solid. Cavalry, artillery, wagon train, and infantry stepped the same tread to the music of the march. His men were not allowed to be butchered for glory, and to have his name and a battle fought, with the number of killed and wounded, go back to Richmond for his own glory. When he fought, he fought for victory, not for glory. . . . His adversaries knew him, and dreaded the certain death that awaited them. His troops were brave; they laughed in the face of battle. He had no rear guard to shoot down any one who ran. They couldn't run; the army was solid. The veriest coward that was ever born became a brave man and a hero under his manipulation. His troops had the utmost confidence in him, and feared no evil. They became an army of veterans, whose lines could not be broken by the armies of the world. Battle became a pastime and a pleasure, and the rattle of musketry and roar of cannon were but the music of victory and success.

General Joseph E. Johnston (left) had few illusions about the daunting decisions facing him in the summer of 1864. But in spite of his failure to relieve Vicksburg and persistent pressure from President Davis, Johnston would once more choose the preservation of his army over the dubious prospects of defeating a determined foe that heavily outnumbered him.

> Dalton Ga
> March 7. 1864
>
> My dear Col
>
> I enclose to you a Copy of a letter I have written to the President. I have written this from my deep interest in our affairs throughout our Country. I am highly pleased with the Condition of our army. My corps is

Within days of his arrival in Georgia, General John Bell Hood sent President Davis the first of a series of confidential letters challenging General Johnston's strategy. A copy, along with a cover letter (above), was forwarded to Colonel James Chesnut, an aide to Davis and husband of the diarist Mary B. Chesnut.

MAJOR JAMES D. PORTER
STAFF, MAJOR GENERAL BENJAMIN F. CHEATHAM

Commissioned a captain on Cheatham's staff in September 1861 and shortly after promoted to major, Porter served under Cheatham throughout the Atlanta campaign. In December 1863 he was given leave to recruit behind enemy lines in Tennessee, and the following summer he was briefly the commander of a "camp for disabled men." After the war he served two terms as governor of Tennessee.

After the battle of Chickamauga, General Bragg dissolved Cheatham's Division and gave him a division of troops from other States, allowing him to retain one Tennessee brigade upon the ground that so large a body of troops from one State in one division promoted too much State pride at the expense of pride in the Confederate States. When General Johnston assumed command of the army at Dalton, one of his first acts was to restore the old organization. The order to this effect created unbounded enthusiasm in the division. With one impulse the men marched to army headquarters with a band

A native of Nashville, Major General Benjamin Franklin Cheatham (above) first commanded his fellow Tennesseans during the Mexican War. By the spring of 1864 this rugged, hard-drinking fighter was leading a division that accounted for more than half the Tennesseans in Johnston's army.

of music and called for General Johnston. General Cheatham escorted him from his room to the front door and presented him to his command with heartiness as genuine as it was unmilitary. Placing his hand upon the bare head of the chief of the army, he patted it two or three times and, looking at the men, said: "Boys, this is Old Joe." . . . That was the happiest presentation speech ever made by any man—happy because General Johnston had the good sense to appreciate it and happy because it touched and thrilled the hearts and minds of soldiers who loved their own chief. General Cheatham was the only man in the Army of Tennessee who could have made such a presentation speech without offending General Johnston, and to my mind it was the supreme test of the good sense of the last named that he received it in the presence of several thousand private soldiers with all the kindly grace of manner that characterized every act of his noble life.

CAPTAIN DAVID P. CONYNGHAM
VOLUNTEER AIDE-DE-CAMP, FEDERAL STAFF

Well aware of Sherman's low opinion of reporters, Conyngham, a correspondent for the New York Herald, secured an officer's appointment and a uniform to give him easier access to military circles. In addition to his work reporting on the campaign, he served admirably on several staffs.

Thomas's headquarters comprised a most gorgeous outlay of tents of all kinds; wall tents, Sibley tents, fly tents, octagon tents, and all kinds of tents. Every officer had a tent; almost every servant had a tent; while the adjutant general's tent was a sort of open rebellion against all restrictory orders. A kind of caravan, full of pigeon holes, and covered over with an immense fly, was one of its most peculiar features. Sherman, on the contrary, had but one old wall tent, and some three or four flies, for his quarters.

Whether it was that General Thomas felt sore at the contrast, or General Sherman did not like the example set by General Thomas, he could never let slip an opportunity to pass a joke at Thomas's expense.

He would frequently rein up his horse in front of Thomas's quarters, and ask, "Whose quarters are these?"

"General Thomas's, general," would be the reply.

"O, yes; Thomastown—Thomasville; a very pretty place, indeed; appears to be growing rapidly!" and he would chuckle and ride off.

Major General George H. Thomas (left) was hailed as the Rock of Chickamauga for his masterful direction of the Federal rear guard on the last day of that battle in September 1863. Disavowed by his family in 1861 when he forsook his native Virginia to serve the Union, Thomas was a West Point classmate of Sherman, who gave him command of the 73,000-man Army of the Cumberland, the largest by far of Sherman's three armies.

In this April 1864 photograph, the Army of the Cumberland's chief of staff, Brigadier General William D. Whipple (standing, center), hands a dispatch to a clerk seated at General Thomas' many-pigeonholed special office wagon, the most prominent feature of his elaborate headquarters.

Following their introduction in the spring of 1863, Federal corps badges soon became cherished emblems of unit pride for Union soldiery. Pictured (from right to left) are those for the Army of the Cumberland: the star and crescent of the XX Corps, the acorn of the XIV Corps, the triangle of the IV Corps, and the crossed-saber badge of the Cavalry Corps.

"Temptation comes to throw up ones commission and stay at home among such jolly lads and lassies."

LIEUTENANT CHESLEY A. MOSMAN

59TH ILLINOIS INFANTRY, GROSE'S BRIGADE

By 1864 thousands of Union soldiers who had joined up in 1861 for "three years or the war" were faced with the decision of whether to stay on or quit the fight. Most, like Mosman, chose to reenlist, lured by cash bounties, 30-day furloughs, and large measures of patriotism and pride.

I didn't keep a regular journal while at home, but I apprehend that the recollections of that visit will not soon fade from my memory. The visiting with relatives, calls on young ladies and attendance on balls and parties during our month furlough will hardly interest those who read this diary and so any account of our doing in the way of social pleasures will be omitted as immaterial. We had a splendid time and the people showed their appreciation of our service and their hearty support of our cause in ways too numerous to mention. But it all went too quickly and even the momentary pleasure of the passing hour was lessened by the knowledge that in a few short days we would have to return to the front and a soldier's life with all its privations and dangers. One feels to question whether these so called pleasures pay. It is too liable to make one dissatisfied with his lot and temptation comes to throw up ones commission and stay at home among such jolly lads and lassies who seem to exist for the fun and frolic of life rather than its serious duties. Of course they do all that can be done to make us enjoy ourselves but right in the midst of it comparisons as to our and their future will unbidden come to the mind of the man on furlough.

Many of the three-year veterans chose to reenlist as a group so they could take their leave and be feted by friends and family together. The invitations and menu cover shown at right are mementos kept by Captain Francis DeGress, the commander of Battery H, 1st Illinois Light Artillery, testifying to the full social schedule observed by him and his men during their visit home in March and April of 1864.

LIEUTENANT THOMAS J. STOKES
10TH TEXAS CAVALRY (DISMOUNTED), GRANBURY'S BRIGADE

A minister who preached and held prayer meetings for his brigade, Georgia-born Stokes witnessed the tide of religious fervor that swept through the Army of Tennessee in the early months of 1864, when hundreds of men were immersed in creeks at mass baptisms. "Men who never shrank in battle from any responsibility came forward weeping," Stokes wrote, describing one Sabbath service.

Near Dalton, April 28th, 1864. My Dear Sister. . . .
The great unexampled revival is fast increasing in interest. I have just returned from the creek, where I saw thirty-three buried with Christ in baptism, acknowledging there before two thousand persons that they were not ashamed to follow Jesus in His ordinance. My soul was made happy in witnessing the solemn scene. . . . I preached for General Polk's brigade night before last, and we had a very interesting meeting. They have just begun there, yet I had a congregation of some 400. . . . The revival in our brigade has continued now for four weeks, nearly, and many have found peace with their Savior. If we could remain stationary a few weeks longer, I believe the greater portion of the army would be converted. This is all the doings of the Lord, and is surely the earnest of the great deliverance in store for us. It is the belief of many, that this is the "beginning of the end."

Affectionately,
Your Brother

A schoolteacher in Corinth, Georgia, Missouri Stokes received many letters from her brother, Thomas, describing "a revival so vast in its proportions." In one letter the preacher-soldier wrote, "The glad tidings may go forth that the Army of Tennessee is the army of the Lord." As the campaign loomed ahead, foot soldiers and generals alike sought God's providence.

DOCTOR CHARLES T. QUINTARD
CHAPLAIN AT LARGE, ARMY OF TENNESSEE

Born and raised in Connecticut, Quintard obtained a medical degree in New York City and in 1848 moved south to practice, eventually settling in Memphis. Six years later he decided to enter the Episcopal priesthood. With the outbreak of war he became chaplain of the 1st Tennessee Infantry and later, at the behest of General Johnston, of the entire army.

On the 8th of May, 1864, while I was in Atlanta in charge of St. Luke's Church and in attendance upon the hospitals, the following telegram came to me from Major Henry Hampton: "Can't you come up tomorrow? General Hood wishes to be baptized." It was impossible for me to go, but it was a great pleasure for me to learn afterwards that General Polk arrived with his staff that day and that night he baptized his brother General. It was the eve of an expected battle. It was a touching sight, we may be sure,—the one-legged veteran, leaning upon his crutches to receive the waters of baptism and the sign of the cross. A few nights later, General Polk baptized General Johnston and Lieutenant-General Hardee, General Hood being witness. These were two of the four ecclesiastical acts performed by Bishop Polk after receiving his commission in the army.

CHAPLAIN THOMAS H. DEAVENPORT
3D TENNESSEE (C.S.) INFANTRY, BROWN'S BRIGADE

Grim camp conditions, homesickness, and a tough new military service law made desertions all too common in the Confederate ranks. Chaplain Deavenport was present when the ultimate penalty was meted out to 14 North Carolinians from Brigadier General Alexander W. Reynolds' brigade, just days before the opening of the campaign.

May 4th. . . . Today I witnessed a sight, sad indeed, I saw fourteen men shot for desertion. I visited them twice yesterday and attended them to the place of execution. Most of them met death manfully. Some, poor fellows, I fear were unprepared. I saw them wash and dress themselves for the grave. It was solumn scene, they were tied to the stake, there was the coffin, there the open grave ready to receive them. I have seen man die at home surrounded by loved ones, I have seen him die on the battle field among the noble and brave, I have seen him die in prison in an enemy land, but the saddest of all was the death of the deserter, but even there Christ was sufficient. "Tell my wife," said one but a few minutes before the leaden messengers pierced his breast, "not to grieve for me, I have no doubt of reaching a better world." Let me then continue to hold up that savior and point sinners to him. I think they were objects of pity, they were ignorant, poor, and had families dependent upon them. War is a cruel thing, it heeds not the widow's tear, the orphan's moan, or the lover's anguish.

CAPTAIN FRANCIS HALSEY WIGFALL
STAFF, LIEUTENANT GENERAL JOHN B. HOOD

The spring of 1864 saw increasingly stringent conditions wrought by the Union's tightening grip on the South. The loss of farmland and restrictions on transportation prompted the Confederate States to enact legislation reducing the already dwindling rations a soldier was allotted. In a letter to his mother, Wigfall, son of Texas senator Louis T. Wigfall, expressed the frustration experienced by soldiers over their meager provisions.

Tell Papa that the army is very much "down on" Congress for the ration bill and ask him to be sure and have it remedied as soon as the session begins. I have heard several plans proposed by officers for inviting one or two members of Congress now with the army to a "one ration a day dinner." Something of this sort, for instance: The entertainer would be very generous and have the whole day's ration served for dinner. He would divide the pound and a quarter of meal, the quarter of a pound of hominy and the third of a pound of bacon into three parts and give his guest one, take one himself and set one aside for his servant. However, we all live in hope of the better time coming. . . .

We are barely managing to exist on the third of a pound of bacon. We keep up our spirits however, and hope for the time when Congress shall intervene in our behalf and satisfy the Oliver Twists of the Army. A friend of one of our mess the other day sent a turkey and you should have seen our countenances as we prepared to devour him.

CAPTAIN GEORGE W. F. HARPER
58TH NORTH CAROLINA INFANTRY, A. REYNOLDS' BRIGADE

Writing home to his wife on April 7, Harper tells of one of the mock battles staged by Johnston to stir up his men's martial vigor. Harper, whose Colt Navy revolver and holster are shown at right, was wounded at Resaca on May 15 and sent home. He returned in August and served until surrendering with his regiment in April 1865.

ave just ret'd from witnessing the grand sham battle of Hardee's Corps. It was a magnificent sight. The spectators alone numbered thousands if not more. Many ladies from Atlanta & other places were present adding to the beauty of the scene. Wish you could have seen it. The boxes were recv'd this morning. I thank you all a heap for mine. My appetite was good enough to enjoy our rough fare and I hope it will not be spoiled by your "goodies." My messmates recv'd a number of color'd eggs with their wifes names &c. &c. on them. You probably forgot that it was Easter so will excuse you especially as I prefer to cook 'em myself & don't care much for the shells. We had plenty of fine music from the bands to day . . . "Marsalaise," "Mockingbird" "Dixie" "Bonnie Blue Flag" &c. The last named is favorite in Hardee's Corps his battle flag being of blue with a full moon in the center. Ours is the red cross. Infantry artillery & cavalry participated in the fight to day & the firing at times was pretty heavy.

This distinctive style of Rebel battle flag, carried by many regiments in Hardee's corps, was probably designed by General Hardee himself early in 1862. The soldiers were fiercely proud of their blue banners and resisted attempts by military authorities to force them to adopt the more familiar Southern Cross. The flag shown here, now faded, was issued to the consolidated 8th and 19th Arkansas in the spring of 1864, only to be captured on September 1 at Jonesboro.

"The poor man and the rich man, fathers alike of men fighting the same battles in defense of the grandest principle that ever inspired mortal man to combat."

MARY A. H. GAY
RESIDENT OF DECATUR

An impassioned Confederate loyalist, Gay made the trip from her native Decatur, outside Atlanta, to the front lines at Dalton to bring her half-brother, Lieutenant Thomas Stokes, some of the comforts of home. Later, as the fighting grew nearer, she frequently traveled to Atlanta to help with the wounded in the city's hospitals.

From Atlanta to Dalton, $7.75. From the 23d to the 26th of April, 1864, to Mrs. John Reynolds, for board, $20.00. From Dalton to Decatur, $8.00. . . .
This trip was taken for the purpose of carrying provisions and articles of clothing to my brother and his comrades in General Joseph E. Johnston's command. In vain had our mother tried to send appetizing baskets of food to her son, whose soldier rations consisted of salty bacon

and hard tack; some disaster, real or imaginary, always occurred to prevent them from reaching their destination, and it was, therefore, determined at home that I should carry the next consignment.

After several days' preparation, jugs were filled with good sorghum syrup, and baskets with bread, pies, cakes and other edibles at our command, and sacks of potatoes, onions and peppers were included. My fond and loving mother and I, and our faithful aid-de-camps of African descent, conveyed them to the depot. In those days the depot was a favorite resort with the ladies and children of Decatur. There they always heard something from the front—wherever that might be. The obliging agent had a way, all his own, of acquiring information from the army in all its varied commands, and dealt it out galore to the encouragement or discouragement of his auditors, as his prejudices or partialities prompted. On this occasion many had gone there, who, like myself, were going to take the train for Atlanta, and in the interim were eager to hear everything of a hopeful character, even though reason urged that it was hoping against hope.

I was the cynosure of all eyes, as I was going to "the front;" and every mother who had a darling son in that branch of the army hoped that he would be the first to greet me on my arrival there, and give me a message for her. And I am sure, if the love consigned to me for transmission could have assumed tangible form and weight, it would have been more than fourteen tons to the square inch.

Helpful, willing hands deposited with care my well-labeled jugs,

Civilians who wanted to travel by train in wartime Georgia had to seek official military approval. This travel pass, much like one Mary Gay would have used, shows the date of issue, the traveler's name, the points of origin and destination, and the authorizing officer's signature. Later in the campaign, when the Federals took over the railroads, civilian rail travel was all but eliminated.

baskets, etc., and I deposited myself with equal care in an already well-filled coach on the Georgia Railroad. Arrived in Atlanta I surreptitiously stowed the jugs in the car with me, and then asked the baggage-master to transfer the provisions to a Dalton freight train. Without seeming to do so, I watched his every movement until I saw the last article safely placed in the car, and then I went aboard myself. Surrounded by jugs and packages, I again became an object of interest, and soon found myself on familiar terms with all on board; for were we not friends and kindred bound to each other by the closest ties? Every age and condition of Southern life was represented in that long train of living, anxious freight. Young wives, with wee bit tots chaperoned by their mothers and sometimes by their grandmothers, were going to see their husbands, for, perhaps, the last time on earth; and mothers, feeling that another fond embrace of their sons would palliate the sting of final separation. The poor man and the rich man, fathers alike of men fighting the same battles in defense of the grandest principle that ever inspired mortal man to combat, on their way to see those men and leave their benedictions with them; and sisters, solitary and alone, going to see their beloved brothers and assure them once more of the purest and most disinterested love that ever found lodgment in the human heart. . . .

Those were days of slow travel in the South. The roads were literally blockaded with chartered cars, which contained the household goods of refugees who had fled from the wrath and vandalism of the enemy, and not unfrequently refugees themselves inhabited cars that seemed in fearful proximity to danger. Ample opportunity of observation on either side was furnished by this slow travel, and never did the fine, arable lands bordering the Western & Atlantic road from the Chattahoochee river to Dalton give greater promise of cereals, and trees in large variety were literally abloom with embryo fruit. Alas! that such a land should be destined to fall into the hands of despoilers.

LIEUTENANT JOHN M. DAVIDSON
39TH NORTH CAROLINA INFANTRY, ECTOR'S BRIGADE

Davidson, a merchant who owned shops in Tennessee and Georgia when he volunteered for service in 1861, by the spring of 1864 was plagued by illness. Chronic pain drove him to seek the less physically demanding position of adjutant and to repeatedly apply for a furlough. In a letter to his wife, Davidson writes of his longing for the joys of hearth and home.

Camp Lee Near Pollard Ala
April 22d, 1864
My Own Dear Julia. . . . I was at Town & some person told me a letter had gon to camps for me. I attended to business with dispatch and hurried out as I began to think the time long in hearing from my several epistles that I had sent and my joy was complete when I received it and recognised the familiar hand writing. . . . I am fearful I am going to suffer considerably from Rhumatism this Spring. some days I can scarcely walk. . . . I feel greatly distressed some times for fear I will yet loose the use of my limbs. it is Chronic and perhaps last me as long as I live. if I could remain at home I would resign but if I do so soon as I got better I would be conscripted. We are moving to Town

"I hope this cruel war will end this year and I be spared to enjoy uninterruptedly the society of Wife children & friends."

to day. 2 Regts are gone and ours & the 25 will go in the morning. all the Troops from here have been ordered to Dalton but our Brigade and we are left here to Guard the Road to Mobile &c. I hope we will get to remain here as there is not much danger of a fight here. . . . We have not drew a cent of money since I returned. I have been borowing all the time. . . . Lt Whitaker will return about the 10 of May and I will then make an application for a Furlough and bring you all the Money I can spare. I feel distressed about your condition and fear that you would suffer if it was not for Mother. . . . When I get my Debts paid I will have a better chance of sending you more as our Rations are now given to us. we are now at our new camp near Town and evy thing is bustle & confusion putting up Tents making scaffolds beds &c. . . . I think I will be at home in May & June. . . . I would be so glad to see you and the children. I can imagine I see you flying arround attending to your little domestic affairs this evening preparing & fixing your-self & children for Sabbath School in the Morning. I would be so glad to be with and accompany you to church once more. it reminds me of by gon days when our cup was overflowing with happiness & pleasure and I read thos eyes of affection and trace your thoughts and with what pride you strove to render your-self agreeable & pleasant to the man that had promised at the sacred Alter to Cherish & protect you. I hope this cruel war will end this year and I be spared to enjoy uninterruptedly the society of Wife children & friends. We have been so successful this spring. if matters continue so this summer we certainly will have peace. Forrest took Fort Pillow Paduca Ky and our Armies was victorious in La recently and their is a great Battle now preparing at Dalton & in Ga. so if God only prosperous us their it will prevent Lincoln from being elected and perhaps bring about an armistis. . . . If I succeed in getting the Adjt position I will let you know. good evening Dear Julia. may Heavens richest blessings be yours. As ever your loveing & devoted Husband.

Jno M D

PS. Save a chicken for me if you [can] as we get none in the Armey.

JULIA DAVIDSON

A schoolteacher before she married, Julia Davidson moved to Atlanta to be near her parents when her husband, John, left their home in Ducktown, Tennessee, to fight in the war. Aware of her husband's poor health, she once wrote: "I wish (is it right or wrong) you would get sick enough to come home." In this letter she describes the struggle to maintain a household under harsh economic conditions.

Atlanta Ga May 1st 64 . . .Well times do not get any better. I cannot see that the new issue has done any good. Bacon is $4.50 to $6.00 pr lb butter is $5.00 to $6.00 & $7.00 per lb. I hear beef steak was $8.00 per lb. at the market, though as I have plenty of butter & milk I do not buy much meat. I settled up the milk account with Sasseen received $95.00. I then went to the city relief store where meat was selling at $3.50. when I presented the money which was $5.00 bills, he refused to take them saying the board had so ordered him. I could not say a word. I thought the 5s were as good as the new issue. I went back to Sasseen got him to charge part of it give me some new money and some change besides. I had an order for $21.00 and so I fixed it up and bought me one shoulder. I would have laid out more then but my money was all in 5s. Oh! I could not keep my feelings down a *great big lump would come up in my throat which I tried in vain to swallow.* the water would come in my eyes & my lips quiver in spite of me. not that he had insulted me, but he is so *cross* so *harsh* so *grim* never has a pleasant word or smile for any one and acts & talks as though he thought soldiers wives were *no bodys.* And I could not think it was much benefit to the poor, at least when they refused 5 dollar bills. I wish he were in your place and you in his. I could not help contrasting him with you in his dealings. you so kind, so pleasant endeavoring to please your customers, he so *cross* so *angry looking* so *unsympathising* so unpitying—maybe it will all work right. I heard also that he was a *Yankee.* if true does it not look well for the people of Atlanta to give the situation of distributing provisions to the poor and to the soldiers families to a Yankee.

CAPTAIN LEMUEL P. GRANT
Engineer Corps, C.S.A.

Formerly the chief engineer of the Georgia Railroad, Grant was assigned in 1862 to oversee the repair and rebuilding of railroads wrecked by Federal raiders. Later he was charged with the construction of defensive works around Atlanta and Augusta.

Engineers Office
Atlanta April 12th 1864
Col. M. N. Wright
Comdg. Troops & Defenses of Atlanta
Colonel

I have the honor to comply with the request contained in your note of the 31st ult.

I beg leave to call your attention to the accompanying sketches of "The City of Atlanta and line of Defences" and plan of redoubt "with section of rifle" pit to the former of which it will be necessary for me to refer in this brief report.

The length of line marked in red is 10 2080/5280 miles. To fully man this line will require Fifty five thousand (55,000) Troops.

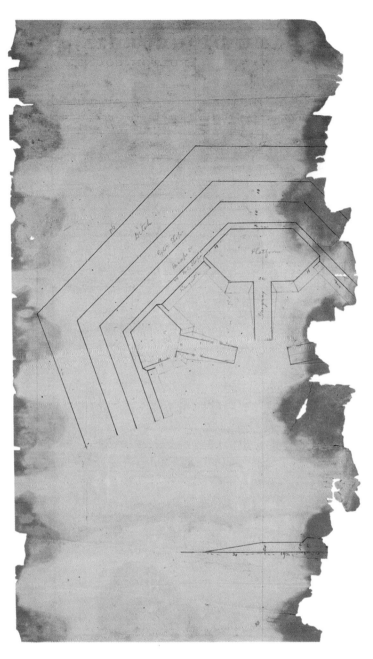

A fragment of Grant's drawings for the fortifications around Atlanta (above) shows the layout of one of the forts. Grant began construction of the works in July of 1863, using slave labor provided by their owners for $25 per day. By April 1864 the city was encircled by a system of berms, ditches, and parapets that would later offer refuge to General Hood's beleaguered troops. Drafting tools used by Grant appear at left.

PRIVATE
JOHN W. COTTON
10TH CONFEDERATE CAVALRY, ANDERSON'S BRIGADE

Although more liberal than Bragg, General Johnston still granted furloughs reluctantly. Only 1 in 30 enlisted men, selected by lot, could take a furlough, and Private Cotton was numbered among the unlucky. The father of seven children, Cotton returned home to Alabama in 1865 only to die the next year, probably of measles.

MARY S. MALLARD
RESIDENT OF ATLANTA

Mallard, the wife of a Presbyterian minister, wrote to her mother describing the apprehension felt by all Atlantans as word of impending hostilities reached the city. With the front only a hundred miles away, citizens feared the worst but nevertheless remained steadfastly confident of General Johnston's leadership.

Tunnel hill Ga. aprile 23th 1864

Most dear beloved wife and children I take my pen in hand to try to rite you a few lines to let you no that I am well in body but not in mind I am very much troubled about not getting my furlough Dave Martin and bill got there furlough and started home yesterday evening I never have had nothing to hurt my feelings as bad in my life general Johnson has passed order for no more furloughs to be granted for the present so there ant no chance now to get a furlough I would give anything in the world almost to bee at home with you now but as long as I cant my prare is that you may do well in delivering your der little babe do the best you can and take good care of your self and the baby I dont no that I will ever live to see it but I still live in hopes that I will live til the war will end so we can live in peace and harmony once more I think if this war was ended I would bee the happiest man living we are looking for a fite here every day some of our regiment is gone now to run in some of the yankey pickets one of our men that went with them has just got in he says they got 23 prisoners and killed 10 or 12 they are all comeing in we never got nary man killed and but 2 wounded rite as soon as you get this letter and let me no how you are comeing on and how manuel is getting on with his crop and how your wheat looks nothing more at present I remain your true devoted husband til death

John W. Cotton

Atlanta, Thursday, May 5th, 1864

Dear Mother,

We all fear the next terrible struggle, and I trust our people will not be so lifted up by our recent successes as to be led to vainglory and forgetfulness of our merciful Heavenly Father, the source of all these blessings. A battle is daily expected at the front, though some persons think this will be chiefly a diversion to prevent the troops being sent to General Lee. The Yankees are thought to have about eighty thousand men at Chattanooga, and General Johnston has about sixty thousand, all in fine spirits and expecting victory. I trust the battle will be decided very soon. No one seems to apprehend any danger for this place, for falling back is not General Johnston's policy. The committees here are getting ready and preparing themselves to go up to the relief of the wounded should a battle take place. . . .

Your affectionate daughter,
Mary S. Mallard

"You must not feel any uneasiness if you receive no letters from me for several weeks. The Army is expected to move soon."

LIEUTENANT JOSEPH F. CULVER
129TH ILLINOIS INFANTRY, WARD'S BRIGADE

Toward the end of April, Sherman began issuing orders to his various commands to prepare for battle, stressing among other things a stricture on outside communications. Many men, including Joseph Culver, dashed off what they thought might be, at least for a while, a last letter. But Culver continued to write to his wife, Mary (above, right), often several times a week. They had been married in December 1861. Joseph went off to war the following August, shortly before the birth of their first child, who died not long after while Culver was serving in Tennessee. Promoted to captain on June 28, 1864, Culver survived the war to return home and raise seven children.

Head Qurs., 129th Regt. Ills. Vols.
Wauhatchie, Tenn., April 30th 1864
My Dear Wife

I recd. no letter from you this morning, but recd. one from Henry Greenebaum in which he says you are well. My health is very good. Dr. Johnson is quite sick with dysentery. Lum Hill is much better. We are mustering for pay to-day and expect pay next week.

I have but a moment to write before the call sounds for muster. I will try and give you a long letter to-morrow (Sunday). Connelly handed me an ambrotype of himself taken on horseback; I will send it as soon as I get time to put it up carefully. Bro. Johnie gave me a set of sleeve buttons which I will send you to have them fixed; get a gold link and some device on the top.

You must not feel any uneasiness if you receive no letters from me for several weeks. The Army is expected to move soon, and all mails going North will be stopped. I look for it every day. In the meantime, keep a brave heart and write often. Your letters will still reach me. I may get an opportunity occasionally to send a letter by private sources to be mailed north of the lines, but you must take it for granted that all is well and trust in God. May he bless you with health and happiness and kindly watch over you.

We are forbidden henceforth to furnish any army news, and we feel that it is all right and proper. You may confidently expect to hear a good account of us if an opportunity offers. Remember [me] in love to Mother and Maggie and kindly to all our friends. May holy Angels guard thee and peace and contentment dwell with thee. With much love, I remain,

Your Affectionate Husband
J. F. Culver

Smoky Range.

Smoke of Enemy's Ca[...]

THE ADVANCE SIGNAL-STATION NEAR RINGGOLD, GEORGIA.

RINGGOLD, GEORGIA.—[See Page 283.]

HARPER'S WEEKLY.

285

APRIL 30, 1864.]

"I picked up a skull which had a smooth, round hole through it; small it was, but yet large enough to let a life pass out."

Buzzard's Roost Gap.

The pair of newspaper engravings at left give two views of the no man's land that separated the two armies as of December 1863. After the Federals drove the Rebel army off the heights around Chattanooga in late November, Union forces kept up the pursuit into northwestern Georgia as far as Ringgold Gap, where they drew up after a sharp fight with the Confederate rear guard. In the top image, Federal signalmen keep watch over distant, enemy-held Rocky Face Ridge and Mill Creek Gap, here labeled Buzzard's Roost Gap. The town of Ringgold (bottom) still lies partially in ruins months after its rail yard, factories, and warehouses were put to the torch by retreating Rebels.

PRIVATE CHARLES E. BENTON
150TH NEW YORK INFANTRY, RUGER'S BRIGADE

Most of Sherman's army spent the winter camped in and around Chattanooga, well back from the front lines and close to the railhead and supply depot that sustained the growing Federal presence in the area. When orders went out in late April to move to the front, many units had to march 20 miles or more. Some troops, including Charles Benton, crossed the seven-month-old Chickamauga battle ground, a grisly prelude to the killing fields of Georgia that lay ahead.

On our way we passed the battlefield of Chickamauga. The battle was fought in the autumn before and resulted in a severe defeat to our army there engaged. There is a certain gruesomeness about an old battlefield, not yet so old that nature has claimed her own and covered the scars. Trees and branches that were torn were still hanging, though shrivelled and dead, and there was still a stench of decaying flesh in the air.

Some of the slain had been buried, though it had been hastily and imperfectly done. Protruding shoes here and there showed the bones of the foot inside, the flesh having disappeared, and not infrequently a hand would be seen extended above the ground, with the skin dried to the bones and weathered to the color of granite. The fingers would be curved as if beckoning, but in one instance I noted that the index finger was pointed upward. In one locality many hundreds had been left unburied, and the bones were peeping through the clothing. I picked up a skull which had a smooth, round hole through it; small it was, but yet large enough to let a life pass out.

March to the Chattahoochee

Sherman launched his offensive on May 7, 1864, and within hours Thomas' troops had cleared the Confederates from Tunnel Hill. Schofield's Army of the Ohio linked up with Thomas, and the combined force continued to advance on Johnston's main position at Dalton, only to be stymied by the formidable defenses on Rocky Face Ridge. Meanwhile McPherson was leading his Army of the Tennessee south to Snake Creek Gap, threatening to envelop the Confederate flank and rear. Sherman was confident that the bold maneuver would succeed, exclaiming to his aides, "I've got Joe Johnston dead!"

Sherman's elation was short-lived, however. When the vanguard of McPherson's army passed through Snake Creek Gap on May 9, they found several thousand Confederate troops blocking the approaches to Resaca, where the Western & Atlantic Railroad crossed the Oostanaula River. Fearing that the Confederates were already there in strength, McPherson pulled back into the gap after a short fight and awaited orders. In fact McPherson vastly outnumbered the enemy troops to his front. His caution allowed the newly arrived Army of Mississippi troops led by Leonidas Polk to bolster the defenses at

Resaca, while Johnston, alerted to the presence of enemy troops in his rear, began withdrawing from Dalton. By May 13 Johnston had united with the bulk of Polk's corps and was preparing to make a stand at Resaca.

Disengaging most of Thomas' force and sending them on the route McPherson had taken through Snake Creek Gap, Sherman was disappointed to find Johnston entrenched at Resaca. "Well, Mac," Sherman told McPherson, "you have missed the opportunity of a lifetime." When Sherman attacked on May 14, his troops were driven back with heavy losses. The next day, Sherman again assaulted Johnston's line and again was repulsed. But when Brigadier General Thomas W. Sweeny's division crossed the Oostanaula at Lay's Ferry, threatening Johnston's left, the Confederate commander saw no alternative but to abandon the bridgehead at Resaca and continue his withdrawal southward.

After a sharp rearguard action at the Rome

This desolate vista, looking down the wagon road leading into Mill Creek Gap toward the wooded mountains on the horizon, greeted the Federals as they set out in early May on their march to Atlanta.

crossroads on May 16, Johnston halted his army three days later near the town of Cassville. Meanwhile, Sherman directed Thomas and McPherson to converge on Kingston, where Sherman believed he would find the Rebel army, leaving Schofield and Hooker to proceed on alone toward Cassville. The Confederate commander had set in motion an ambush to destroy this exposed left flank on the morning of May 19, but the unexpected presence of Federal cavalry, the failure of Hood to carry out orders, and the approach of other Federal forces that afternoon caused Johnston to again disengage and withdraw to the commanding ridges astride Allatoona Pass.

Sherman decided to keep on flanking, bypassing the Rebel strongpoint and shifting the bulk of his army to Dallas, 15 miles southwest of Allatoona. From there he could turn east and gain the line of the Western & Atlantic at Marietta, severing Johnston's line of retreat. On May 23 Sherman crossed the Etowah River, which he grandly proclaimed "the Rubicon of Georgia." But rough terrain slowed the Yankee columns, and when the vanguard of Sherman's force—Hooker's XX Corps—reached Dallas, Johnston had beaten them to the punch.

Hooker attacked on May 25, but his columns were cut to pieces by the well-placed soldiers of Hood's corps covering the New Hope Church crossroads. Two days later, Major General Oliver O. Howard's IV Corps assaulted the Confederate right at Pickett's Mill, only to be hurled back with great loss by Cleburne's division. "This is surely not war," one Federal wrote, "it's butchery."

Seeking to follow up his success, on May 28 Johnston ordered Hardee to counterattack the Yankee right flank near Dallas. But when Hardee sent Brigadier General William B.

Bate's division forward, the charge foundered against the breastworks of Major General John A. Logan's XV Corps. Unable to pierce the strong enemy line, Sherman once again sent McPherson on a flank march around the Southern left. On June 4 Johnston evacuated the war-ravaged landscape that men of both sides dubbed the Hell Hole and fell back to the Lost Mountain Line that covered the Western & Atlantic Railroad near Big Shanty.

Taking advantage of the rough, mountainous terrain and aided by nearly two weeks of heavy rain, the Confederate commander slowed Sherman's advance to a crawl. While surveying Federal positions from the top of Pine Mountain on June 14, Lieutenant General Polk, the highest-ranking Confederate officer to fall in the campaign, was killed by a Federal shell. When continuing Union probes threatened him again, Johnston withdrew to a position two miles to the south along a line buttressed by Kennesaw Mountain, a natural fortress known as the Gibraltar of Georgia.

Sherman shifted Schofield and Hooker to the south in an attempt to bypass the Rebel strongpoint. But Johnston dispatched Hood's corps to counter the threat, and on June 22 the fiery Southern commander lashed out at the Yankee force near Kolb's Farm. Massed Federal artillery mowed down the charging Southern ranks, but for the time being Hood had stymied the enemy effort to get in the rear of Johnston's army.

"I am now inclined to feign on both flanks and assault the center," Sherman wired the War Department. "It may cost us dear, but the results would surpass any effort to pass around." On June 27 Sherman committed the bulk of his force in a massive attack on the Rebel defenses of Kennesaw Mountain. Advancing with suicidal gallantry, the blue-

clad columns charged time and again against the impregnable enemy line. But the Yankee soldiers' bravery proved futile in the face of devastating fire that scythed down entire ranks of men. By day's end 3,000 Union troops had fallen, and the fighting petered out in a grim standoff.

Seeking to break the impasse, Sherman shifted McPherson's army from the left to join Schofield on the right of the extended Union line. This maneuver pried Johnston out of his entrenchments on Kennesaw Mountain and compelled the Southern commander to continue his retreat to a new position near the Western & Atlantic at Smyrna. Following another brief standoff on July 4, Sherman again began sidling to Johnston's flank, and the Confederates once more withdrew, this time to a powerful series of earthworks north of the Chattahoochee River—the last great barrier between Sherman and Atlanta.

A force of military engineers and slaves had worked feverishly under the direction of Johnston's chief of artillery, Brigadier General Francis A. Shoup, to construct a virtually impregnable defensive line. In addition to the usual rifle pits, the works boasted diamond-shaped redoubts made of logs and packed earth. A stockade of sharpened vertical logs linked the redoubts. Emplacements for artillery were also built into the stockade halfway between each redoubt.

Johnston had such confidence in his new line that he predicted it would hold Sherman back "a long time." Sherman as well admired the Rebels' Chattahoochee defenses. Riding down from Smyrna on the morning of July 5, he viewed the Confederate works from a hill about two miles from the river. He thought the line "one of the strongest pieces of field fortification I ever saw."

From that same hill Sherman saw a vista that excited him more. For the first time in his two-month campaign the ultimate objective came into view—Atlanta, beckoning from a distance of no more than eight miles.

Enticing though the target must have been, Sherman had no intention of launching the type of head-on assault that had bloodied his armies at Kennesaw Mountain. While Thomas demonstrated against the Chattahoochee defenses and McPherson continued to feint to the south, on July 8 a full division from Schofield's Army of the Ohio crossed the river six miles beyond Johnston's right flank. The next day Brigadier General Kenner Garrard's cavalry division gained the south bank of the Chattahoochee near Roswell, 16 miles northeast of the Confederate position.

With Federal forces threatening to cut him off from Atlanta, on the night of July 9 Johnston abandoned his defenses. That night another enactment of the now familiar rituals unfolded: the withdrawal across bridges strewn with green cornstalks to muffle the sound of retreat, the burning of the spans, the dismantling of the pontoons.

With the Chattahoochee behind him, General Johnston marched his army a few miles back to Atlanta's outer defensive line on the high ground south of Peachtree Creek, a tributary of the river. The new line faced north to cover the city, now just a few miles away.

Sherman celebrated by taking a much-needed bath in the Chattahoochee. The next morning, July 11, he wired Washington, "We now commence the real game for Atlanta."

The worst fears of Jefferson Davis had come to pass. In two months the Yankees had succeeded in maneuvering Joe Johnston into the defenses of Atlanta, and a siege of the Gate City seemed a foregone conclusion.

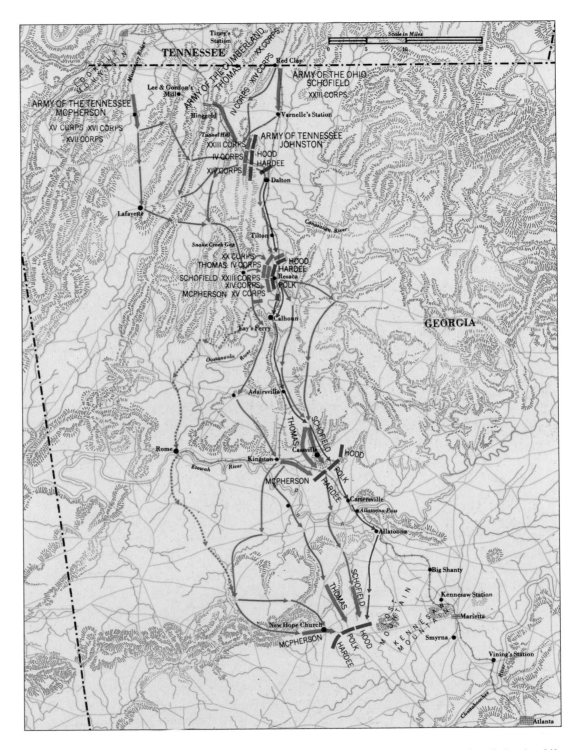

During the first month of the campaign, the outnumbered Confederates bloodied the pursuing Federals while deftly avoiding their flanking maneuvers. But in doing so, the Rebels lost about 75 miles of territory.

"A blinding flash before my eyes, a sensation as if a hundred pound rock had struck my right shoulder."

LIEUTENANT LOT D. YOUNG
4TH KENTUCKY (C.S.) INFANTRY, LEWIS' BRIGADE

Young's unit was one of the five regiments in the all-Kentucky brigade led by Brigadier General Joseph H. Lewis. Because of their service in the Confederate army, the soldiers were cut off from their homes in Union-held Kentucky and Lewis' command became popularly known as the Orphan Brigade. Here Young recalls watching the Federals mass for a feint against Dug Gap. Later, a leg wound at Jonesboro on August 31 put him out of the war.

While contemplating the future, news came that the enemy were now moving Daltonward. We indulged the hope and wondered whether Sherman would undertake to force the pass in Rockyface Mountain through which the railroad and wagon road both ran. We thought of Leonidas and his Spartans and hoped for an opportunity to imitate and if possible to eclipse that immortal event at Thermopylae. But not so the wily Sherman. That "old fox" was too cunning to be caught in that or any other trap.

We were ordered out to meet him and took position in the gap and on the mountain, from which we could see extending for miles his grand encampment of infantry and artillery, the stars and stripes floating from every regimental brigade, division and corps headquarters and presenting the greatest panorama I ever beheld. Softly and sweetly the music from their bands as they played the national airs were wafted up and over the summit of the mountain. Somehow, some way, in some inexplicable and unseen manner, "Hail Columbia," "America" and "The Star Spangled Banner" sounded sweeter than I had ever before heard them, and filled my soul with feelings that I could not describe or forget. It haunted me for days, but never shook my loyalty to the Stars and Bars or relaxed my efforts in behalf of our cause.

LIEUTENANT COLONEL EDWARD HAYES
29TH OHIO INFANTRY, CANDY'S BRIGADE

Mustered in as a captain in 1861, Hayes was captured in his first campaign by Thomas J. "Stonewall" Jackson's men at Port Republic in June 1862 and later exchanged. During the attack up Dug Gap on May 8, 1864, a bullet shattered his right shoulder. It took three years for the wound to heal and even then, as his wife recalled, the arm remained useless and "hung as a heavy weight against his body."

Twenty minutes more of climbing and the enemy opened with a few dropping shots intended to draw our fire. Some of the recruits brought their pieces to a "ready," but a word from their officers checked them and we still pushed upwards, and in five minutes more a gleam of fire ran along the crest of the ridge and the minnies came slashing through the brush all about us. We had drawn the enemy's fire and although it had cost us something it "counted us one for game." There, and not 'till there did our Colonel order the fire returned, which was promptly done, by division, and hardly checked our advance. A few moments more and we could fairly see the nature of the position we were trying to storm.

The ridge was capped by a palisade of perpendicular rock from ten to thirty feet high, with only two or three breaks in its fortress-like line.

The thing looked hopeless and our men taking in the situation at a glance, instantly availed themselves of such cover as could be had, but still worked forward until we were within forty or fifty yards of the crest. And now began a singular fight. No foolish volley firing, but sharp, close, and for us at least, terribly deadly work.

Our artillery now sent in a few shots, but as the chances of hitting us and the enemy were about equal, soon desisted. It may be asked why we did not withdraw. For several reasons. There was a deep ravine on our right, and as we could not see how the rest of our lines were making it, we hoped they might find better ground and possibly carry the position, if we could only keep the enemy in our front so busy as to prevent his doubling on our right. There was another reason. It was our boast that in nearly three years service we had never "limbered to the rear" without orders. . . .

It was equally certain that we could not stay where we were, and we therefore decided to make an attempt to carry the ridge at points where the breaks in the palisade of rocks suggested the possibility of doing so. I had just gone to the left to give the order, when a blinding

Some twenty years after the war, the Western & Atlantic Railroad, connecting Chattanooga and Atlanta, was anxious to increase ridership. Realizing that no line had more battlefield sites along its route, rail officials produced a guidebook, *The Mountain Campaigns in Georgia.* Most of the illustrations, whose accuracy was underscored by testimonials from Sherman and Johnston, were done by artist Alfred R. Waud, "who personally visited all the battlefields depicted." Waud first prepared colored sketches (left) which were then rendered into engravings for publication (below). Shown here is the Federal advance into Mill Creek Gap.

BATTLE OF MILL CREEK GAP.
On the line of the Western & Atlantic Railroad, near Dalton, Ga.
May 9, 1864.
Johnson's and Butterfield's Federal divisions assaulting portions of Bate's and Stewart's Confederate divisions.

In another Waud sketch, Federals from Geary's division brave withering fire from Daniel H. Reynolds' Arkansas brigade and Joseph Wheeler's cavalry in a forlorn attempt to force their way through the narrow defile at Dug Gap. Geary suffered 357 casualties—some caused by boulders rolled from the heights by the Rebels.

flash before my eyes, a sensation as if a hundred pound rock had struck my right shoulder; followed by a tumble down hill, admonished me that my share in that fight was over.

With no very clear idea of what had happened I attempted to get up; finding that my right arm would not respond, I took a look in that direction and seeing a hole in my coat between the strap and the collar, began to think I was hit. Then, feeling myself bleeding I passed my hand inside my vest and drew out a handful of blood to see the color, and remember saying to myself that it was venous blood.

Two men stepped out to pick me up, but just as they raised me from the ground a dozen balls whistled by and one of the men pitched headlong down the hill. I had afterwards the pleasure of knowing that he was not killed, although very severely wounded. Of the next ten minutes I have no distinct recollection, but afterwards learned that I passed along to the center of the regiment, reported to the colonel that I was hit, and requested him to send another officer to the left.

LIEUTENANT ANDREW M. SEA
Marshall's Tennessee (C.S.) Battery, Hood's Corps

On May 9 Sherman ordered another feinting attack, this time up Crow Valley on the north side of Rocky Face Ridge. Confederates of Major General Carter L. Stevenson's division were rushed into position in the nick of time and again the Federals were cut down trying to scale the slopes—but not before Lieutenant Sea and his battery mates felt themselves left in a most vulnerable position.

My section of artillery was encamped by the side of the main road, which led up the valley and was halfway between Dalton and the gap. The battery boys were lounging about the guns in rather a listless, lazy sort of way, unsuspicious of danger. I was lying under the shade of a small tree, aimlessly gazing across the open ground in my front, when I became interested in the movement of a rapidly approaching horseman. Upon his nearer approach I at once recognized Maj.-Gen. S[tevenson], who briefly informed me that a division of Federal troops was driving our small command through the gap, and would soon be upon me on its way to capture the town of Dalton and the supplies of our army. He ended his hurried information by ordering me to put my guns in position for action and "fight them to the muzzle of the guns." Meanwhile he would hurry any command he could find to my support.

Well, this was an eye-opener sure enough! Just think of it! "Fight them to the muzzle of the guns" simply meant to die or be captured in your tracks; sacrifice yourselves and guns to gain a little time, and that, too, absolutely without support. Why the order fairly took my breath. I was not one of those men who never felt the sensation of fear. Still I had hitherto summoned courage enough to go in and stay when comrades were around me and I felt that I had a fair chance; but with two pieces of artillery and without support to fight a division of the enemy flushed with success seemed preposterous. I confess that I was decidedly rebellious, and my thoughts while preparing for action were not the most pleasant. Still the order was peremptory, and left me no discretion. What could not be helped must be endured.

The enemy did not approach as rapidly as I anticipated, and our little band was disputing every inch of ground; but the firing was perceptibly getting nearer and nearer. Just then my attention was called to another rider coming directly from the front. He was kicking with both feet and beating his jaded horse with his saber-scabbard. He was a badly demoralized, straggling cavalryman. On he came to the battery, and, checking up his horse, breathlessly asked what command that was. Upon being informed, he partially turned in his saddle, and, looking in the direction of the enemy, he said, "Now, d——n you, I reckon you'll stop!" and away he went, kicking and spurring for dear life. The incident was so supremely ridiculous that my poor boys forgot their own peril in their jeers and laughter. Looking at the figure of the retreating cavalryman, our eyes were gladdened by the sight of a body of infantrymen coming from Dalton at a double-quick, and riding at the head of the column was Gen. [A.] Reynolds, who commanded a small brigade of Virginians and North Carolinians. He was a small, delicate-looking man, calm and absolutely fearless; a stouter heart never beat in human breast. These qualities had been apparent on many a bloody field. Early in the war, on Gauley River, W. Va., his splendid judgment and dauntless courage had saved the day, and ever since he had been known as "Old Gauley." My relief at seeing him may be imagined, and I said: "Well, General, you never saw a man so glad to see another."

"Why, what's the matter? Had you in a tight place, didn't they? But it's all right, Lieutenant. If I can't take my fleet-footed Virginians and my 'tarheels' and whip any division of Yankees that ever lived, my name ain't Gauley Reynolds, and I want you to see me do it."

Brigadier General Alexander W. Reynolds commanded a brigade that included the only two Virginia regiments serving in Johnston's army. A wound at New Hope Church removed him from further field command, but after the war he saw service as a colonel in the army of the khedive of Egypt.

CAPTAIN ROBERT S. CHAMBERLAIN
64TH OHIO INFANTRY, HARKER'S BRIGADE

Chamberlain was one of the 88 casualties suffered by his regiment during the May 9 attack on the north side of Rocky Face Ridge. A ball from Edmund W. Pettus' Alabama brigade shattered Chamberlain's chin and jaw and led to his discharge in September.

We moved forward under a murderous fire and got so close to their line of works that I could see the buttons on their coats. . . . Sergeant Patterson with the colors was standing with his face nearly against my right shoulder, as I stood up on the incline of the root of the tree, his forehead about on a line with my chin, as near as I can tell. The tree was not more than 10 inches in diameter and that distance from the works made us quite a prominent mark for the enemy.

We could hear the bullets hit the tree and see the bark fly as they shot at us. Patterson remarked, "Captain, they might come over and take us in out of the wet." I started to look around the tree to see if anything of that kind was likely to occur. I had not more than looked when a ball—shot from an Enfield musket in the hands of an Alabama soldier—struck me on the left side of my chin in front of the stomach tooth, passed through the jaw, coming out on the right side three teeth forward of the angle of the jaw, cutting off my chin, except about three quarters of an inch at the corner of my mouth on the left side, and about a half inch on the right side, making an opening in which the small end of an ordinary broomstick could have been laid horizontally against the underside of my tongue.

After being struck I faced to the right to start to the rear and as I did so, Patterson settled back, grasping the flag and staff with both hands in front of him, falling to the ground straight and stiff, apparently as if he had been laid there, and the colors arranged or draped over him as tastefully as if done by the tenderest of female hands.

SHERMAN'S DEPARTMENT—ENGAGEMENT AT SNAKE CREEK GAP, GEORGIA, FROM A SKETCH BY THEODORE R. DAVIS.—[SEE PAGE 355.]

THE WAR IN GEORGIA.

We give on this page two illustrations of recent events in Georgia, sketched on the spot by our artist, THEODORE R. DAVIS. The capture of Dug Gap by General GEARY'S Division of HOOKER'S Corps was an achievement worthy of the veterans who had already earned renown by their bravery at Mission Ridge. The assault was made on the 8th instant. Ridge after ridge was carried by the fearless veterans, who climbed the perpendicular crags with steady feet, often crossing rocky gorges where a single false step would have been instantly fatal, and at last swept the enemy from the heights as so much chaff. Mr. DAVIS writes: "Captain BARTLETT, commanding a storming party of the Thirty-third New Jersey, was killed on the last crest. The Thirty-third behaved with splendid valor. Our loss was 250 killed and wounded. Some of our troops, after they had actually climbed the last ridge to the crest of the pall ade formation, were hurled from the top by the rebels, who, instead of taking them prisoners, preferred to mangle the brave boys among the rocks beneath. The place was defended by STEVENSON'S Rebel Division. Colonel CLARK, of the 145th New York, was among those thrown from the top." For an account of the engagement at Snake Creek Gap see news page.

SHERMAN'S DEPARTMENT—GENERAL GEARY'S ASSAULT ON DUG GAP, GEORGIA.—[FROM A SKETCH BY THEODORE R. DAVIS.]

This page from the June 4, 1864, edition of Harper's Weekly illustrates the two phases of Sherman's opening movements. The lower engraving shows Brigadier General John W. Geary's Federal division moving up to attack the Rebel-held rock palisades on either side of the narrow passage at Dug Gap. Despite the claim of the newspaper caption that the troops "swept the enemy from the heights as so much chaff," the attack itself was a total failure. The upper engraving shows McPherson's Federals on the attack after their successful flanking movement around Rocky Face Ridge. Horsemen from the 9th Illinois Mounted Infantry, the vanguard of McPherson's column, engage Confederate cavalrymen at the southern entrance of Snake Creek Gap, in the rear of Johnston's main force.

PRIVATE THOMAS W. MOFFATT

12TH ILLINOIS INFANTRY, BURKE'S BRIGADE

Six days after passing through Snake Creek Gap, Private Moffatt celebrated his 20th birthday. Born in Orillia, Ontario, Moffatt moved with his family to Amboy, Illinois, when he was three. After the war, he returned to Ontario, where as a constable he was credited with the capture of a number of "desperados."

*I*t was pitch dark, and a few minutes after we joined the regiment our cavalry proceeded up the Gap. They had not gone very far before they met and engaged the enemy in combat. We were right behind them, sloshing along over the stones and water of Snake Creek Gap. The road over which we were passing was probably the finest in the world as far as dustlessness was concerned for it was the flat bed of Snake Creek. We splashed along in this, sometimes stumbling and falling and always feeling for the man in front of us, so dark was it. Occasionally we would halt and stand breathless while our pickets drove back the pickets of the enemy. At times we would see the flash of a gun in the hills on either side and hear the zing of the bullet as it passed somewhere near us.

The boots I was wearing that night were not the regulation army boots but were a pair I had purchased while in the north on furlough. The long marches had weakened them and this jaunt up Snake Creek was the last straw. At the toe the upper parted company with the sole and on account of the thinness of the latter it bent back exposing the whole fore part of my foot to the stones over which we were stumbling. If I had happened to have stood in the path of a rebel bullet that night I do not think the rebels would have found much to interest them in the way of loot, at least on my feet, when they found me in the morning. . . .

In this way we carried on during the rest of the night and daylight found us well advanced toward the southern end of the gap. During all this time the cavalry up ahead was driving back the enemy.

As soon as it was daylight we lay down on each side of the road or the creek, (whichever you prefer) and other troops passed toward the front between the ranks of our tired feet. This marching continued for hours; artillery, infantry and cavalry passing with their commanders.

In this way I had the pleasure of reviewing almost the whole of the Army of the Tennessee moving into battle as I lay resting at the side of the road. I saw McPherson and Logan with their staffs as they passed by.

COLONEL JAMES COOPER NISBET

66TH GEORGIA INFANTRY, STEVENS' BRIGADE

Nisbet spent the first two years of the war as a company officer in the eastern theater. After the Battle of Fredericksburg he was given permission to return home to Georgia and raise a regiment. In the fall of 1864 Nisbet and his year-old 66th Georgia found themselves directly in the path of McPherson's army.

*O*n the first of May I received an order to go to Resaca, to guard the Western and Atlantic Railroad bridge across the Oostenaula River, relieving the 1st Florida Regiment. On the march Hamilton said: "Well, Nisbet, what would our leader, Stonewall, think of us? Going eighteen miles to the rear to guard a bridge, at the beginning of a campaign? Let's beat our swords into ploughshares and pruning hooks and make a garden; the time and opportunity seem to be favorable."

. . . In a few days, the cavalry scouts brought to me a Negro girl who stated that she lived . . . on the Snake Creek Gap road; that she was on her way to Resaca to get medicine for "old mistiss" when she was overhauled by some mounted soldiers in blue who took her horse. . . .

The cavalry officer who brought the girl to me said he was sure that they were Yanks, so I informed General Johnston that there was a force of the enemy's cavalry in Snake Creek Gap. . . .

I was very uneasy that night, and the next morning, for I realized that McPherson could capture Resaca if he advanced in force. After a while I was informed that there was a train at the station loaded with troops. I hastened down there and met Brigadier General James Cantey, who [had with him] about two thousand strong. . . .

We rode out about a mile on the Snake Creek Gap road. I stopped and informed him that it was as far as we could go with safety. . . . I advised him to keep all of our little force concentrated in the works around the bridge; that if we could hold it against McPherson's Corps of twenty-three thousand men until Johnston could send us reenforcements we would do well.

Resaca

Determined to make a stand at Resaca, on May 13 Johnston positioned his forces along a ridge that lay between the Conasauga and Oostanaula Rivers and protected the line of the Western & Atlantic Railroad. Rather than launch an immediate assault, Sherman deployed four of his corps to pin Johnston in place while McPherson's Army of the Tennessee moved south to probe for an opening in the enemy left flank.

On the afternoon of May 13 Major General John A. Logan's XV Corps arrived just west of Resaca and drove in the outlying Confederate skirmish line. Logan discovered that Johnston had anchored his southern flank—Leonidas Polk's corps—on a bend in the Oostanaula, thus preventing any flank attack at that point.

Temporarily frustrated on the right, Sherman decided to strike at Johnston's center on the morning of May 14. The Federal attack began at 9:00 a.m. with a division of Major General John M. Palmer's XIV Corps pushing eastward across the valley of Camp Creek, toward the crest held by Hardee's corps. Slowed and disorganized by the swampy lowlands along the creek, the troops of the XIV Corps did not near Hardee's position until afternoon, and then they were hurled back by heavy Confederate fire.

Before the rest of the XIV Corps was fully deployed to resume the assault, Brigadier General Henry M. Judah launched a reckless charge with his division of Schofield's XXIII Corps. One brigade of the XIV Corps joined Judah's dash, but the Federals were torn apart by Rebel artillery salvos and the musketry of Hindman's and Bate's divisions.

Schofield, who four days later would relieve Judah of command for his "incompetency," committed Cox's division to support the attack on Hindman. Three times Cox gained a point within 75 yards of the Rebel line, but he was unable to breach the entrenched position, and his battered units withdrew.

On the Federal left, Howard's IV Corps came into action against the northern flank of Johnston's line, where it angled east to the banks of the Conasauga River. Howard's assault was no more successful than Schofield's had been, and his troops only managed to carry an advanced line of rifle pits before recoiling with heavy losses.

Seeking an opportunity to flank the Yankees, Johnston lashed out at Howard's wavering ranks with two divisions of Hood's corps in the early evening. Major Generals Carter L. Stevenson and Alexander P. Stewart wheeled against the Federal left flank and were about to overrun a battery of artillery when the timely arrival of troops from Hooker's XX Corps restored the Union line.

The only substantial Federal success on May 14 came at 6:00 p.m., when several brigades of Logan's XV Corps managed to clear Polk's troops from high ground on the southern left flank. Polk pulled back to a new position closer to the railroad and the town of Resaca, while the Yankees dug in along the former Confederate line.

As Sherman tried and failed to break Johnston's line, McPherson's troops discovered a way to pry the Confederate army out of its formidable defensive position. Sweeny's division of the XVI Corps moved several miles south of Resaca to Lay's Ferry, where the Oostanaula made a loop to the west. On the late afternoon of May 14, Sweeny brushed aside a handful of Confederate cavalry and

crossed two regiments in pontoon boats to the river's southern shore. Learning that Major General William H. T. Walker's Confederate division was en route to secure the vulnerable bridgehead, Sweeny pulled his troops back across the river. But when Walker arrived to find the enemy gone, he drew back to the east, leaving the ferry unguarded. At Sherman's order, Sweeny recrossed the Oostanaula on May 15 with his entire division.

With Sweeny in position to cut the Western & Atlantic Railroad and block Johnston's line of retreat to Atlanta, Sherman shifted Hooker's XX Corps to bolster a renewed assault on the Confederate right. At 11:30 a.m. on May 15, Hooker's three divisions launched their attack, and Brigadier General William T. Ward's brigade managed to overrun an outlying Confederate earthwork, capturing a battery of Georgia artillery. But Hooker's attack stalled in front of Stewart's entrenchments, and when friendly troops mistakenly fired into the backs of Ward's men, the Federals abandoned the captured Rebel guns.

As the Yankees fell back in confusion, Johnston ordered Stewart out of his works in a counterattack. Johnston attempted to call off the maneuver when he learned that the Yankees had again crossed the Oostanaula at Lay's Ferry and were advancing toward the rear of his army. But Stewart was already heavily engaged. He lost nearly a thousand men before he was able to get back to his entrenchments.

Just after sundown Johnston summoned his senior officers and informed them that the army had no choice but to abandon the position at Resaca. Having failed to prevent Sweeny's troops from gaining the Confederate side of the river, Walker's division battled to hold the Federals at bay long enough for

Johnston to evacuate the Resaca defenses.

Under cover of darkness Johnston's troops disengaged and fell back to a tight perimeter just north of Resaca. From there the Rebel soldiers crossed the Oostanaula River on a temporary pontoon bridge, and in the early morning hours of May 16 they set fire to the railroad span to prevent it from falling into Yankee hands. They also ignited the nearby wagon bridge, but advancing Federal skirmishers managed to douse the flames.

Sherman was not aware of the full extent of Johnston's withdrawal until all but a handful of Rebel stragglers had made it safely across the Oostanaula River. Having successfully accomplished the risky evacuation of the Resaca line, Johnston continued to fall back southward along the line of the Western & Atlantic toward Adairsville, Kingston, and Cassville.

By the early afternoon of May 16 General Sherman's troops had repaired the damaged bridges at Resaca, and Howard's IV Corps was advancing in the wake of the retreating Confederate army.

The fighting at Resaca cost the Federals some 4,000 casualties, 600 of whom were killed or mortally wounded. Confederate losses totaled nearly 3,000, more than 500 of whom were captured. Bloody as the fight was, it was only the beginning of a grueling series of hard-fought engagements on the road to Atlanta.

For two bloody days, the Rebel army, positioned atop a commanding ridge overlooking Resaca, withstood furious Union assaults. The Rebels abandoned their defenses only when a Federal division threatened Johnston's line of retreat.

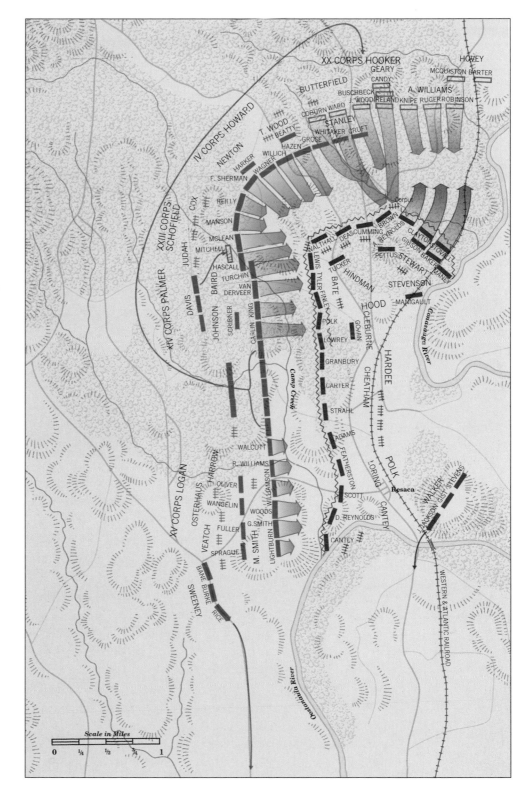

43

LIEUTENANT LOT D. YOUNG
4TH KENTUCKY (C.S.) INFANTRY, LEWIS' BRIGADE

The Federal attack at Resaca on May 14, poorly coordinated from the start, bogged down in the swampy ground that lay around Camp Creek at the base of the Rebel-held heights. The slaughter of the blue-coated ranks—joyously described here by Lieutenant Young—led four days later to the dismissal of General Henry Judah, who bore the blame for the fiasco.

When Sherman's columns four or five deep debouched from their positions—a long, heavily wooded ridge—into the narrow valley, on the East side of which we had constructed rifle pits, he found us ready to receive his gay and awe-inspiring columns, who moved in perfect step, with banners flying and bands playing, as though he expected to charm us.

The eagerness of our own men could scarcely be restrained until they had reached the point to which our orders had been given, seventy-five to eighty yards, when our lines opened almost simultaneously a deadly and murderous fire from both infantry and double-shotted artillery, that flesh and blood could not withstand. Retiring in disorder to their original position in the woods, they rallied and reformed, while their artillery was busy playing upon our batteries, from which they received no response whatever, a mystery at the time to many of us, but which we understood a little later on when they again moved down to the attack, to be met in the same manner with both infantry and artillery, and with similar results. Three times during the morning and early afternoon were these attacks made upon our lines, with the same results. It was a veritable picnic for the Confederates and was the second time in the history of the war, up to this time, that we had presented such a glorious opportunity, protected as we were by earthworks, with clear and open ground in front. Had Sherman continued this business during the entire day (as we hoped he would) the campaign would have ended right here, as we had not called into requisition any of our reserve force. The principal part of the afternoon was spent by the artillery—after the infantry had gotten enough of it—on both sides pounding away at each other in a lively and entertaining fashion.

One of the hardest hit units at Resaca was William P. Carlin's brigade, part of the XIV Corps contingent attacking on the right. Carlin's advancing men quickly suffered more than 200 casualties, and the brigade was forced to fall back to the feeble shelter of the creek, where some companies had to stand waist deep in water until darkness could cover their retreat. Among Carlin's dead was Captain E. Irvine McDowell (left), the commander of Company I, 15th Kentucky Infantry.

LIEUTENANT RALSA C. RICE
125TH OHIO INFANTRY, HARKER'S BRIGADE

Rice began the war with the 2d Ohio Cavalry, but after a few months he contracted measles and was discharged. In November 1862 he returned to the colors, this time with the 125th Ohio Infantry. That regiment was held in reserve during the fighting on May 14 but was forced to endure shelling through most of the day.

The first line of works, simply a pile of old logs thrown up, was now held by our men. The line was constructed by the enemy with an evident purpose of abandonment as they were enfiladed by their artillery in the second line. On our way in we followed the low ground which was covered with brush and an occasional

"Sherman's columns . . . moved in perfect step, with banners flying and bands playing, as though he expected to charm us."

GEN. JOSEPH E. JOHNSTON.
Commanding Confederate States Army.

BATTLE OF RESACA, GA.
On the line of the Western & Atlantic Railroad.
May 15, 1864.
The attempt against Gen. Hindman's position by a portion of the Army of the Cumberland.

GEN. WM. T. SHERMAN,
Commanding United States Army,

A Confederate battle line from Hindman's division pours murderous volleys into a mass of Federals struggling up a slope at Resaca. Though artist Alfred Waud rendered the terrain accurately, he took a bit of dramatic license by placing the Rebels out in front of their earthworks, an unlikely position unless they themselves were attacking.

"My head was full of a buzzing din, and the sound of that blood falling on the ground seemed louder than a cataract."

tree. The first thing of note was a cannon shot coming down our line, out of reach, but near enough for discomfort. A trio of officers, Generals Manson, Cox and Harker, was sitting on a log near where we were then passing. The next shot followed the first one on nearly the same line, lower and more to the right of us. It found these officers and the middle one, General Manson, was struck by it. I was then a Lieutenant, following along on the flank of the company, and was just opposite the log mentioned. General Cox was nearest me. He was thrown on the ground by the concussion. On regaining his feet he seemed bewildered. I said, "General, this is a warm place!" "Yes," he replied, "you are right about that." I could not stop to inquire further. I did not see General Cox again until many years after the war. I then reminded him of this incident. Needless to say, I needed no further introduction to him.

SERGEANT JAMES L. COOPER
20TH TENNESSEE (C.S.) INFANTRY, TYLER'S BRIGADE

Recovering from a wound received at Missionary Ridge in November 1863, Cooper returned to his regiment in March, only to be hit again at Resaca. This time a Minié ball passed through his neck, miraculously missing his spine and major blood vessels. On his return in July he was given a commission and an appointment on the brigade staff. After the war, he went back to his home in Nashville and eventually became a top breeder of Jersey cattle.

During the night of the 13th we worked at the fortification, and on the 14th, about 12 o'clock the enemy advanced in force, and began a heavy attack. We repulsed several assaults, and about three o'clock we were sitting behind our rail piles waiting for another charge. At this time I was shot by a sharpshooter who had crawled within a short distance from the works. I was sitting down, closely wedged in by my companions on every side, for the position was very exposed, when all at once I felt a terrible shock and with a sinking consciousness of dying, became insensible. In an instant I recovered my senses, and found myself with my head fallen forward on my breast, and without power to move a muscle. I could hear the blood from my wound pattering on the ground, and thinking I was dying, almost thought I saw eternity opening before me. I felt so weak, so powerless, that I did not know whether I was dead or not. The noise of the battle seemed miles away, and my thoughts were all pent up in my own breast. My system was paralyzed, but my mind was terribly active. My head was full of a buzzing din, and the sound of that blood falling on the ground seemed louder than a cataract. I finally recovered the use of my tongue and still thinking I was dying, told the boys that it was no use to do anything for me, that I was a dead man. All this time I could hear remarks around me, which, although very complimentary, were not at all consoling. When first shot one man exclaimed, "By God, they killed a good one that time," another "My God! Cooper's killed," and several other equal to these. Finally Capt. Lucas directed the man directly behind me, J. Gee, of Co. D to catch hold of the wound and try to stop the blood. To my surprise he succeeded, and in half an hour, or less time, I had sufficiently recovered my strength to start to the rear. I walked half a mile through perfect showers of balls, and reached the ambulance perfectly exhausted. I was taken to the hospital, and after being exposed to some danger from shells, that night we were taken to the railroad, and then to Atlanta. I suffered some from my wounds before I reached Atlanta but was well cared for when I was taken to the hospitals. I was about the most forsaken looking object that came to that place, I know, and when I got off the cars felt pretty sheepish. The entire "crystal of my pants" was gone, and I was covered with blood and dirt, so I had reasons for feeling sheepish, being exposed to the sharp eyes of about four hundred ladies. If their eyes were sharp, their hands and hearts were tender as I soon experienced.

PRIVATE ROBERT H. STRONG

105TH ILLINOIS INFANTRY, WARD'S BRIGADE

After a year and a half on garrison duty, Strong's regiment got its first taste of front-line fighting as part of Hooker's attack on May 15. The Yankees overran Captain Maximillian van den Corput's Georgia battery but were soon forced to withdraw. That evening a Federal work party returned and hauled away the Rebel guns.

We first had to cross a small field and then go through a scattered peach orchard. Then, on a hill beyond, the fort sat waiting. As soon as we skirmishers moved out of the woods onto the field, the Rebs began shooting at us. Someone cried out that there was a sharpshooter in a tree sniping at us. So, in spite of our orders not to fire, a dozen of us fired into the tree. The man came tumbling down, legs spread out, and struck the ground with a thud. I remember thinking as he fell he resembled a big squirrel.

We advanced with no more shooting on our part. The bugle sung out "Skirmishers, lie down," and in the next minute, "Charge!" and the rest of the boys went over us with a yell. Most of the skirmishers, I among them, got up and joined the charging column and went up the hill with the rest. We were driven back from the works once, but in a moment we rallied and without waiting for orders—men were dropping all around us, but we had no time to look after them—with a rush and a cheer, which I can imagine I hear now, we drove the Rebs from the first line of works back into the second line, where their cannon were. . . .

A great many amusing and pathetic incidents happened during and after our charge, only a few of which I will repeat. Undoubtedly you remember the massacre of the prisoners captured at Fort Pillow, Kentucky, by the Rebel General Nathan Bedford Forrest. Well, when we rushed from the first line that we captured to the second line, where the Rebel cannon were, we of course captured a good many prisoners.

Some of the enemy who refused to run or surrender were killed there. Some crawled under the gun carriages to escape the storm of bullets and bayonets.

One big red-headed man, a cannoneer, crawled out and begged for quarter. He had his shirt off, and on one arm was tattooed in big letters, "Fort Pillow." As soon as the boys saw the letters on his arm, they yelled, "No quarter for you!" and a dozen bayonets went into him and a dozen bullets were shot into him. I shall never forget his look of fear.

Captured on May 15, probably while deployed as a skirmisher, Private James M. Stedham of the 25th Alabama (above) was sent to prison at Camp Morton, outside Indianapolis. There he languished until March 5, 1865, when he succumbed, like so many fellow prisoners, to "acute dysentery," just weeks before the war's end.

CORPORAL EDMUND R. BROWN
27TH INDIANA INFANTRY, RUGER'S BRIGADE

Brown mustered in as a 17-year-old private in September 1861. Hit at Antietam, he later declined promotion to sergeant "over those absent wounded." Brown spent his last months of service as a clerk and later wrote the 27th's regimental history. Here he relates his unit's part in the repulse of Hood's attack against the Federal left on the afternoon of May 15.

At length, when the rebel force was only thirty-five yards away, the Colonel, speaking in slow, distinct tones, said, "Now, boys. Ready, aim, fire!" Then he fairly shrieked the one word "Charge!" and all the other officers repeated the word, with deeply surcharged feelings, "Charge!" Poor men of the misguided South! It was all over in one terrible minute of time, and the story is soon told. Thirty-three of those men who, a moment before, were advancing so confidently, lay dead at our feet! Fully as many more were too badly wounded to be able to move without assistance; thirty-five others, including the colonel, were in our hands as prisoners; while the balance simply turned and ran so promptly and swiftly that we were not able to get them. Many of them must have thrown down their guns to facilitate their flight, as the ground was covered with them. . . .

Colonel Lankford, the officer captured . . . was a short, stout-built man, and when taken, was sweaty, red in the face and puffing like a wood chopper. Of course he could not be otherwise than greatly crestfallen over the way matters had turned. He came very near losing his life, partly through a misapprehension. It happened, naturally, that the first members of the Twenty-seventh to reach him were enlisted men. They did not think of the point of honor involved in a person surrendering to one of his own class; while it seemed that Colonel Lankford was quite strenuous about it. Before he could make himself understood more than one soldier would have shot him, if others had not prevented them. They thought he was too slow in giving up his sword. When it was ascertained what his contention was, it required but a moment for one of our commissioned officers to step forward and receive the sword.

Although the Rebel assault on the Union left met with some success on May 14, a follow-up attack the next afternoon by Stewart's division brought only heavy losses. Among the captured were both the commander, Colonel A. R. Lankford, and the battle flag (above) of the 38th Alabama. Issued earlier that spring, the flag bears the crossed cannon awarded for the capture of enemy artillery.

CAPTAIN JAMES COMPTON
52D ILLINOIS INFANTRY, RICE'S BRIGADE

The action that finally pried the Rebels out of their earthworks around Resaca was the crossing of the Oostanaula River at Lay's Ferry by Sweeny's division, which included the 52d Illinois. The Federals got across using portable wood-framed canvas boats that were assembled well back from the river and then brought up under the cover of woods. Sweeny's men laid down heavy covering fire to keep the enemy from making short work of the flimsy craft.

Early in the morning of the 15th, the Second Division was again in motion. The passage of the river and the laying of the bridge were to be again attempted. The troops were again deployed and a line advanced to the river. The enemy at once opened from their side, and the fire seemed to be hotter than ever. I presume it so seemed because I was ordered to take three pontoons and in them cross with my command. As I was about to get into the leading boat, I felt as if

Abandoned Confederate earthworks, once manned by soldiers from Polk's corps, stand silent watch over the small town of Resaca (left background). Barely visible just beyond the town are the bridges over the Oostanaula River erected by the Federals to replace the spans burned by Johnston's retreating army.

I were between "the devil and the deep sea." In front were rebels, in the rear, General Sweeney, while, not Jordan, but the Oosta[n]aula, "rolled between." I was not anxious to cross to the opposite shore, for my "possessions" did not "lie there;" and moreover, I was always a little "gun shy". . . .

I was not so much afraid of being killed as of being drowned afterwards; I had early been taught to "shun the second death."

But General Sweeney (the boys called him "the Corporal") had a manner of giving his orders in staccato, reminding one of electricity or dynamite, and if any hesitancy was shown in obeying, his comments were rendered in three languages, English, Irish-American and profane, thickly punctuated with exclamation points—making it decidedly unpleasant for the person addressed. Therefore it took me but a moment to decide to face the "rebs," and I gave the command,

"There is something terrible to me in this nameless resting place, this unknown burial."

"steady, boys," and jumped into the boat. Every officer here knows why I gave that command, for you all know that the more "shaky" an officer was, the greater was his anxiety to "steady" the boys.

All being in readiness, we started and the oarsmen pulled with a will. The Oostenaula is only a hundred yards wide, but at that time I would have certified that it was the broadest river in the [world]! The enemy did not discover us until we were well under way, and we crossed with the loss of only two men wounded, in my boat. We deployed under the bank and advanced into the woods, driving the enemy before us. Other companies soon followed, and it was not long until our whole regiment, the 52nd Illinois, was over and the enemy driven far enough from the ferry to allow the laying of the pontoons. As soon as the bridge was ready, both brigades of the division crossed and formed, the first brigade on the right, or West of the road, and the second on the left. Earthworks were thrown up and we were there to stay. Johnston's flank had been turned.

PRIVATE HIRAM S. WILLIAMS
Pioneer Corps, Army of Tennessee

Born and raised in New Jersey, Williams completed his carriage maker's apprenticeship in 1854 but spent the next few years stumping for the nativist Know-Nothing party in the Midwest. In 1861, two years after moving to Alabama, Williams enlisted in the Confederate army. On the night of May 15, 1864, temporarily detached from his construction duties, he was assigned to help get the wounded across the Oostanaula during the retreat from Resaca.

How shall I describe the past night? If I live to the allotted period of man's existence, I can never forget the scenes I have witnessed for they are indelibly stamped on my memory. Limbs mangled and torn, much suffering and pain—Oh, Lord! It was truly horrible. About two o'clock last night we were ordered to assist our Division Surgeons about getting the wounded men on board the train bound for Atlanta. The wounded for the whole Corps were scattered about on every side. Some in a deserted house, some under rough shelters of brush, some in tents, and others on the cold ground with no covering but their blankets. By passing once through the grounds, we could find men suffering from all kinds of wounds. Here on a rough table the surgeons were amputating a leg, on another one's arm was being taken off, while a score of others just taken from the ambulances were awaiting their turn, with all manner of wounds claiming attention. There one could see what ever was. In the hospital after the wounds are dressed it is bad enough, but it is no comparison to the battle-field hospital. I saw one poor fellow belonging to a Texas Reg who had his leg almost torn off by a cannon ball just above the knee, the bones crushed and torn out, only adhereing to the trunk by a few pieces of skin, who had been bounced for nearly 6 miles in an old wagon of an ambulance over roads far from being good. Yet he was still alive and perfectly reliable in his speech.

In moving the wounded, it was really heart rendering to listen to their groans and cries. Several had been shot directly through the bowels, and the least movement caused them to suffer intensely. After loading three trains with the wounded, we were called upon to bury three men who had died since being brought to the hospitals. We dug a shallow grave some three feet deep by 4 feet wide and laid the three poor soldiers in it side by side and covering them with their blankets. We covered them up as hastily as possible for day was fast approaching, and the enemies guns at Resaca, the light of burning bridges, and the reports of soldiers all told us that the enemy would soon be upon us. What a burial! Unknown, they were inhumanly, *treacherously,* buried by stranger hands. Yet, no doubt that they had fast and loving friends and relatives, who if they could, would have closed their eyes and performed the last sad rites of the dead, with tears in their eyes and sighs of true grief. But now their friends will never know where they sleep "the last unwaking sleep," for no rough board even marks their resting place. There is something terrible to me in this nameless resting place, this unknown burial, I trust it may never be my lot to die and be buried thus.

PRIVATE JOHN F. BROBST

25TH WISCONSIN INFANTRY, SPRAGUE'S BRIGADE

By the spring of 1864 Brobst's regiment, like many other western units called up in the second year of the war, had spent most of its time in miserable camps along the Mississippi River, losing far more men to disease than to the enemy. As Brobst explains to his friend and future wife, Mary Englesby, after Resaca, a soldier's life demands more than just standing up to the enemy's guns.

Now, Mary, I have always said I never would discourage any person in regard to enlisting, but if I was in your father's place I should not enlist, for he has a family and there is enough that has none, that can go better than he can. If I had a family I should never [have] enlisted. There are plenty of ways to get clear of a draft, and make money while he is doing it. Go and hire out for a government teamster or a brakesman on the cars, get thirty-five or forty dollars per month while they are drafting, then quit and go home about your business and it [is] nobody's business. I should not try to stop or say one word to keep any other man from enlisting. It is very hard to be a soldier. No matter how bad the weather is you must go. If it rains you must stand or sleep out, with not as much as a leaf to shelter you from the storm. Perhaps have about half a meal for two days, and that the poorest kind of living. . . . This is not the case at all times, for when we are where we can get it we have plenty, and that which is good, but the most of the time we are on the move and then we cannot get such as is fit for a man to eat.

Now, I will tell you as near as I can what the load is that a soldier has to carry, and march from 15 to 25 miles a day. He has a gun that weighs 11 pounds, cartridges and cartridge box about 6 pounds, woolen blanket 3 pounds, rubber blanket 5 pounds, two shirts, two pairs of drawers about 3 pounds, canteen full of water which they oblige you to keep full all the time, which is about 6 pounds, then three or five days' rations, which will weigh about 8 pounds, and then your little trinkets that we need, perhaps 2 pounds, makes a total of about 45 or 50 pounds. That is what makes us think of our homes in these hot days.

Well, I must tell you what I have been doing today. I have been washing all the forepart of the day. You would have thought I was some old maid washing away there all alone, no one to bother me at all. I can wash, cook, sew, do anything as well as any of the girls. I will be all ready to keep a bachelor's hall when I get home. Then my sign over the door will be, "Positively no admittance for ladies."

I wish the people up north would send them tormented old baches off to the war up there, or they will steal all the girls away from us by the time that we get back, and we will have to wait for the young ones to grow up. Oh, if I really knew that this would be the case I should try and get shot, I do believe. What a good thing it is that we cannot read the future, do you not think so?

Well, I must stop and go and see if I can't find a secesh sheep that is playing the spy on us, and will have to be shot and have his bones picked. Oh, I am one of the lowest grade of men. I go right in a man's yard, steal a sheep, hog or chicken, cow or anything that I can find, take off a corpse before the eyes of the owner, and if [he] says anything tell him to dry up or he will get his wind shut off for a year or two. I expect all such kinds of animals will run and yell as soon as they see us coming home.

KATE CUMMING
CONFEDERATE NURSE

Over her family's objections, Scottish-born Cumming left her home in Mobile, Alabama, in 1862 to join a corps of volunteer nurses formed to care for the wounded from Shiloh. Later, as a matron of the Confederate hospital at Newnan, Georgia, Cumming wrote of the frustration and heart-ache brought about by the lack of adequate supplies and facilities.

May 24. . . . We have a number of the sick and wounded from the Twenty-ninth Alabama Regiment. One lad, in his sixteenth year, is very ill; he requested me to write to his father, and let him know where he is. I said why not write to your mother. After hesitating awhile, tears filled his eyes, and with a quivering lip he told me she was deranged on account of her sons all leaving her for the army; he had run away two years ago. Dr. Hughes intends sending him home as soon as he is able to travel. . . .

We daily see soldiers who have come from the front, ragged, barefooted, and half-starved, while right along side of them men dressed in the best the land can afford, and eating the best of fare. To get all of this they are defrauding soldiers of the comforts provided for them by the government.

I have been told of one man who a year ago was not worth a cent; he was made commissary of a hospital post, and is now worth thousands.

We are badly off for dishes, spoons, and knives and forks; of the last we are much in need. The men have to eat with their fingers. A hospital is all very well when we can get what we want, but to live as we do—with just half enough of food and furniture—it is a very trying place.

Defended by a Rebel fort on the hilltop at left, the narrow gorge at Allatoona Pass offered dismal prospects for any direct assault. The repulse at Resaca was enough for Sherman. On May 20 he ordered his columns to leave the railroad, bypass Allatoona, and head southwest toward the small town of Dallas.

New Hope Church, Pickett's Mill, and Dallas

Johnston continued to retreat south across the Etowah River to the high ground at Allatoona Pass. Sherman, in pursuit, declined to risk a costly frontal assault; instead, he decided to cut loose from the railroad, cross the Etowah, and bypass Johnston's position from the west.

All three Union armies moved out on May 23. Schofield skirted Johnston's left flank, while Thomas, in the center, marched on New Hope Church, southwest of Allatoona. McPherson's army swung farthest to the west and marched on Dallas, a crossroads southwest of New Hope Church. If all went according to plan, Johnston would be forced to fall back from Allatoona in order to secure his vulnerable railroad lifeline to Atlanta, and Sherman would win a bloodless strategic victory.

But as the Federal armies closed in on their objectives, Confederate cavalry alerted General Johnston, who moved quickly to counter the threat. Johnston ordered a series of westward shifts, and by May 24 a solid nine-mile front blocked Sherman's line of march—Hardee on the left, Polk in the center, and Hood on the right. Johnston's army dug in and prepared to meet the Yankees.

On the late morning of May 25 Hooker's corps was approaching New Hope Church when the leading division, commanded by General Geary, met sudden and unexpected resistance from Stewart's Confederates. Geary deployed his men in line of battle and began throwing up log breastworks, hoping to maintain his position until the rest of Thomas' army arrived.

At 4:00 p.m. all three of Hooker's divisions renewed the advance, attacking in parallel columns as the skies opened in a torrential downpour. "It was simply slaughter," one Federal recalled; "scores and hundreds of men surged right up to the breastworks and died there." Within minutes Hooker's corps was repulsed with nearly 1,600 casualties.

Having failed at New Hope Church, Sherman decided two days later to shift Howard's IV Corps to Pickett's Mill, a mile beyond the Confederate right flank. From there Howard could advance southwest, rolling up Johnston's line and breaking the stalemate. But Johnston had again guessed Sherman's intentions, and as Howard neared Pickett's Mill he found Hindman's and Cleburne's divisions dug in along a ridge and ready to meet him.

At 4:30 p.m. on May 27, Howard launched the divisions of Brigadier Generals Thomas J. Wood and Richard W. Johnson in a head-on assault against the Confederate position. Once again the Federals advanced in compact columns of brigades, and just as at New Hope Church, the blue-clad ranks were savaged by canister and musketry. Wave after wave of Federal troops pressed on only to be hurled back with staggering losses. Cleburne's division mounted a series of counterattacks that further demoralized the bloodied Yankee brigades, and the fight continued well past sundown. At 10:00 p.m. a final charge by Brigadier General Hiram B. Granbury's Texas brigade drove Howard's men from the field. Some 3,000 Federals fell at Pickett's Mill, nearly 10 times the Confederate loss.

Following this second costly reverse, Sherman began to shift his armies back to the line of the Western & Atlantic. On May 28, when Johnston realized Sherman was again on the move, he ordered a reconnaissance of the Federal lines at Dallas to determine if McPherson's army was withdrawing.

Shortly after 4:00 p.m., a reconnaissance by Bate's division discovered that McPherson's army had not moved. And Bate's Rebels found their way blocked by Logan's XV Corps. Frank C. Armstrong's brigade of Mississippi cavalry, fighting dismounted, attacked first and briefly penetrated Logan's lines, capturing a battery of artillery. But the Yankees quickly rallied and recaptured the guns. Hearing the firing, General Lewis impetuously launched his Kentucky brigade and, joined by Jesse J. Finley's brigade, briefly made some headway against the Yankees. But the attack was unsupported, and the Rebels fell back after heavy losses.

Determined to prevent Sherman from shifting eastward, Johnston kept up the pressure on the Federal right in a series of assaults that pinned McPherson's army in place for nearly three days. By now many of the weary Yankees had taken to calling the battle-scarred area the Hell Hole. But by June 1 McPherson had managed to reach New Hope Church, enabling Thomas and Schofield to pull their armies out of the entrenchments and gain the line of the Western & Atlantic at Acworth. From there Sherman shifted south along the railroad to Big Shanty, midway between Allatoona and Marietta.

By mid-June Johnston had taken a new position along the rugged slopes and ridge lines that connected Lost, Pine, and Brush Mountains. Beyond these crests lay the still more formidable Kennesaw Mountain, and within this natural fortress the Army of Tennessee prepared to meet Sherman's next move.

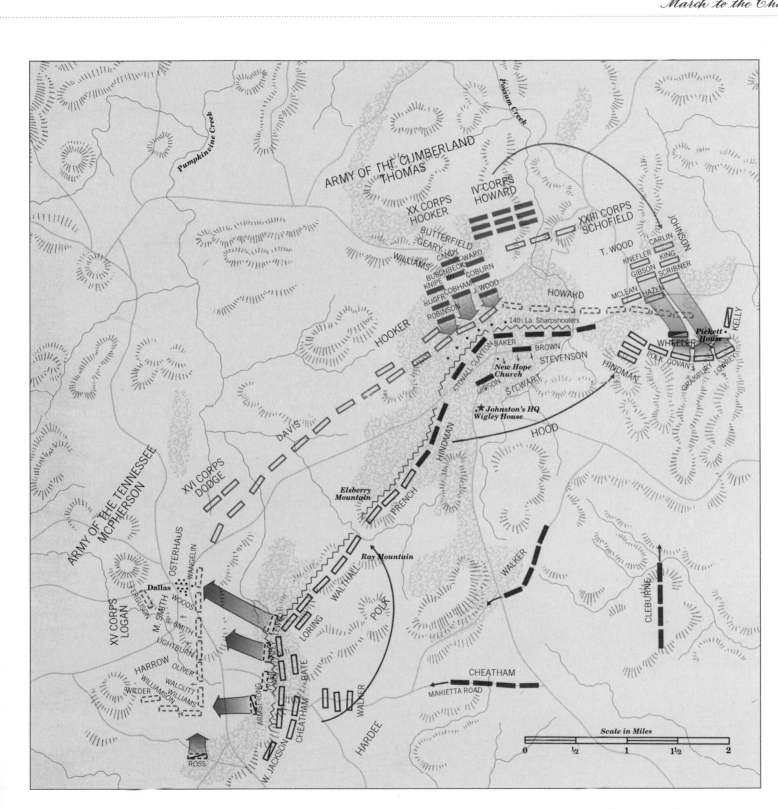

After the Confederates shifted west to block a Federal flanking movement, the two armies found themselves locked in a furious week-long engagement.

PRIVATE CHARLES E. BENTON

150TH NEW YORK INFANTRY, RUGER'S BRIGADE

Benton's regiment had served in Alpheus Williams' division since the Gettysburg campaign in 1863, ample time for its members to become familiar with the general's revealing mannerisms. After the battle at New Hope Church, Benton, a 23-year-old farmer from New York, apparently had seen enough of the front line. For the next three months he secured temporary duty as a nurse in a field hospital.

If "Pop" Williams ever had any emotions, he took good care not to let them show in his face, for through all times and places it wore an expression of impenetrable good nature which was a closed book to the would-be mind-readers. But there was one thing which he failed to mask, and that was the cigar which was carried in his mouth most of the time. Was it lighted and emitting a cheerful cloud of smoke? All would be quiet for the day. Had it been allowed to go out, while the end was being violently chewed? Then plans were maturing and some new movement was on foot. But when it was frequently shifted from side to side in his mouth and kept rolling over and over between the lips, "like a log in the peeler," as the paper-pulp man said, then there would surely be a fight before dark.

This battle near New Hope Church was a surprise to many, for it opened with the suddenness of a cyclone descending from a clear sky, without the usual prelude of skirmish firing. But those mind-readers who had carefully noted his cigar that morning as the General rode past with his staff said that it had not been lighted at all, but was rolling between his lips with unusual vigor.

Alpheus S. Williams received his commission as brigadier general in 1861 on the basis of his service with the Michigan militia. Despite commendable performances in several battles, he was consistently passed over in favor of Regular Army officers and never rose in rank during the war, a predicament that left him embittered but unshaken in his resolve to finish the fight.

CORPORAL EDMUND R. BROWN

27TH INDIANA INFANTRY, RUGER'S BRIGADE

At New Hope Church, Williams' division charged into the fire of Stewart's Confederates, who 10 days before had charged the Federals at Resaca. Reflecting on his regiment's loss of 50 men at Resaca, Brown noted that "conditions being more than reversed, it is not surprising that results should, in a measure, be reversed also."

Suddenly, a most terrific fire of both musketry and artillery was opened upon us. We were at the foot of, or passing up, a gentle slope. On the crest, barely a few rods distant, was a long parapet blazing with fire and death. The undergrowth was so dense that few, if any, of us were aware of what we were coming to, until the storm burst. It came with so little premonition on our part, that it almost seemed as if the position had been purposely masked, and that we had been decoyed to our death. This impression may have prevailed among us to some extent afterwards. It is scarcely necessary to say that such was not the case. The timber which, for lack of time and means, the enemy could not cut away, had, until now, prevented them from seeing us, as well as us from seeing them.

It would be impossible to conceive of a more appalling, terrifying, if not fatal, rain of lead and iron than this one, which our line met at New Hope Church. The canister and case shot in particular, hissed, swished and sung around and among us, barking the trees, glancing and bounding from one to the other, ripping up the ground, throwing the dirt in our faces and rolling at our feet, until those not hit by them were ready to conclude that they surely would be hit. Milton's words were none too strong to apply to the situation:

"Fierce as ten furies and terrible as hell."

Yet the boys only cheered the more defiantly, and, while loading and firing with all their might, gained ground to the front. Just in the hottest of the fight there was a downpour of rain. In the damp and murky

BATTLE OF NEW HOPE CHURCH — "THE HELL HOLE."
May 25, 1864.

GEN. ALEX. P. STEWART,   "New Hope" * * * from the bloody fighting there for the next week, was called by the soldiers "Hell Hole."—   GEN. JOSEPH HOOKER,
Commanding Confederate States Forces.   SHERMAN'S MEMOIRS, VOL. II., page 44.   Commanding United States Forces.

atmosphere the smoke from our muskets, instead of rising and disappearing, settled around us and accumulated in thick clouds. The woods in which we were immersed became [weird] and spectral. Eventually it became almost a battle in the dark. When we were finally brought to a standstill it was impossible to make out with any distinctness even the position of the enemy. Our aim was directed almost wholly at the flashes and reports of their guns.

The landscape for this Waud engraving was based on a photograph taken of the shattered New Hope Church battlefield not long after the fighting there on the afternoon of May 25, 1864. As the Yankees stumbled through the dense undergrowth toward a barely visible Rebel line, "the shot and shell from the enemy's batteries crashed through the timber," one survivor recalled, "cutting off limbs, blazing and splitting trees, like tremendous bolts of lightning."

PRIVATE ISAAC N. RAINEY

7TH TENNESSEE (C.S.) CAVALRY, ESCORT, W. JACKSON'S DIVISION

The second of eight sons, Private Rainey joined up on March 20, 1863, 16 days shy of his 18th birthday. His father gave him a good horse and a captured Yankee saddle, and his mother sewed him a uniform, cap, and overcoat. In April 1864 his unit was assigned to Johnston's army, giving Rainey the chance to spend time with his older brother, Captain Joseph Rainey of the 48th Tennessee Infantry.

I was sent with a message to an officer somewhere near New Hope. Message delivered and too far to go back, I begged shelter at a farm house within half a mile of the church. About daylight there was heavy cannonading and musketry. I got up, dressed and saddled my horse. I knew Joe's command was in it. Cannon shot and bullets were flying thick over and about the house. The farmer,

Immediately after graduating from the University of Alabama in 1861, Captain John G. Finley (above) raised a company, the Montgomery Cadets, and subsequently served with the artillery before transferring to the 22d Alabama Infantry. Wounded in the shoulder at New Hope Church, Finley took a short leave before returning to duty for the rest of the war.

his wife and two pretty daughters were much alarmed. One of the girls ran to me and begged me to save her and threw her arms around me. I didn't object to that but it was embarrassing especially as mammy and pappy were looking on. I told them to go inside the big log house. I galloped toward the church, and met wounded soldiers walking away from the battle. The very first man I noticed was Joe sitting in the church yard on a flat tombstone. He looked tired. He said his company had just come in from the line of fight for a rest. That he had fired forty rounds. As we sat "spat" struck the stone, then another and another. I said: "Joe let's get away from here!" "Oh what's the use? One place is as good as another!" Just then the company was called to "fall in" and I left him.

PRIVATE BENJAMIN T. SMITH

51ST ILLINOIS INFANTRY, HARKER'S BRIGADE

Shortly before the Atlanta campaign Smith received an appointment as a personal orderly to Brigadier General John Newton, commander of the 2d Division, IV Corps. Near midnight on May 25, Smith returned from a courier mission "ready to drop off my horse, for the want of sleep." He and a companion had just lain down between a pair of logs, using saddles for pillows, when chaos erupted.

A bout the time we had settled down, one of our pickets posted only a short distance in front of our works, thought he saw something suspicious moving in front of his vision, and fired his gun off at it; a dozen shots followed. The rebels thinking a night attack was on foot opened fire from behind their works all along our front, not five hundred yards distant from our line. The way their shot and shell came tearing over was a caution, our men thinking the rebs were coming, opened fire from the batteries, and the infantry pored in their lead; all the rattle of ten thousand rifles and fifty cannon, made a pandemonium of sound and awoke the echoes of the more than Egyptian darkness. All the boys ran down to get behind the works, yelling to Morse and I to hurry up. But we just lowered our heads from off the saddles and lay still, by mutual agreement; Mitchell commenced to utter a long string of curses, as he usually does when excited, but we paid no heed to him, we concluded we were as safe there as any where. We could hear the bullets sing over us, and now and then "zip" one would bury it self in our logs, or glance over its top; the shells all passed over too high to hit anything but the trees, or sail through their branches.

Both sides wasted little time digging in after the opening clash at New Hope Church on May 25. Stretches of the densely wooded landscape were transformed into complexes of log traverses, rifle pits, and dugouts (above). The narrow no man's land kept marksmen in both armies busy until the line was abandoned on June 4.

For the thirty minutes it lasted the air was pretty well filled with flying lead and iron. It finally dawned upon the enemy, and our men, that there was not going to be any assault from either side; firing ceased, almost as suddenly as it had commenced, when quiet reigned again. The contrast, of the stillness was so great, from the thunderous roar, that one could almost hear a pin drop, but the air seemed to quiver or vibrate, or the drums of our ears caused the feeling. The boys all returned to their evacuated positions, and finding us all safe, turning in I went to sleep in no time.

"Suddenly there came a ringing rattle of musketry, the familiar hissing of bullets, and before us the interspaces of the forest were all blue with smoke."

LIEUTENANT AMBROSE BIERCE

STAFF, BRIGADIER GENERAL WILLIAM B. HAZEN

After distinguished military service, Bierce went to California to embark on a journalism career and soon established himself as one of the country's most popular writers. Several of his pieces were drawn from his wartime experiences, such as the selection here, excerpted from "The Crime at Pickett's Mill."

We moved forward. In less than one minute the trim battalions had become simply a swarm of men struggling through the undergrowth of the forest, pushing and crowding. The front was irregularly serrated, the strongest and bravest in advance, the others following in fan-like formations, variable and inconstant, ever defining themselves anew. For the first two hundred yards our course lay along the left bank of a small creek in a deep ravine, our left battalions sweeping along its steep slope. Then we came to the fork of the ravine. A part of us crossed below, the rest above, passing over both branches, the regiments inextricably intermingled, rendering all military formation impossible. The color-bearers kept well to the front with their flags, closely furled, aslant backward over their shoulders. Displayed, they would have been torn to rags by the boughs of the trees. Horses were all sent to the rear; the general and staff and all the field officers toiled along on foot as best they could. "We shall halt and form when we get out of this" said an aide-de-camp.

Suddenly there came a ringing rattle of musketry, the familiar hissing of bullets, and before us the interspaces of the forest were all blue with smoke. Hoarse, fierce yells broke out of a thousand throats. The forward fringe of brave and hardy assailants was arrested in its mutable extensions; the edge of our swarm grew dense and clearly defined as the foremost halted, and the rest pressed forward to align themselves beside them, all firing. The uproar was deafening; the air was sibilant with streams and sheets of missiles. In the steady, unvarying roar of small-arms the frequent shock of the cannon was rather felt than heard, but the gusts of grape which they blew into that populous wood were audible enough, screaming among the trees and cracking their stems and branches. We had, of course, no artillery to reply.

Our brave color-bearers were now all in the forefront of battle in the open, for the enemy had cleared a space in front of his breastworks. They held the colors erect, shook out their glories, waved them forward and back to keep them spread, for there was no wind. From where I stood, at the right of the line—we had "halted and formed," indeed—I could see six of our flags at one time. Occasionally one would go down, only to be instantly lifted by other hands.

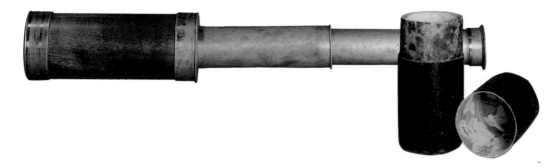

In February 1863 Ambrose Bierce was assigned to General Hazen's staff as his topographical engineer, duty that required special tools, such as his field glass, shown at left with its case. On June 23, 1864, a sharpshooter's bullet put Bierce out of action until after the fall of Atlanta.

SERGEANT ANDREW J. GLEASON
15TH OHIO INFANTRY, WILLICH'S BRIGADE

The original commander of the 15th Ohio's brigade, General August Willich, was wounded at Resaca and replaced by Colonel William H. Gibson; Brigadier General Samuel Beatty fell sick on May 23 and was succeeded by Colonel Frederick Knefler. Then came the "slaughter-pen" at Pickett's Mill that left nearly 1,500 vacancies in the ranks, one of which was filled by Gleason, who was promoted to lieutenant shortly afterward.

The line advanced into a ravine close to the rebel works, where it met with a decided check, and having little protection was in a literal *slaughter-pen.*
Here fell gallant Sergeant Ambers Norton, our color bearer, with his life blood staining the flag a deeper crimson. One by one all the color guard, with one exception, were either killed or wounded. Company H, the left color company, seemed almost annihilated. Orderly Murnaugh, Sergeant Miller, Corporal Updegrove and several others were killed, while Capt. Updegrove and many of his men were wounded.

The only protection available was to lie close to the ground or seek cover behind trees and rocks—by no means plenty—until fire had slackened. No supports had come up and our bugle had sounded the recall as soon as it was apparent the works could not be carried. A galling cross fire scorched the ravine and ridge alike, rendering it almost useless to seek shelter of tree or rock.

I noticed two men taking shelter behind a medium-sized tree on the brink of the ravine, and when one of them was hit in the hand by a minie ball and retired to the rear, I crept to his place behind the other. He was leaning against the tree and would not lie down, although he was not firing. In a few minutes a ball came from the left and struck him squarely in the temple with that peculiar "spat" which once heard is at once recognized as the passage of a bullet through flesh and bone. It killed him so suddenly that he never changed his position, and had I not heard the shot strike and been spattered by his blood and brains I might have believed him still untouched. He was a stranger to me, evidently from another regiment, and being past all human aid I soon left him, going to another tree where I could get a better view of the front.

To my surprise not a soul was visible. The woods were full of smoke and I thought the line could not be far away. The rebel fire still swept the ground like a hailstorm and I deemed it better to quietly await further developments than to try to get away, although our bugle kept blowing the recall.

It was now past sunset and the woods were growing dark, when a wounded man belonging to Company I of our regiment came from the left front, painfully limping toward the rear and, seeing me, asked me to help him as he was nearly exhausted. I arose and taking his roll of blankets in one hand and his arm in the other, led him to the rear as rapidly as his condition would permit. He was severely wounded in the thigh.

Passing on to the right I soon gained the shelter of the ridge and near its foot passed Major McClenahan with a bugler, watching for stragglers from the front and having the recall blown at intervals. Alas! Too many of our brave comrades lay up that bloody ravine, forever beyond the sound of the bugle; many more were so badly wounded as to be helpless, and others were so close to the rebel works that they dared not stir until darkness shielded them.

Like so many battle sites of the Civil War, the field of Pickett's Mill was left blanketed with the residue of the fighting. This canteen lay rusting where it was dropped until a souvenir hunter picked it up long after the battle.

"They all say that the dead are strewn thicker on the ground than at any battle of the war."

CAPTAIN SAMUEL T. FOSTER

24TH TEXAS CAVALRY (DISMOUNTED), GRANBURY'S BRIGADE

Probably because two of his divisions were so badly mauled by Cleburne's men, including the 24th Texas, Sherman omits any mention of Pickett's Mill in either his official report or his memoirs. Many Texans, like Captain Foster, began the war as cavalry, but the more pressing need for infantry soon forced most to give up their horses. The 24th Texas was dismounted in the summer of 1862, and though the regiment kept its name, it fought on foot until the end of the war.

About sun up this morning we were relieved and ordered back to the Brigade—and we have to pass over the dead Yanks of the battle field of yesterday; and here I beheld that which I cannot discribe; and which I hope never see again, dead men meet the eye in every direction, and in one place I stoped and counted 50 dead men in a circle of 30 ft. of me. Men lying in all sorts of shapes . . . just as they had fallen, and it seems like they have nearly all been shot in the head, and a great number of them have their skulls bursted open and their brains running out, quite a number that way. I have seen many dead men, and seen them wounded and crippled in various ways, have seen their limbs cut off, but I never saw anything before that made me sick, like looking at the brains of these men did. I do believe that if a soldier could be made to faint, that I would have fainted if I had not passed on and got out of that place as soon as I did. . . .

Genl Joseph E Johnson, and Genl Hardee and Genl Cleburn and Genl Granbury all ride over the battle ground this morning and Genl Johnson compliments us very highly on the fight. They all say that the dead are strewn thicker on the ground than at any battle of the war; but it don't seem to be so funny now as it was when it was going on. I feel sick every time I think of those mens brains.

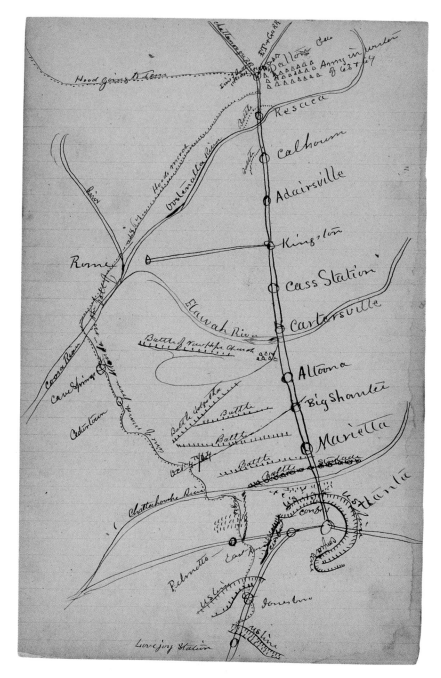

Foster began his diary in September 1862 and faithfully continued his entries even during a stint at prison camp in the first months of 1863, after his capture in Arkansas. Exchanged shortly afterward, he saw action throughout the rest of the war and added to his journal a few maps, like this one showing northern Georgia with some of the camps and positions that figure in his narrative.

PRIVATE JOHN K. DUKE

53D OHIO INFANTRY, LIGHTBURN'S BRIGADE

Near Dallas on May 28, Bate's Confederate division launched a spirited but fruitless assault against Logan's corps on the Federal right. The charge of Finley's Florida brigade "was an extremely gallant one," Private Duke recalled; "they came with heads bowed down and hats pulled over their eyes as if to hide from view their inevitable death." But even with the repulse of the enemy, the Yankees took more than a few casualties themselves. Among them was one of Duke's officers, Major Ephraim Dawes.

It was the evident intention of our enemy to force their way through . . . and capture our trains. In the heat of the fray Major Dawes apprehended that our line might give way at this point and rushed to the road just as their line was within about 50 feet of ours. Their color-bearer was shot down and immediately the colors were caught up by one of the color-guards. The line began to waver.

Just prior to this, Major Dawes received a severe facial wound. The bullet struck the left side of the lower jaw, carried away the body of the inferior maxilla to near the angle. It took off his lower lip, tore the chin so that it hung down, took out all the lower teeth but two and cut his tongue. It was the most horrible looking wound I saw during my entire army service.

While in the ambulance going to the rear for treatment, he wrote in the dust upon the opposite side, "Good for a 60 days' furlough."

Just prior to his receiving this awful wound he was struck in the back of the head by a glancing ball. This, however, was so small in comparison to the other that but little attention was paid to it. As to the nerve of the major, and how he survived this terrible ordeal, the reader may judge.

Graphically showing the severity of Major Dawes' wound are the two photographs above, the one on the left taken in March 1864 and the other in July, after he had undergone the first round of surgery on his shattered jaw. At right, heavily stained with his blood, is the frock coat Dawes was wearing when he was hit. Discharged on August 31, he endured several more operations, all without anesthesia for fear he might suffocate on his own blood while unconscious.

SERGEANT JOSEPH J. HUNTER
1ST MISSISSIPPI CAVALRY, ARMSTRONG'S BRIGADE

In the Rebel assault on Logan's heavily entrenched corps at Dallas, the first to attack was Armstrong's cavalry, fighting on foot and carrying their pistols. With a rush they overran the 1st Iowa Battery, but unsupported they were forced to fall back. Sergeant Hunter survived the battle and the war, but his cousin Willis Hunter was mortally wounded going over the breastworks.

Our regiment had a skirt of very thick undergrowth of wood to go through on the side of the hill in front of the battery. When all things were ready and a signal given, both commands jumped over the works and with a yell moved forward, the Yanks pouring shot and shell; but on we went, and when within seventy-five yards of the battery all drew their navies and on to them we went. The men left their guns, running over the breast-works which were about twenty steps in the rear of the guns, so right on their breast-works we went; some mounting on top of them, pouring pistol balls into the Yanks as they ran down the hill in front of us. So we had their guns and works, but our infantry on our right failed to go to their works but returned to their works, leaving our regiment alone. The Yanks to our right gave us a cross-fire which we could not stand. We accordingly spiked the guns and fell back in good order, carrying wounded and some of the dead with us.

In a letter home, written the day after the costly Rebel charge at Dallas, Lieutenant Colonel Frank Montgomery of the 1st Mississippi (left) voiced an opinion, shared by many in Armstrong's brigade, that "somebody blundered." Though the accusation never went anywhere, he had already had a couple of rows with his superiors, the latest in March 1864, when he was brought up on charges after some of his men hissed at a passing general.

MARY S. MALLARD
RESIDENT OF ATLANTA

With the front now only 30 miles from Atlanta, the fighting had come home to the city's inhabitants. As scores of wounded soldiers streamed into town, the residents of Atlanta turned out in numbers to feed and tend them. Mallard and her husband, the Reverend Robert Quarterman Mallard, joined their fellow humanitarians in doing what they could to ease the pain and suffering all around them.

Atlanta, Friday, June 3rd, 1864
My dearest Mother,
. . . We are passing through so much anxiety and perplexity that days sometimes seem weeks, and I scarcely realize how time is passing. We have been expecting a general engagement for the past two weeks, and it has not come yet, so that everyone has given up conjecture and now quietly awaits the issue. Our army is about thirty miles from this place, and the Yankees just in front of them. They have made several night attacks recently, and in every instance our men have driven them back with great slaughter. I presume you saw by the papers that seven hundred Yankee dead were left upon the field the night they attacked Cleburne's division. We too are losing many noble lives, though few in comparison with the enemy, for our men fight almost entirely behind breastworks.

Our town is rapidly filling up with the wounded. Some of the hospitals are entirely filled. Stores are being fitted up for hospitals, and I presume the city hall and other buildings will soon be impressed for the same purpose. I have been unable to go to the hospitals myself, as they are very far off, and I have not the strength to walk; but I prepare and send food to them. I have been sending for a week past to a ward filled with Texas men. They often send and beg me to send more arrowroot; sometimes requests come for onions, lettuce, and all manner of things.

As the fighting drew near, the Reverend Robert Mallard (right), pastor of Atlanta's Central Presbyterian Church, ministered to the wounded and the homeless. It was a daunting task; as the war progressed, drugs and medical supplies at Confederate hospitals became even more scarce. In August of 1864 a notice placed by a Macon hospital in the Daily Intelligencer, an Atlanta newspaper, made an appeal for rags, to be used as bandages.

"In a word a line of battle is no respecter of property for lives are at stake, men, women and children, and the interest of the Confederacy."

The bundle of rags and box of arrowroot came quite safely this evening, and will be very acceptable. I will keep the arrowroot and prepare it myself, for it is generally so badly prepared at the hospitals that the men will not eat it.

Mr. Mallard goes down tonight at two o'clock to the cars to assist in having the wounded carried to the various hospitals. There is a great deal of work to be done here now, not only with the wounded but with the refugees, who are here in great numbers. Mr Mallard works constantly with the committee, and they are doing a great deal of good. They have quite a village of refugees dependent upon them for provisions, and many of them for clothing. The citizens of Savannah have been very generous in sending up rice and corn for them.

. . . Mr. Mallard has been constantly called on the street by his engagements with the committee, and he says everyone seems to him to be earnestly at work trying in every way to alleviate the sufferings of those around. . . .

Your affectionate daughter,
Mary S. Mallard

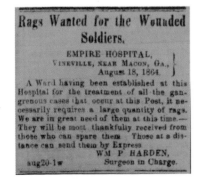

CAPTAIN
SAM C. KELLY
30TH ALABAMA INFANTRY, PETTUS' BRIGADE

On June 4 Johnston shifted his army back to the east to counter Sherman's move to Allatoona. In what was becoming a familiar pattern, the Rebels masterfully avoided the Federal flanking maneuvers and soon were sitting behind a new line of earthworks. On June 9 Kelly wrote to his wife after completing work on the Lost Mountain Line.

We may fight here; no skirmishing within hearing. All seemed confident of success should we attack. Some lament the desolation we are making, but all say "better that than for us to run on their breastworks and be cut to pieces and be whipped" then all behind would be gone. The truth is they flank and we follow on the inner track, form line and offer battle; they refuse and in a day or so are moving (flanking) to our right. We follow and let them go round to the end of our line and get in our rear to where ever they choose. So it does not make any difference how good our works are, with no foe in front, they are no use to us. We have the advantage of the inside track, and greatly in the choice of ground. I say Johnston has the confidence of nine-tenths of the army, and if our battle line was formed in your back yard, I should say to you "Take what you can to the rear; the wheat to be fed, fences to be made into breastworks, gardens trampled, and roads and paths in every direction through the fields of corn." In a word a line of battle is no respecter of property for lives are at stake, men, women and children, and the interest of the Confederacy.

SERGEANT FENWICK Y. HEDLEY

32D ILLINOIS INFANTRY, SANDERSON'S BRIGADE

Born in England, Hedley immigrated to the United States and eventually settled in Illinois. He mustered in as a fife player but was reassigned to regular ranks when regimental bands were eliminated. Beginning in the summer of 1863, Hedley spent most of his time on detached service as a clerk. During the Atlanta campaign he was attached to the headquarters of the 4th Division, XVII Corps.

*Y*e never gazed upon a grander scene than that spread before the vision from the summit of Ackworth's rugged hill that bright June day. . . . To front and rear, the valleys stretched away in wide expanse of field, and orchard, and grove. The air was laden with the incense of flower and fruit. Fleecy clouds floated athwart the blue expanse above, intercepting here and there the bright sunshine, and mottling the landscape with alternate patches of light and shadow, which chased each other from field to field, across hillock and stream.

Through this fine setting passed a magnificent panorama. Following the meanderings of numerous roads, hither and thither, to right and to left, up hill and down dale, in sunshine and in shadow, long lines of blue, tipped with shining steel, threaded their way. Here, borne by a mounted orderly, a yellow guidon, inscribed with the familiar devices belonging to general headquarters, spoke the presence of the supreme chief and his staff. At intervals, similar banners emblazoned with arrow, or cartridge-box, or acorn, designated the places of corps commanders; others with these emblems in red, white, or blue, told of the presence of division and brigade generals, enabling the practiced eye to recognize and name each command as far as the devices could be discerned. Between and among these, behind and in front, as far as the eye could reach, floated countless national colors, each marking a regimental organization. So far did they lie below the point of observation on Ackworth, that regiments seemed to be but companies, and no sound came up from the mighty host. In rear of each division followed the artillery, the bright brass of the Napoleons alternating with the dull color of the steel Rodmans. And then, away in the background, rising and falling with hill and valley, outlined against the bright green of field and wood, or the clear blue sky, the long wagon train stretched out, the white canvas covers seeming, in the distance, like the sails of ships at sea.

Far to the front, bounding the entire southern horizon, rose majestic Kenesaw, "the Twin Mountain," and its adjacent peaks, as if planted there to stay the steps of the onward pressing hosts, bidding them go thus far and no farther. But already, almost at their very base, white puffs of smoke rose in defiance from the rifles of the federal advance; while high overhead, at Ackworth, waved the tell-tale flags that bore the directions of the great war-chief to the troops opening the conflict.

LIEUTENANT JOHN W. COMER

45TH ALABAMA INFANTRY, LOWREY'S BRIGADE

Many Confederates went off to war accompanied by black servants, who despite their status as slaves proved to be immensely loyal to their masters. Born in 1845 to a prominent family from Barbour County, Alabama, the young Comer, pictured above with his servant, Burrell, saw his first active campaigning in the summer of 1864. Shortly after he penned this letter, dated June 14, he received a minor wound but returned to duty until paroled in May 1865.

I am glad to say I am still safe & well. I never enjoyed better health in my life, I have a few soars on one of my feet, caused I think from such hard and continual marching. We have been on the pad since we left Montivallo the 5th day of May. When we lie down at night we do not know how long we will be permitted to sleep, all the principal manuvers are made in the night. I never think of pulling off my clothes or shoes when I lie down. I have not pulled off my Pants or Shoes to lie down more than twice since the 5th of May. I sleep with my belt around me & my sword & haversack under my head so as to be ready to move in a moment when called upon. Local service is a paradise compared to active service. I do not believe there is a Soldier in this army but what has got lice (Body lice I mean). I have my clothes boiled but to no purpose. it is useless to try to get rid of them as long as we have to fare as we do, they plague me half to death, keeping me scratching & feeling . . . While I am writing our Pickets are fighting in front & the Enemy are cannonading heavily. But I have become accustomed to the sound and it does not bother me at all. We are ready and anxiously awaiting the attack of the Enemy. The army is in fine spirits and confident of success in the end. . . .

Burrell is now with the wagon train. I sent him to the rear to wash some clothes. one of our men has just got in from the train [and] says he is well & will come to the Regt. in a few days. If Burrell holds out just full to the end & stick[s] to me as well as he has done heretofore & I come out safe, a mint of money could not buy him. There are very few negroes in the army that are not worth anything to their masters at times like this. Burrell is not afraid of anything. he came to us the other day while we were on Picket & borrowed some of the boys guns & shot at the Yankees. said he wanted to kill one Yankee before the war ended.

LIEUTENANT WILLIAM M. POLK
STAFF, LIEUTENANT GENERAL LEONIDAS POLK

On the morning of June 14 General Leonidas Polk was felled by a Yankee shell on Pine Mountain. His son, Lieutenant Polk, had served under him as assistant chief of artillery. After the war Polk moved to New York City and eventually became one of the country's prominent gynecologists.

On reaching the crest of the hill the spectators had a full view of the surrounding country, over which sunshine and shadow moved, keeping pace with the slowly drifting clouds. Both lines of battle were plainly visible. Bodies of men could be seen, busy with axe and spade. Guns were being placed in position. Groups of officers could be distinguished moving about behind the lines. The adjacent fields were white with the covers of a thousand wagons. In the distance, to the front, lay the hills of Etowah; to the right, the peaks of Kenesaw.

The constant firing of the heavy lines of skirmishers, reinforced here and there by the guns of some battery, whose position was marked by the white smoke which in the still air settled about it—all combined to make the scene one of unusual beauty and grandeur. In the enthusiasm of the moment some of the officers stood on the parapet and exposed themselves to the sharp gaze of hostile eyes. The men of the battery vainly warned them of the danger. While they were speaking there was a flash, a puff of smoke, a sharp report, and in an instant fragments of splintered rock and flying earth scattered around them, as a shot was buried in the parapet. The officers separated, each seeking some place of greater safety. General Johnston and General Polk moved together

At the time of his death, General Polk carried in his pocket copies of Doctor Quintard's popular devotional tract, Balm for the Weary and the Wounded (left), intended as gifts for Johnston, Hood, and Hardee.

to the left, and stood for a few moments in earnest conversation behind a parapet. Several shots now passed together just above the parapet and touched the crest of the hill. Generals Johnston and Polk, having apparently completed their observations, began to retrace their steps. General Johnston fell a few paces behind, and diverged to the right; General Polk walked to the crest of the hill, and, entirely exposed, turned himself around, as if to take a farewell view. Folding his arms across his

Moving to take cover from Federal artillery, Johnston and Hardee look over their shoulders just as a shell strikes Polk, who had held back for one last glance at the enemy's positions. The unknown artist of this sketch downplayed the severity of Polk's fatal wound—in reality he was practically disemboweled.

breast, he stood intently gazing on the scene below. While he thus stood, a cannon-shot crashed through his breast, and opening a wide door, let free that indomitable spirit. Amid the shot and shell now poured upon the hill, his faithful escort gathered up the body and bore it to the foot of the hill. There, in a sheltered ravine, his sorrow-stricken comrades, silent and in tears, gathered around his mangled corpse.

Hardee, bending over the lifeless form, said to Johnston, "General, this has been a dear visit. We have lost a brave man, whose death leaves a vacancy not easily filled"; then, kneeling by the side of the dead body, he exclaimed: "My dear, dear friend, little did I think this morning that I should be called upon to witness this." Johnston, with tears in his eyes, knelt and laid his hand upon the cold brow of the fallen hero, saying, "We have lost much! I would rather anything but this."

CAPTAIN DAVID P. CONYNGHAM
Volunteer Aide-de-Camp, Federal Staff

At the foot of Pine Mountain on the morning of the 14th, General Sherman himself observed the group of Confederates on the crest of the prominence. Remarking "how saucy they are!" he ordered the nearest battery, Captain Peter Simonson's 5th Indiana, to fire a few salvos at the enemy party. Two days later a Rebel sharpshooter put a bullet through Simonson's head.

Skirmishers were thrown out in order to cover the advance of our lines, and a few sections of artillery were placed in position. The skirmishing was pretty brisk towards evening, and the batteries opened a dropping fire on the rebel position. Sherman rode up to a battery, and turned his glass towards Pine Mountain.

After taking a good view he turned to the officer in command, saying, "Captain Simonson, can you send a shell right on the top of that knob? I notice a battery there, and several general officers near it."

"I'll try, general."

The captain fired, and the general looked on with his glass.

"Ah, captain, a little too high; try again, with a shorter fuse;" and up went the glass to his eye. Away went the shell, tearing through General Bishop Polk in its course.

"That will do," said Sherman, shutting down his glass.

It is said that Johnston and Hardee were on their horses beside Polk when he fell, and when the first shell came they remarked,—

"It is safer to alight."

Polk smiled, and still staid surveying our position, and thus met his death. We knew that night that he was killed, for our signal officers had discovered the system of the rebel signals, which enabled them to read the despatches along the enemy's lines.

When we took that hill, two artillerists, who had concealed themselves until we had come up, and then came within our lines, showed us where his body lay after being hit. There was one pool of clotted gore there, as if an animal had been bled. The shell has passed through his body from the left side, tearing the limbs and body in pieces. Doctor M—— and myself searched that mass of blood, and discovered pieces of the ribs and arm bones, which we kept as souvenirs. The men dipped their handkerchiefs in it too, whether as a sacred relic, or to remind them of a traitor, I do not know.

SARAH "SALLY" CLAYTON
RESIDENT OF ATLANTA

A young woman in the summer of 1864, Clayton had already been touched by war. Her brother, William, of the 7th Georgia, was wounded in Virginia. In July Sally and her sister Caroline were sent away to Alabama to escape the scourge of typhoid fever that would later claim the life of her sister Gussie. Before she left Atlanta, Clayton saw the entire city mourn the death of General Polk.

I have already told of what was considered about the greatest day Atlanta had ever seen and now we come to one of the saddest, the bringing into the city the remains of General Polk, soon after he was killed on Pine Mountain the middle of June 1864, and then lying in state in St. Luke's Church in Walton street. The train came in quite early, and the body was taken to the "Little Refugee Church" as it was called. . . .

. . . I could not begin to say how many, many thousands marched through the little church on that occasion or how sad their mien.

The good old Bishop's death seemed a personal loss to every one who looked upon his bloodless face that day. Tears were shed by hundreds of those present, but very silently, not a sound was heard in the entire church but that of footsteps as the crowd passed through. Many, very many of the throng paused long enough when the casket was reached to stoop, for it was quite low, and take a leaf, or flower or twig. There was no cessation of the stream of humanity: except for a short religious service, until the time came to remove the remains to the noon day train to start for Augusta where the remains were to be buried in St. Paul's churchyard.

The crowd made way in the street for the passing of the hearse and the carriages of the pallbearers, then quietly fell in line, and with bowed heads followed in their wake, while all the time the beauty of the morning seemed a mockery to the gloom and sorrow of Atlanta that day.

BRIGADIER GENERAL ALPHEUS S. WILLIAMS
DIVISION COMMANDER, XX CORPS

In many ways a bloody rehearsal of his costly attacks around Atlanta a month later, Hood's assault at Kolb's Farm on June 22 was both poorly planned and badly executed. Ordered only to block Sherman's attempt to turn the Confederate left, Hood impetuously set his corps against a numerically superior and well-positioned foe. Participating in the repulse was General Williams' Federal division, which inflicted heavy casualties on the attacking Rebels.

We had just begun to pile rails when the heavy skirmish line of the enemy poured out of the woods all along the open and advanced at a run. Three columns, massed, followed close and deployed in three and four lines. Our artillary opened upon them a most destructive fire. The infantry columns opposite Knipe and Ruger's left moved forward, but as they reached the brow of a ravine which ran parallel to our front, the whole line opened a withering volley. Some Rebs. went back, some scrambled down into the deep ravine, but none ever passed beyond it. One heavy column got hold of the woods in front of Knipe's left, and upon it I turned twelve pieces of artillery, sweeping it with canister and case shot until the devils found sufficient employment in covering themselves behind trees and logs.

Farther toward our left a huge mass of Rebels moved out to attack Robinson's brigade, but three rounds from the rifled guns set the whole mass flying in the greatest disorder. They never reached the fire of our infantry. The attack was kept up from 4 P.M. until near dark. The numbers were formidable, but the attack was indeed feeble. The Rebs. had been badly shaken by our artillery fire before they left the woods. All the prisoners say this. Indeed, after the first half-hour the men considered the whole affair great sport. They would call out to the Rebels who had taken shelter in the woods and in the deep ravines in our front, "Come up here, Johnny Reb. Here is a weak place!" "Come up and take this battery; we are Hooker's paper collar boys." "We've only got two rounds of ammunition, come and take us." "What do you think of Joe Hooker's Iron Clads?" and the like. . . .

Altogether, I have never had an engagement in which success was won so completely and with so little sacrifice of life. Considering the number of the enemy sent against my single division, the result is indeed most wonderful and gratifying. Dory Davis (T.R.) has been here making a sketch of the ground for *Harper's;* but he says that *Harper's* don't put in half he sends and those are bunglingly and incorrectly copied. He sketches beautifully and the pictures he has sent give a most correct idea of the field of fight, so far as landscape is concerned. We are now lying in the woods and have possession of the ground the enemy charged over. They have strong works not a mile in our front and our pickets keep up the usual popping of small arms.

GENERAL SHERMAN'S CAMPAIGN—GENERAL WILLIAMS'S DIVISION OF HOOKER'S CORPS DRIVING THE REBELS THROUGH THE

One of the Rebels who fell before Williams' guns was Lieutenant Colonel Calvin H. Walker of the 3d Tennessee, pictured at far left in prewar militia uniform next to his brother James. In a report of the battle on June 22, Walker's division commander, Carter Stevenson, expressed deep regret at the officer's death, referring to him as a "model of the Southern soldier and gentleman." Shown above is the belt and "C.S." plate worn by Walker.

CORPORAL BENJAMIN F. MCGEE
72D INDIANA INFANTRY, WILDER'S BRIGADE

Known as the Lightning Brigade, Wilder's command consisted of four regiments of mounted infantry, all of which were armed with seven-shot Spencer repeating rifles, giving the men unsurpassed firepower. Although they traveled as cavalry, they usually dismounted before a fight and fought as infantry. And like any foot soldier, they found the sight of the Confederate works along the Kennesaw Mountain Line deeply troubling.

On emerging from this forest we could see, for the first time during our service, nearly the entire field of strife. The panorama was terribly grand and awe-inspiring. Had we the time, and the power of Homer, we should like to describe it. What was most repugnant to our feelings, and made us shrink back a little on emerging from the dark woods, was to see on the north end of Kenesaw an eight-gun battery, of largest calibre, which seemed within a stone's throw of us, and ready to drop death and destruction amongst us. The battery was really four miles away, but so clear was the air that the grim guns seemed very near. The truth is, as we swept our eyes over the scene, horrible with devices and enginery of death, the prospect for a speedy termination of the conflict was not at all encouraging. Every mountain and hill, in front and away to the right, fairly bristled with artillery and swarmed with rebels. Never before had we seen so many rebels at one time.

ED BY THEODORE R. DAVIS.—[SEE FIRST PAGE.]

This engraving of Williams' division at the battle of Kolb's Farm appeared in the July 2, 1864, issue of Harper's Weekly, just a little more than a week after the artist, Theodore R. Davis, produced the sketch from which the engraving was taken. Davis was no doubt pleased by the rapid turnaround, a process that usually took several weeks. But like all the special artists, he was probably less than satisfied with the rendition from his original.

Kennesaw Mountain

On June 14 General Sherman began testing the strength of Johnston's new defensive line, which covered a 10-mile front extending from Lost Mountain in the west to Brush Mountain in the east. Elements of three Federal corps attempted to pinch off William Bate's division, which held a northward-projecting salient at Pine Mountain. A round fired from an Indiana battery claimed the life of General Leonidas Polk, who was touring the position in company with Johnston and Hardee. But the Yankees were held off, and Bate was able to evacuate the mountain under cover of darkness. Over the next four days Sherman kept up the pressure in what he described as "one grand skirmish extending along a front of eight miles." The Federals gained no clear advantage, and by the morning of June 19 Johnston had drawn his troops into a formidable network of batteries and rifle pits centered on the 700-foot crest of Kennesaw Mountain. Less than 30 miles from the outskirts of Atlanta, Kennesaw was, in Sherman's words, "the key to the whole country." But the Union commander was unwilling to attack without first attempting to find a means of flanking the natural fortress.

Sherman sent Hooker and Schofield to secure the Powder Springs road, which seemed a promising route around the Confederate left. Johnston anticipated the move, and on June 22 Hood's corps was in place to block the Federals at Kolb's Farm. The impetuous Hood mounted a poorly conceived attack and was repulsed with heavy loss. For the time being Sherman gave up on his effort to flank Johnston and turned his attention back to the Confederate center.

The strongest part of the Confederate line extended south along the slopes of Kennesaw Mountain to Little Kennesaw—300 feet lower than its sister peak—and on to Pigeon Hill, which covered the Burnt Hickory road to Marietta. At dawn on June 25, Major General Samuel G. French, whose division held Pigeon Hill, observed blue columns shifting to his left and ordered his batteries to open fire. "The enemy replied furiously," French reported, "and for an hour the firing was incessant." The artillery duel flared up again that afternoon, as Sherman continued to mass his forces in front of the Kennesaw Mountain Line.

Remarking that "flanking is played out," Sherman ordered that a two-pronged assault be launched on the Rebel center at 8:00 a.m. on June 27. While Schofield continued to threaten the enemy left flank, Logan's XV Corps would advance on Little Kennesaw and Pigeon Hill. But the main attack would be made by Thomas one and a half miles farther south. There the enemy-held crest was lower and the gentler western slopes better suited to infantry deployments.

Three of Logan's brigades moved out at 8:30 a.m., and Brigadier General Joseph A. J. Lightburn's troops overran an outlying line of rifle pits held by the 63d Georgia. But Lightburn's assault collapsed in the face of artillery fire from French's Confederates on Pigeon Hill. French shifted troops from Brigadier General Matthew Ector's Texas brigade to bolster Francis Cockrell's Missourians and Claudius Sears' Mississippians on the hill, and the defiant garrison stood off the Yankee brigades of Charles Walcutt and Giles Smith.

The steep, heavily wooded terrain slowed the attackers, and the handful of Federals who gained French's breastworks were killed or captured. The survivors took shelter in the swale between Pigeon Hill and Little Kennesaw to the north, only to be caught in a cross fire. Many remained pinned down until darkness enabled them to work their way back to the Union lines.

While McPherson's diversionary attack was being repulsed, Thomas was launching the main effort against a wooded ridge defended by Hardee's corps. Although the ground seemed more promising than did the rugged slopes of Kennesaw Mountain and Pigeon Hill, the Southern line was well entrenched and bolstered with artillery. Cleburne's division held the northern portion of the ridge, and Cheatham's the southern, where the earthworks turned to the east in a salient soon to become known as the Dead Angle.

Two brigades of Brigadier General John Newton's division would advance against Cleburne's defenses, while the brigades of Brigadier General Charles G. Harker, Colonel Daniel McCook Jr., and Colonel John G. Mitchell assaulted the Dead Angle. Thomas directed that the 8,000 troops spearheading the assault be massed in columns of regiments and that they charge at the double-quick without halting to fire: They would carry the Rebel breastworks at bayonet point. One Federal officer called the formation "a human battering ram."

Following a brief preliminary bombardment, two signal guns launched the blue-clad masses toward the enemy line. They were met with a wall of flame that brought down entire ranks of men, while the survivors tried to press on over the writhing bodies of fallen comrades. Everywhere the Federal attack was blunted at great cost, but nowhere was the carnage greater than at the Dead Angle, held by the Confederate brigades of Alfred J. Vaughan and George E. Maney.

Harker's brigade swung against the angle from the north but was hurled back after Harker was shot from his horse with a fatal wound. McCook's and Mitchell's brigades charged the southern side of the Dead Angle but were similarly repulsed. McCook was mortally wounded, as was his successor in command of the brigade, Colonel Oscar F. Harmon. When Sherman suggested that Thomas try another attack, the commander refused with the comment, "One or two more such assaults would use up this army."

By noon the battle for Kennesaw Mountain was over. Sherman's loss of 3,000 was more than three times the number of Confederate casualties, and the armies settled into a grim standoff as Sherman once again shifted his attention to Johnston's left flank. While Johnston was distracted by the assault on his center, Schofield began sidling around the Confederate left. McPherson marched to extend Schofield's line farther south, toward the Chattahoochee River and Atlanta, and on July 2 Johnston withdrew from the blood-soaked slopes of Kennesaw Mountain.

Frustrated by his foe's elusiveness, General Sherman ordered a direct attack on the Confederates dug in along the Kennesaw Mountain Line. The resulting slaughter served only to convince the Federal commander to return to flanking maneuvers.

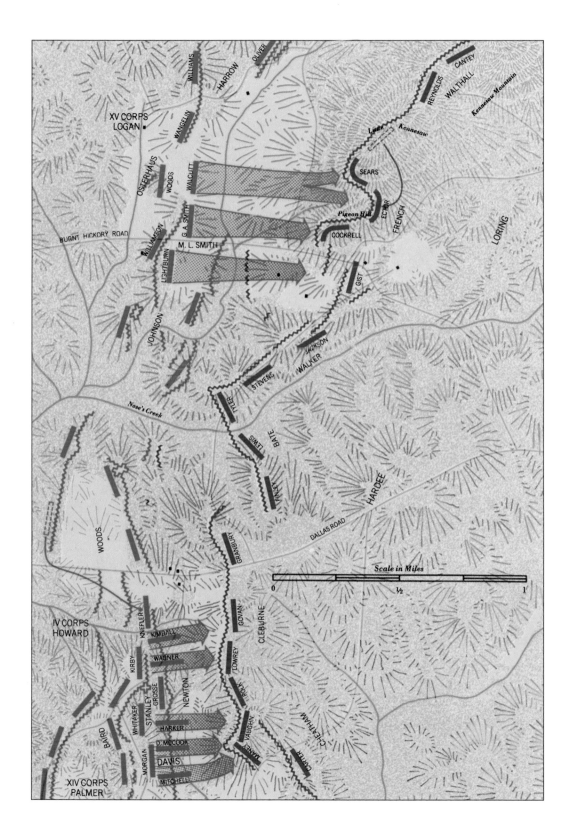

CAPTAIN ALVAH S. SKILTON

57TH OHIO INFANTRY,
G. SMITH'S BRIGADE

Less than a month after surviving the charge at Kennesaw Mountain, Captain Alvah Skilton and 90 others from his regiment were captured at the Battle of Atlanta. Skilton escaped from a South Carolina prison only to be recaptured and sent to Libby Prison in Richmond, Virginia.

The short Southern twilight had suddenly ended and darkness settled down upon the camp, hiding alike under its mantle the rocks, trees and stern implements of war. For a time silence reigned, broken only by the low murmur of the voices of the men as they talked of loved ones at home, dead or absent comrades, or told tales and laugh-provoking jokes to pass the time. And I well remember a group that gathered that night about a camp chest under the shadows of the pines to eat a scanty supper by the light of a single tallow candle.

This little group consisted of Col. A. V. Rice, commanding the 57th Regiment; Lt. Col. S. R. Mott, Adjutant M. M. Newell, Quartermaster T. L. Parker and myself. The meal was nearly finished when an orderly was heard inquiring for Col. Rice. On being directed to him he delivered an envelope, gave a salute and rode away into the darkness.

Col. Rice broke the seal deliberately, read the order and without

comment passed it to Col. Mott, who read it and gave it to me. So it was read in silence and passed around the table.

It was an order for the brigade to move silently out of the works and proceed to a designated spot near the gap, or depression, between Big and Little Kennesaw mountains, and at daylight on the 27th form part of a forlorn hope, or storm column, in an endeavor to make a lodgment inside the enemy's works.

In an hour the regiment was underway and marched a greater part of the night before we arrived at the place assigned us, which was in a dense field of underbrush and close up to the enemy's works. Here we laid down for a little rest. It seemed as though I had scarcely fallen asleep when I was awakened by someone shaking me and whispering in my ear that Col. Rice wanted me. I reported at once and found that Gen. Giles Smith had sent an order requiring the three ranking officers of each regiment of the brigade to report at his headquarters. Cols. Rice

and Mott, and myself as senior captain, proceeded to report at once and were, I believe, the first to arrive.

Gen. Smith had established his headquarters under a hickory tree with a small, circular grass plot about 40 feet in diameter to the south of it. The plot was surrounded by a dense growth of underbrush. In a short time there were assembled here the three ranking officers from each regiment in the brigade and the members of Gen. Smith's staff. When all had reported Gen. Smith addressed us as follows:

"Gentlemen, I have sent for you to advise you of what is expected

Just visible through the haze are the twin prominences of Kennesaw Mountain (below) and Little Kennesaw (below, left), both heavily fortified by the Rebels in the last two weeks of June. This recently discovered composite photograph was taken soon after the battle from a position behind the Confederate right.

of us today and to make such provision as is possible to prevent confusion or misunderstanding.

"This column has been selected as a 'forlorn hope' and we are expected to carry the enemy's works in our front. Should we succeed in doing it, we are to hold them at all hazards for at least 10 minutes when ample reinforcements will be sent to enable us to hold the works.

"Gentlemen, this will be serious business and some of us must go down. I do not say this to frighten you, for I know that is impossible, but to impress on your minds that if I fall you must look to Col. Martin of the 111th Illinois for orders. If he falls you must look to Col. Rice of the 57th Ohio."

Turning to Col. Rice, who stood nearest to him, he said, "Of course, Col. Rice commands his regiment. Should he go down, Col. Mott succeeds and in the event of his falling, Capt. Skilton will assume command."

Gen. Smith addressed the officers of each regiment in like manner, calling each officer by name and rank, thereby showing how perfectly he was acquainted with them and how thorough was his knowledge of his command. When he was finished he said, "Gentlemen, go back to your respective commands, impart this information to your men and when the bugle sounds, charge. And may God bless and protect you all!"

No event of the war has left a more vivid or lasting memory in my mind than this meeting at early dawn under that hickory tree at the foot of Kennesaw. But for how many was it their last meeting on earth, and how few of those who met for that brief consultation are now living and how many of the living are maimed and crippled for life?

At the Battle of Kennesaw Mountain, Colonel Americus Vespucius Rice led his 57th Ohio against Cockrell's Missouri brigade, which was dug in on Pigeon Hill. After closing to within 20 yards of the Rebel line, Rice was wounded three times in quick succession. The most severe of his wounds cost him a leg; even so, he returned to military service in June 1865.

SERGEANT WALTER A. CLARK
63D GEORGIA INFANTRY, MERCER'S BRIGADE

Known as the Oglethorpes, Company A of the 63d Georgia had been serving along the Georgia coast with the rest of the regiment until they were summoned to join Johnston's army at Dalton in April 1864. On July 26 several companies of the 63d were sent out to man the picket line in front of Walker's division. On the following morning, the advance of Lightburn's Federal brigade, masked by trees, caught them by surprise, and Clark's company was thrown into the fray.

The Oglethorpes were in reserve, and Maj. Allen, misled by Capt. Buckner as to the situation and ignorant of the fact that the attacking column had already reached our skirmish line, ordered the company in to fill the gap. Gallantly led by Lieutenants Blanchard and McLaughlin, they advanced at a double quick step and on reaching the open field were met by a murderous fire both from the front and flank, for French's deserted pits were already occupied by the enemy. The woods to the left and front were swarming with blue coats. On a portion of the line held by Co. K, they had reached the pits and a hand to hand conflict ensued. Men fought with clubbed muskets. A short-legged Irishman of that company, with the unusual name of John Smith, had his gun seized by a stalwart Yankee and there was a struggle for its possession. The little son of Erin was game, but he was overmatched in strength and shoving his opponent backward as the gun was wrenched from his hands, he said, "To —— with you and the gun too." Lieut. George A. Bailie, of Co. B, had his ear grazed by a minie and his antagonist, twenty feet away, reloaded to fire again; having no weapon but his sword, Lieut. B. decided to emulate David in his contest with Goliath, and picking up a stone he threw it, striking his foe squarely between the eyes and placing him hors de combat for a time at least. Further up the line and near the vacant pits, another member of the regiment, whose name is not recalled, stood loading and firing as rapidly as his teeth could tear the cartridges and his hands could ram them home. His face was cold and pallid and bloodless, but not from fear. Blackened with powder stain, through which the perspiration trickled in streams, his eyes flashed defiance with every flash from his gun, while disdaining the protection of the pits he stood there a perfect demon of war, with no thought save to kill.

"Gentlemen, this will be serious business and some of us must go down."

The slaughter at Kennesaw Mountain on June 27 began at 8:00 a.m., when the Union batteries opened up on the Confederate positions ringing the high ground to the east. Within minutes the Rebel batteries (left) unleashed their reply. Then as the blue-clad battle lines emerged from cover to begin their advance, Johnston's artillery targeted the Federal ranks with lethal loads of case shot and canister.

LIEUTENANT RALSA C. RICE
125TH OHIO INFANTRY, HARKER'S BRIGADE

Lieutenant Rice had thus far passed through every fight without a scratch. Then came the attack at Kennesaw, where his regiment was chosen to form the vanguard of Harker's brigade. Fortunately, the bullet that finally found him only creased the top of his head, but the blow was enough to knock him out, raise a great lump, and have him left for dead on the battlefield.

Our instructions were brief and to the point: "The 125th is chosen to lead in the charge. You will deploy as skirmishers and at the bugle's signal you are to charge and put yourselves inside the works of the enemy, and then create as much confusion as possible; in the meantime the brigade will come to your support. The 125th Ohio has been chosen a forlorn hope today. Let every man do his best."

My position was on the extreme left of our line, and I had special instructions to keep connection with the line on our left. On the way back to the company I remarked to Captain Moses, "Pretty severe orders, Captain?"

"Yes," he said. "It means death or captivity to all, if we are lucky enough to reach them."

Our men were made acquainted with the orders and the work expected of them. One man had to be left to guard such baggage as we could dispense with in our run. The Captain directed me to detail someone. I saw that he was shirking a dreadful responsibility. I looked the boys over. There was not one wishful look; to do or die was in the face of each and all. I selected the oldest man present. While waiting for the bugle we had time to survey the ground and our prospects in front. My route was to be across an open field for about 200 yards with not so much as a stump to be seen. . . .

With the first blast of the bugle we were over and away. As soon as the line on our left reached the aforementioned thicket those nearest me broke for this cover. I saw no more of them. This disconcerted me very much as I could not now keep our own alignment and connection with them. I had no time to dwell on any side issues so I kept a straight forward course.

We found the enemy's first line was located on the timber line—an old rail fence had been utilized in the construction of light works. So sudden had been our dash that the Johnnies in this line surrendered almost to a man. The main line was plain to be seen, and from the point where I reached the first line was about 75 yards up a steep in-

cline. A halt was made here—our "wind" was gone. Besides, the prisoners had to be looked after. My first thought was that with these prisoners among us we would not be targets for those above us, but in this we were mistaken. Their bullets kept coming regardless of whom they hit. We compelled the captured men to go back over the ground to the rear. An order was sent down the line to remain where we were for the present, to fire as fast as possible and await further developments. It was very evident that with only a skirmish line our efforts to create confusion among such a body of men would be of no consequence unless the brigade was in immediate support. . . .

The brigade made three attempts to come across, but was driven back with severe losses each time. At point-blank range for grape and canister, in solid column, company front, no troops could endure such a slaughter. In the meantime our own muskets were worked as never before. From where I lay by looking through between the rails I could see the enemy reinforcing their line. A traverse was in my front, over which they had to climb like a flock of sheep over a fence. Here was a fine chance to test my marksmanship. My right hand had not forgotten its cunning. Three of the boys loaded and passed me their muskets. While thus engaged one of them misfired. I drew it back and proceeded to recap it. I was compelled to shift my position to kneeling. Just then a bullet found a weak spot in the rail and struck me fairly on top of the head. For a brief period there was a blank spot in my memory. I lay there long enough to be reported among the slain in a dispatch sent to a Cleveland newspaper.

When the attacking Yankees spilled out of a sheltering tree line they were raked by every gun their enemy could bring to bear. The Federal brigade under General Charles G. Harker (left) was pinned down in the triple row of obstacles that fronted the Rebel positions. Mounted on a white horse, Harker had just shouted, "Come on, boys!" to his faltering command when a bullet slammed into his chest and dropped him from the saddle.

SERGEANT SAMUEL A. HARPER
52D OHIO INFANTRY, D. MCCOOK'S BRIGADE

Most of the men who made the charge found out what was in store for them only that morning. The anxious moments for the men in Thomas' corps were prolonged by deployment delays, and some of their officers offered words to steady the nerves of the rank and file. As Sergeant Harper recalls, Colonel Daniel McCook Jr. spent the last moments before the attack among the familiar faces of the 52d Ohio Infantry, his command before he took over the brigade.

The brigade was ordered to lie down as we were in easy reach of the enemy's skirmishers. While passing to the rear, Col. McCook noticed that I was standing up; he stopped, and in a commanding tone said, "Sergeant Harper, don't you know you are unnecessarily exposing yourself, lie down." He . . . was in the act of returning when the officer behind the stump, with whom he had been talking, called out, "Don't be rash, colonel, don't be rash." He answered this by quoting in a very calm manner these lines which, I think, occur in the stanzas from Macaulay's Horatius:

"Then up spoke brave Horatius, the Captain of the gate:
'To every man upon this earth death cometh soon or late
And how can man die better than facing fearful odds,
For the ashes of his fathers and the temples of his gods?'"

He recited these lines as he walked to the front and center of his command, which position he had barely reached when the signal guns to the left fired. He gave the command and dashed forward.

A member of the large Ohio clan known as the Fighting McCooks, Colonel Daniel McCook Jr. (above) was one of eight brothers who, along with their father, donned Union blue. Although Colonel McCook commanded a brigade for nearly two years, he was not promoted to general until July 16, a day before he died of wounds received at Kennesaw Mountain.

PRIVATE S. M. CANTERBURY
86TH ILLINOIS INFANTRY, D. MCCOOK'S BRIGADE

Harker's and McCook's brigades both converged on the so-called Dead Angle, a prominent salient in the Confederate battle line manned by Tennesseans of Cheatham's division. The Federals attacked using a formation with a narrow front and deep ranks, a lamentable tactic that made it difficult for the Rebels to miss. McCook's command alone suffered nearly 500 casualties. Only a few of the Yankees, including Private Canterbury, reached the precarious shelter that lay at the foot of the Rebel earthworks.

At the creek at the foot of the hill I was in the rear, but got to the works as soon as any of the boys. I caught up to the front line as we reached the works. I found the brigade all mixed up in one line. In the space I was in I could not tell what was being done very far on the right or left of me. The rebel musketry fire was terrific; to stand still was death.

I realized the safest place was at the works. Col. Dan was in the lead. He said, "Forward with the colors!" When I first reached the works I fell or laid down, and hugged the works as close as I could for protection and to rest, as in running the distance we did, combined with the intense heat, I was about played out. Col. Dan climbed up on the works. For a moment my attention was taken with a rebel on the opposite side from me who was trying to fire under the headlog. When I looked up, Col. Dan was standing on the headlog above me. I heard him say, "Bring up those colors!" I don't know whose colors they were. He grabbed the colors in his left hand, holding them aloft and using his saber in his right hand, parrying the rebels on the other side of the breastworks who were trying to bayonet him. I reached up and took hold of the skirt of his uniform coat and said to him, "Colonel Dan, for God's sake get down, they will shoot you!" He turned partly around stooping a little, and said to me, "G——d d——n you, attend to your own business." Then the gun was fired; they put the gun almost against him. I know the gun was not more than one foot from his hip when they shot him. I could not tell where he was shot. Had I not pulled on his coat I believe he would have fallen inside the rebel works. Some comrades took him back to the rear; that was the last time I saw him.

"It seemed that the arch-angel of Death stood and looked on with outstretched wings, while all the earth was silent."

THE BATTLE OF KENNESAW MOUNTAIN. — "THE DEAD ANGLE."
On the line of the Western & Atlantic R. R. near Marietta, Ga.
June 27, 1864.

GEN. JOSEPH E. JOHNSTON,
Commanding Confederate States Army.

GEN. WM. T. SHERMAN,
Commanding United States Army.

FROM A PICTURE DRAWN BY A CONFEDERATE PARTICIPANT.

The battlefield guidebook published by the Western & Atlantic Railroad included this engraving from a sketch "drawn by a Confederate participant." Defending a portion of the Dead Angle that had no head logs, members of the 1st Tennessee, part of Maney's brigade, pour a withering volley into the faltering Federal ranks. Printed with the sketch in its original form was a poem that ended, "They come, ten thousand strong and lithe, / They fall like wheat before the scythe."

PRIVATE SAM R. WATKINS

1ST TENNESSEE (C.S.) INFANTRY, MANEY'S BRIGADE

For someone who claimed he "always shot at privates," since "it was they that did all the shooting and killing," Watkins had plenty of targets on the morning of June 27. He figured that by the time the fighting was over, he had fired his musket 120 times, leaving his arm "bruised and bloodshot from my wrist to my shoulder."

It was one of the hottest and longest days of the year, and one of the most desperate and determinedly resisted battles fought during the whole war. Our regiment was stationed on an angle, a little spur of the mountain, or rather promontory of a range of hills, extending far out beyond the main line of battle, and was subject to the enfilading fire of forty pieces of artillery of the Federal batteries. It seemed fun for the guns of the whole Yankee army to play upon this point. We would work hard every night to strengthen our breastworks, and the very next day they would be torn down smooth with the ground by solid shots and shells from the guns of the enemy. Even the little trees and bushes which had been left for shade, were cut down as so much stubble. . . .

Well, on the fatal morning of June 27th, the sun rose clear and cloudless, the heavens seemed made of brass, and the earth of iron, and as the sun began to mount toward the zenith, everything became quiet, and no sound was heard save a peckerwood on a neighboring tree, tapping on its old trunk, trying to find a worm for his dinner. We all knew it was but the dead calm that precedes the storm. On the distant hills we could plainly see officers dashing about hither and thither, and the Stars and Stripes moving to and fro, and we knew the Federals were making preparations for the mighty contest. We could hear but the rumbling sound of heavy guns, and the distant tread of a marching army, as a faint roar of the coming storm, which was soon to break the ominous silence with the sound of conflict, such as was scarcely ever before heard on this earth. It seemed that the arch-angel of Death stood and looked on with outstretched wings, while all the earth was silent, when all at once a hundred guns from the Federal line opened upon us, and for more than an hour they poured their solid and chain shot, grape and shrapnel right upon this salient point, defended by our regiment alone, when, all of a sudden, our pickets jumped into our works and reported the Yankees advancing, and almost at the same time a solid line of blue coats came up the hill. I discharged my gun, and happening to look up, there was the beautiful flag of the Stars and Stripes flaunting right in my face, and I heard John Branch, of the Rock City Guards, commanded by Captain W. D. Kelley, who were next Company H, say, "Look at that Yankee flag; shoot that fellow; snatch that flag out of his hand!" My pen is unable to describe the scene of carnage and death that ensued in the next two hours. Column after column of Federal soldiers were crowded upon that line, and by referring to the history of the war you will find they were massed in column forty columns deep; in fact, the whole force of the Yankee army was hurled against this point, but no sooner would a regiment mount our works than they were shot down or surrendered, and soon we had every "gopher hole" full of Yankee prisoners. Yet still the Yankees came. It seemed impossible to check the onslaught, but every man was true to his trust, and seemed to think that at that moment the whole responsibility of the Confederate government was rested upon his shoulders. Talk about other battles, victories, shouts, cheers, and triumphs, but in comparison with this day's fight, all others dwarf into insignificance. The sun beaming down on our uncovered heads, the thermometer being one hundred and ten degrees in the shade, and a solid line of blazing fire right from the muzzles of the Yankee guns being poured right into our very faces, singeing our hair and clothes, the hot blood of our dead and wounded spurting on us, the blinding smoke and stifling atmosphere filling our eyes and mouths, and the awful concussion causing the blood to gush out of our noses and ears, and above all, the roar of battle, made it a perfect pandemonium. Afterward I heard a soldier express himself by saying that he thought "Hell had broke loose in Georgia, sure enough."

CAPTAIN DAVID P. CONYNGHAM
VOLUNTEER AIDE-DE-CAMP, FEDERAL STAFF

The unsuccessful assaults on Kennesaw Mountain cost the Federals some 3,000 casualties. Between June 28 and 29, a series of truces allowed the Yankees to remove their dead clustered in front of the Confederate earthworks. Newspaper correspondent Conyngham saw the odd, brief camaraderie that ensued as Rebel and Federal soldiers mingled on the corpse-strewn slopes of the Dead Angle.

Next day General Johnston sent a flag of truce to Sherman, in order to give time to carry off the wounded and bury the dead, who were festering in front of their lines. A truce followed, and Rebels and Federals freely participated in the work of charity. It was a strange sight to see friends, to see old acquaintances, and in some instances brothers, who had been separated for years, and now pitted in deadly hostility, meet and have a good talk over old times, and home scenes, and connections. They drank together, smoked together, appeared on the best possible terms, though the next day they were sure to meet in deadly conflict again.

Even some of the generals freely mixed with the men, and seemed to view the painful sight with melancholy interest.

I saw Pat Cleburne, with that tall, meagre frame, and that ugly scar across his lank, gloomy face, stand with a thoughtful air, looking on the work his division had done; for it was his troops that defended the line of works in the centre, and committed such fearful havoc on Newton's and Davis's divisions. He looked a fit type of the lean Cassius. He was cer-

tainly to the western army what Stonewall Jackson was to the eastern. . . .

There were Generals Cleburne, Cheatham, Hindman, and M[a]ney, in busy converse with a group of Federal officers, mostly Tennessee officers, whom they had formerly known. Cheatham looked rugged and healthy, though seemingly sad and despondent. He wore his fatigue dress—a blue flannel shirt, black neck-tie, gray homespun pantaloons, and slouched, black hat. At first he was very taciturn; but this wearing off, he made inquiries about old friends, particularly about those from Nashville.

BRIGADIER GENERAL ALFRED J. VAUGHAN
BRIGADE COMMANDER, CHEATHAM'S DIVISION

Vaughan graduated from the Virginia Military Institute in 1851 and worked as a surveyor in California before returning east to farm in Mississippi. In 1861, finding that his home state of Virginia had filled its quota of troops for the Confederacy, Vaughan gained a commission as colonel of the 13th Tennessee. In the early morning of July 5, as he directed the withdrawal of his brigade from its works near Vining's Station, he was struck in the left foot by a Federal shell fragment.

Major General Patrick Cleburne, a native of Ireland, served in the British army before coming to America in 1849. A successful Arkansas lawyer, he was appointed colonel of the 1st Arkansas when his state seceded in 1861. His reputation as a fierce fighter and capable brigade commander earned him the rank of major general in December 1862; he was one of two foreign-born officers so honored in the Confederate army.

A shell from the enemy's battery came whizzing through the air over my line and exploded just as it struck my foot and the ground, tearing off my foot and making a hole almost large enough to bury me in. My staff were lying around under the shade of the tree, but none of them were struck by the shell or any of its fragments. Col. Dyer, who was standing over me at the time, had nearly all his clothing torn off, not by the shell or its fragments, but by the gravel that was thrown up against him. He received seventeen flesh wounds, none of which proved very serious. As soon as the shell exploded he involuntarily started to run to get behind a tree. . . .

The shock from the explosion of the shell was very severe, yet the tearing away of my leg was accompanied by neither pain nor the loss of much blood. In addition to the loss of my foot I received another wound on my other leg which was rather remarkable. I had a cut below the knee about four inches long and down to the bone, as smooth as if it had been cut with a sharp knife, yet neither my pants nor underclothing were torn. It was so smooth a cut that when pressed together it healed by first intention. None of us were able to conjecture what made this cut. Before I would allow my removal I made my staff find my sunglass and my pipe. The rim of my sunglass was broken.

As soon as it was known that I was wounded, the surgeons of my brigade and division came to my assistance, and bound up my wounds as best they could, and gave me some morphine and whisky. I was then put in an ambulance and started to the field hospital. In going to the hospital I passed by Gen. Cheatham's headquarters, who, hearing that I was wounded, came out to sympathize with me, and suggested that as I was looking very pale he thought that some stimulant would do me good, and gave me a stiff drink. I then began to feel pretty good and proceeded on my way to the hospital.

I had not gone very far when I passed Gen. Hardee's headquarters. He had heard of my misfortune and came out to see me. He also said I was looking very pale and that I ought to have some stimulant, and gave me a big drink.

I continued to feel better, and again started toward the hospital, and in a short time passed Gen. Joseph E. Johnston's headquarters. He came out to see me and also said that I was looking very pale, and that some stimulant would do me good. He happened to have some very fine apple brandy, and gave me a big drink, and down it went. From this time on I knew nothing until I awoke on the platform in Atlanta at sunrise the next morning.

LIEUTENANT HAMILTON M. BRANCH
54TH GEORGIA INFANTRY, MERCER'S BRIGADE

In May 1862 Hamilton Branch was elected lieutenant in the 54th Georgia Infantry, part of the Army of Tennessee. After the Confederate withdrawal from Kennesaw Mountain in July 1864, his brigade fell back behind the Chattahoochee River into formidable field fortifications. Branch wore the officer's shell jacket above during his service with the 54th Georgia.

In Reserve of Walkers Division
1/2 Miles of Chattahoochee River
July 6th 1864
My Very Dear Mother
After writing to you on yesterday we were moved one mile to the left and placed in position behind a portion of the stockade erected by Genl Shoop Genl Johnstons chief of Artillery this was the strangest sight we have seen since we have been here, it put me in mind of the fortifications I have read of in the account of the first American settlers lives, it was made thus on every little rise and commanding every little valey there were built redouts and block houses and all between these there were rails and logs about 12 feet in length stuck up in the ground close together, the whole forming (as some of the men remarked) a wall between the cornfeds and wheatfeds, and I would have liked it better

if the wall had been 1/2 mile in height and had been built farther north, we remained at that place doing nothing until dark when Bill arrived and we went to work with a good will, after eating we were ordered to pull down the stockade and build a breastwork instead, this we did working all night and until 9 oclock this morning when we were ordered to stop work and fall in this we did and were moved back into the woods about 200 yds where we dined immediately after dinner (or in fact before Capt. Anderson had finished for he had to eat as he was marching) we were ordered off and marched about 1 mile to this place and were put in reserve of our division, as soon as we stopped I put for the river and took a nice bath and put on my clean cloths. I then went back and just as I had arrived and was sitting down writting to you, we were ordered off again and are now (after having marched 1/2 mile to the left) in the trenches, and ready for a fight, we do not know how long we will stay here, and would not be at all surprised if we were moved in five minutes—thus it is we work all night and march all day and rest all the other time therefore we soldiers have plenty of rest and time to spare. We have not had a gun fired at us now for thirty-six hours in fact there is very little firing along the lines now, the enemy are shelling our pontoon bridges both on the right and left, and we are now putting some in the center. I do not know whether we will cross the river or not. Old Joe knows what he is at and will take care of us and do what is best. Praying Gods blessings on you I remain your devoted son

Hammie

In June 1864 Brigadier General Francis A. Shoup (left), Johnston's chief of artillery, directed the construction of an innovative line of defense along the Chattahoochee. Gangs of slaves, impressed from local plantations, built a series of diamond-shaped log and earth redoubts, dubbed Shoupades in honor of their designer. The Shoupades were connected by palisades, with artillery redans situated to provide point-blank enfilading fire across the face of each fort.

LIEUTENANT CHARLES H. COX
70TH INDIANA INFANTRY, WARD'S BRIGADE

On July 5, while Sherman's armies pressed toward the Chattahoochee River, Federal cavalry rode into the manufacturing town of Roswell, Georgia, and burned several large cotton and woolen mills—disregarding claims of neutrality by the mills' operator, Theophile Roche, a French national.

The latest Atlanta papers are at hand—They give gloomy accounts of the condition of the city—Many inhabitants have concluded to remain and be subjected to Yankee rule, with full confidence (so the editor says) the city will soon be wrested again from our infamous hordes. 'I can't see it' in that light and what Mr Sherman takes he generally *freezes* to—Roswell Cotton factory was taken by our forces the other day—and with it 700 girls who were working in it— The girls were somewhat alarmed at first, but were soon pacified and seemed pleased at being transferred for the Confed'cy to Uncle Samuel —and said they believed they liked the Yanks the best anyhow, as they wore the best clothes and were the best looking men—A dance was proposed by some of the boys, and agreed upon by the girls who went to work and cleaned out and scrubbed the floor of the largest room— some of our *army* fiddlers were engaged—the dance commenced and all 'was merry as a marriage bell'—when Mr Sherman put a finis to their fun by detaching a squad with a pocket full of matches and soon the buildings were no more. The factories were worth over $1,000,000— The girls were sent . . . to be shipped north I suppose . . . mostly are destitute of home . . . some lately arrived from England—Some one proposed that they be issued to Officers on 'Special Requisitions,' certifying they are for our own use—

SERGEANT WILLIAM R. CARTER

1ST TENNESSEE (U.S.) CAVALRY, DORR'S BRIGADE

Carter's regiment was one of the 20 or so Federal units raised primarily from the eastern part of Tennessee, where Union sentiment ran high. Among the first Federal troops to reach the Chattahoochee, the 1st Tennessee was charged with crossing the river on July 9 just below its confluence with Soap Creek. Faced with an impatient brigade commander and a trigger-happy enemy on the opposite bank, the Yankees adopted a novel strategy.

Soon thereafter, a few of the boys were called to the rear—there were just nine men in all—and Colonel Brownlow said, "Boys, we are going to cross that river. It is plain we can't ford it here, and as we have no pontoons, and can't very well make a swimming charge, we'll find another way or break the breeching."

Then, giving directions for the men at the ford to keep up an incessant fire so as to divert the attention of the enemy from the move about to be made, the colonel led his little squad through the brush to a point about a mile up the river, behind a bend, where, lashing a couple of logs together and placing their carbines, cartridge-boxes and belts thereon, they stripped to the skin and, leaving their hats, boots and clothing behind, swam the river, pushing the raft in front of them.

The appearance of nine naked men with belts on, as they stood in line, was somewhat ludicrous, and while Brownlow was giving, in undertones, the directions and plan of attack, it was difficult to repress the humorous remarks interjected by the boys, witty expressions, some of them, that would make the gravest soldier laugh, but would not be appreciated by civilians unfamiliar with military terms. "I'll be durned if this ain't baring our breasts to the foe, for a fact," said one. "I reckon the rebs will climb them trees when they find out we're a lot of East

So unusual was the 1st Tennessee's nude river crossing that it earned a mention in the August 13 issue of Harper's Weekly, along with an illustration entitled Colonel Brownlow on a Picket Hunt *(below). The "Yankee trick" so infuriated the Rebels that they suspended their amiable cross-river transactions, exchanges that were doomed anyway once the Federals began crossing the river in strength.*

GEN. SHERMAN'S ADVANCE.

On this and the preceding, as well as on our first page, we continue our illustrations of General SHERMAN's great campaign. One of these, on page 524, represents THE FOURTH CORPS—General HOWARD'S—CROSSING THE CHATTAHOOCHEE. This corps was one of the last to cross; it reached the Atlanta side without opposition, taking its position in the centre of SHERMAN's lines after crossing the river.

TURNER'S MILL, illustrated on the same page, is on Nickajack Creek, which is an affluent of the Chattahoochee, from the northern side, emptying into that river a little above Sandtown. It was near its mouth that the rebel army made its last stand before crossing the Chattahoochee. The illustration is chiefly valuable for its rural rather than its military feature.

Another pleasant scene, which we give our readers on the same page, is that representing the soldiers engaged in setting Fish-traps in the Chattahoochee.

On this page we give a view of the MILITARY COLLEGE near Marietta, formerly the first in the South. The area, as seen in the sketch, is filled with rebel prisoners.

Another illustration on this page represents Colonel JIM BROWNLOW, with a small party of men in Georgia costume, crossing the Chattahoochee to capture the rebel pickets. The expedition was a successful one, but it broke up the friendly communication which had been several days established between the pickets across the river. This was before SHERMAN had crossed. The morning after the occurrence notice was given of the changed situation by a Reb yelling out across the stream:

"Hello, Yank!"

"What do you want, Johnny?"

"Can't talk to you 'uns any more!"

"How is that?"

"Orders to dry up!"

"What for, Johnny?"

"Oh! JIM BROWNLOW, with his d—d Tennessee Yanks, swam over upon the left last night, and stormed our rifle-pits naked—captured sixty of our boys, and made 'em swim back with him. We 'uns have got to keep you 'uns on your side of the river now."

More interesting, as connected with later and more stirring events, is the illustration given on our first page representing General HOOKER riding along his lines on the morning after the great battle of the 20th. This battle was very severe. The rebels, by their own account, lost over 5000 men, while our loss was less than one-third of that number. The attack was made by the enemy shortly after our troops had crossed Peach-tree Creek. NEWTON's division of HOWARD's corps had found time to protect itself by a slight rail-barricade. HOOKER was attacked while yet in column, his "family," as he calls the Twentieth Corps, getting into order almost without an order. The heaviest attack fell on General WILLIAMS's division. WARD's and BUTTERFIELD's divisions were more successful. They had for trophies seven rebel flags. When HOOKER rode along the lines the next morning, as represented in the sketch, to greet his troops and to congratulate them on their success, these flags were all brought out for his inspection, the men being engaged in burying the rebel dead lying thickly around.

We also give on this page portraits of General A. S. WILLIAMS and of the late General HARKER.

Brigadier-General CHARLES G. HARKER, killed in the assault on Kenesaw, June 27, was a native of New Jersey. He entered West Point in 1854, at the age of seventeen. He entered the regular army as Brevet Second Lieutenant of the Second Infantry July 1, 1858. He was made First Lieutenant of the Ninth May 14, 1861, and a Captain in October of that year. He entered the war as Lieutenant-Colonel of the Sixty-fifth Ohio Volunteers in the fall of 1861, and afterward became its Colonel. He participated in the battle of Shiloh and the siege of Corinth, and helped chase BRAGG out of Kentucky, being then in command of a brigade. His brigade joined General ROSECRANS's Army of the Cumberland. In the official report of the battle at Stone River he was recommended for promotion, which he only received last April, when he was made a Brigadier-General of Volunteers. He was under THOMAS when the latter made his gallant stand at Chicamauga.

COLONEL BROWNLOW ON A PICKET HUNT.—[SKETCHED BY THEODORE R. DAVIS.]

Tennessee bear hunters," put in another. "Talk low, talk low!" said Brownlow, "for the success of this attack depends upon our quietness until we close in with the game, and then you may yell like ———." Well, they started, with trailed carbines, into the cedar thicket, which concealed them from the enemy's view, leaving one man to guard the raft, and moved as rapidly as the nature of the ground would permit, but the funny expressions soon gave place to some that were in violation of the Third Commandment.

They were all "tenderfoots," and as the sharp stones and dry twigs harrowed their soles, and their naked bodies were scratched and punctured by the cedar brush and stung by insects, some vigorous profanity was naturally indulged in. "Curse low, men," ordered Brownlow as he turned his head, and in doing so he nearly stumbled to the ground, but as he recovered himself and went limping along he continued, in a very loud voice, "The occasion is worthy of considerable profanity, but cuss low, cuss low!" Coming to a road that led to the ford, about four hundred yards in the rear of the enemy, and reconnoitering the location and number of the rebel reserves, they formed for the charge, and moved quietly forward, unseen by the rebs, until they got within forty or fifty yards of them.

Then, turning their carbines loose and rushing on them with a yell, in a very few minutes most of those Confederates were awaiting the orders of the Tennesseans. Some of them got away, but they bagged twelve. One of the last to give up was a freckled-faced fellow, half con-

Well versed in unorthodox tactics after his experiences in the brutal "bushwhackers war" that raged between pro-Confederate and Unionist factions in east Tennessee, Colonel James P. Brownlow (left) was mentioned in his division commander's report for July 9 as having "performed one of his characteristic feats to-day." Son of a pro-Union preacher, Brownlow left college in Virginia to go to war and three years later took command of the 1st Tennessee when he was only 21.

cealed behind a tree. When he was covered and surrendered, he threw down his gun and said: "I surrender, but dog-gone my skin, Yanks, 'taint fair to come at us in that way. If we'uns had been strong enough to take you'uns, the Confederate government 'ud hung you all for spies, as you hain't got no uniforms on."

BRIGADIER GENERAL ARTHUR M. MANIGAULT
BRIGADE COMMANDER, HINDMAN'S DIVISION

When the architect of the Chattahoochee River defenses, General Shoup, heard of the order to fall back, he could not help but think that "the days of the Confederacy were numbered." But at the time, few in the army seemed to share his disappointment. Like many officers, General Manigault was anxious for a little rest and eager to put some distance between his troops and the enemy.

To retire without giving any alarm or bringing on an attack was a very delicate operation, but every precaution being taken by wrapping the wheels of our artillery with such material as would muffle and deaden the sound, and by strewing the pontoon bridges with green corn stalks, etc., the result was that the whole army drew out, saving everything in the way of material and without the loss of a man. Everything having crossed to the left bank, the pontoon bridges, of which there was three, were removed and safely in rear before the enemy began to make his appearance on the opposite side. Leaving about a fourth of our force on picket or outpost duty near the river, the remainder retired towards Atlanta, distant from the river about eight miles, and, encamping around the city about three miles from it, made the most of the few days of comparative quiet which succeeded.

From the morning of the 10th of July to that of the 17th, the brigade and Army remained in a state of comparative quiet, and undisturbed rest. The clothing of the men stood greatly in need of careful washing and cleaning, and the rest that all obtained during this short respite was much needed and enjoyed. Still the time was not passed in idleness. Rigid inspections were made, and as far as practicable, many deficiencies were supplied, and everything got in a state of readiness for future action. During this period, we performed as a brigade, one tour of picket duty, lasting forty-eight hours. It was by no means arduous, and but little picket firing took place. The stream separated us from the enemy, who were similarly posted on the opposite bank of the river. I do not believe that we lost a single man on this occasion.

"As the soldiers caught the announcement that Atlanta was in sight, such a cheer went up as must have been heard even in the entrenchments of the doomed city itself."

MAJOR JAMES A. CONNOLLY

123D ILLINOIS INFANTRY, WILDER'S BRIGADE

James A. Connolly, a 22-year-old lawyer from Charleston, Illinois, joined the 123d Illinois Infantry in 1862. Rapidly promoted to major, Connolly served for three years with the Army of the Cumberland. In a letter to his wife, Mary, dated July 12, Connolly recounts his pleasure at his first sight of the Federal goal—the city of Atlanta.

t Chattahoochee River, July 12, 1864.

Dear wife:

Mine eyes have beheld the promised land! The "domes and minarets and spires" of Atlanta are glittering in the sunlight before us, and only 8 miles distant. On the morning of the 5th, while riding at the extreme front with the General, and eagerly pressing our skirmishers forward after the rapidly retreating rebels, suddenly we came upon a high bluff overlooking the Chattahoochee, and looking southward across the river, there lay the beautiful "Gate City" in full view, and as the soldiers caught the announcement that Atlanta was in sight, such a cheer went up as must have been heard even in the entrenchments of the doomed city itself. In a very few moments Generals Sherman and Thomas (who are always with the extreme front when a sudden movement is taking place) were with us on the hill top, and the two veterans, for a moment, gazed at the glittering prize in silence. I watched the two noble soldiers—Sherman stepping nervously about, his eyes sparkling and his face aglow—casting a single glance at Atlanta, another at the River, and a dozen at the surrounding valley to see where he could best cross the River, how he best could flank them. Thomas stood there like a noble old Roman, calm, soldierly, dignified; no trace of excitement about that grand old soldier who had ruled the storm at Chickamauga. Turning quietly to my General, he said: "[Baird], send up a couple of guns and we'll throw some shells over there," pointing to some heavy timber across the River.

In a moment I was off down the road, to the rear, to order up some artillery; the infantry column separated and opened the road, the artillery came thundering along through the long lines of men, and in fifteen minutes from the time our line of skirmishers reached that hill top, a Parrott shell went screaming from the high point, and burst beautifully on the south side of the Chattahoochee—the first since the war began. That was a glorious moment, and I felt proud that I belonged to this grand army, and that I was at the front instead of at the rear, doing "fancy duty." Many a long fatiguing day has passed since I first crossed the Ohio River as a soldier, and the Chattahoochee River then seemed a long way off; many a time since then have I almost felt like giving up in despair, confessing myself unequal to the stern requirements of my time, but fortunately better counsels prevailed. . . .

Your cheerful, hopeful spirit has encouraged and animated me, and I know you would not have me shrink from the ordeal or return home until I can do so honorably.

Closing the Ring

As the Federal juggernaut descended upon Atlanta, Jefferson Davis dispatched General Braxton Bragg to the scene to assess the deteriorating situation. When Bragg arrived on July 13, he received a predictably cold reception from Johnston, and he reported to Davis, "I cannot learn that he has any more plans in the future than he has had in the past." But the president's chief military adviser had no trouble eliciting opinions from John Bell Hood. "We have had several chances to strike the enemy a decisive blow," Hood informed Bragg. "We have failed to take advantage of such opportunities." This, Hood declared, was "a great misfortune to our country." Bragg and Hood agreed: "There is but one remedy—offensive action." Johnston, meanwhile, insisted to the Confederate chief executive that his next move would have to "depend upon that of the enemy."

Jefferson Davis had had enough: Joe Johnston would have to be replaced. And though Hardee was the senior corps commander serving with the Army of Tennessee, his tendency toward caution promised no change in the distressing course of events. Hood, not Hardee, would receive the appointment.

On the night of July 17 Johnston received an official communiqué from the War Department notifying him of his removal from command. The soldiers of the Army of Tennessee were stunned by the news. Brigadier General Arthur M. Manigault noted that his troops "received the announcement with very bad grace, and with no little murmuring."

"By this act the army was *outraged,*" Captain Elbert Willett of the 40th Alabama noted in his diary, "so unexpected, so undeserved."

Despite Johnston's withdrawal to Atlanta, his subordinates had come to trust in their general's strategic vision, and they felt he had displayed great skill in fending off a numerically superior foe. Sam Watkins shared the affection most of the fighting men cherished for Old Joe, stating, "He was more popular with his troops day by day."

Word of the change soon reached the Union lines across Peachtree Creek. Attempt-

Abandoned Rebel earthworks lie along a bluff above the Chattahoochee River near a railroad bridge rebuilt by Federal engineers. General Johnston razed the span when he pulled his army back across the river on the night of July 9.

ing to get an impression of his new opponent, Sherman sought the opinions of two of Hood's acquaintances from West Point. "He is a stupid fellow," General Howard remarked, "but a hard fighter." Schofield, who had roomed with Hood at the military academy, told Sherman, "He'll hit you like hell." The remarks would prove prophetic in the climactic battles that would decide the fate of Atlanta.

On July 20, only three days after taking command, John Hood put his offensive-minded strategy into practice with a vengeance, lashing out at Thomas' isolated army on the south side of Peachtree Creek. The spirited attack by Hardee's and Stewart's corps drove back the Federals in several places, but Union reinforcements and heavy artillery fire finally stopped the Rebels in their tracks. Hardee was about to launch another attack at about 6:00 p.m. when he received orders from Hood to detach a division to meet another Federal threat: McPherson's army was approaching Atlanta from the east and had begun to bombard the city.

Shortly before noon, a 20-pound shell exploded at the corner of Ivy and East Ellis streets, killing a little girl and injuring her parents. The Yankee guns continued to pound the city and its surrounding earthworks well into the evening. "Citizens were running in every direction," a Southern cavalryman recalled. "Terror-stricken women and children went screaming about the streets seeking some avenue of escape from hissing, bursting shells."

The next day Hood saw another chance to smash the Federals when McPherson's troops occupied Bald Hill, a crest commanding the eastern approach to the city. Hood detected that McPherson had failed to protect his left flank at Bald Hill, and the Confederate com-

mander rushed Hardee's corps to the attack on the morning of July 22. The Rebel onslaught nearly succeeded in rolling up the vulnerable flank. But Hood had miscalculated the time needed to make the march, so the attack was delivered at noon, not at sunrise, and the assault was stalled by Federal reinforcements. That afternoon, Benjamin Cheatham's fresh corps broke through the Federal line north of Bald Hill. Sherman himself organized the artillery support for the counterstrike that sent the Confederates reeling.

In two battles, Hood had suffered 8,000 casualties—more men than Johnston had lost in 10 weeks. More than 5,000 Confederates and 4,000 Federals had been killed, wounded, or captured in the fighting on July 22, what would come to be called the Battle of Atlanta. Sherman also lost one of his best commanders. General McPherson was killed by a Rebel skirmisher's bullet.

While Hood admitted that "the grand results desired were not accomplished," his surprise attack around Bald Hill had very nearly succeeded, and it caused many citizens of Atlanta to believe that Sherman might abandon his siege. But though loath to launch an assault on the formidable defenses of the city, the grimly determined Yankee commander was not about to loosen his stranglehold.

In the last days of July Sherman sent his cavalry on a series of raids intended to cut what he called "a circle of desolation" around Atlanta. While the mounted operations were singularly unsuccessful, they paved the way for Sherman's next offensive move—an attempt to sever the city's last remaining lifeline, the Macon & Western Railroad. General Howard, the devout one-armed West Pointer who was now commander of the Army of the Tennessee, swung his troops southwest of

Atlanta to seize control of the vital rail line. "Tell Howard to invite them to attack," Sherman instructed an aide; "they'll only beat their brains out."

Stephen D. Lee, at 33 the youngest lieutenant general in the Confederacy, did just that on July 28. Having only recently arrived at Atlanta to take command of Hood's old corps, Lee lashed out at Howard's positions near Ezra Church. Some 3,000 Rebel troops were cut down in the hail of musket and artillery fire, while the defending Federals suffered only 650 losses. By now many Southerners had lost their enthusiasm for head-on assaults, and the attack was disjointed and half-hearted. "If all the troops had displayed equal spirit," Lee reported, "we would have been successful."

Frustrated in his efforts to sever the Macon & Western, Sherman escalated his bombardment of Atlanta in an attempt to further erode Southern morale. On one day alone, some 5,000 shells fell on the city. "One thing is certain," Sherman informed his superiors in Washington, "whether we get inside Atlanta or not, it will be a used-up community by the time we are done with it."

While the siege ground on through August, the Federal commander had not abandoned his designs on the Macon & Western. On the 25th of the month Sherman set in motion what he styled a "grand movement by the right flank," with Howard's entire army and two of Thomas' corps marching on a broad arc to the west and south, to join Schofield in a three-pronged attack on the coveted railroad.

With Wheeler's cavalry off raiding, Hood was unsure of what the move portended, and he briefly entertained the notion that Sherman had called off his siege. But when Hardee's and Lee's corps arrived at Jonesboro, 15 miles south of Atlanta, they realized the magnitude of the Yankee threat. Hardee attacked the vanguard of Howard's army on August 31 but was repulsed with a loss of 1,700 men, 10 times the number of Federal casualties. With the situation deteriorating rapidly, Hood ordered Lee's corps back to Atlanta, leaving Hardee to wage a rearguard fight at Jonesboro.

On September 1 Howard and Thomas closed in on Hardee's isolated corps. A Mississippi artilleryman remembered, "It was a grand and fearful sight to see that great army coming like a monster wave to engulf us." The result was a foregone conclusion. The Southern line was overrun and, as Sherman put it, rolled up "like a sheet of paper." Hardee led his surviving troops toward Lovejoy's Station, six miles south of Jonesboro.

The debacle at Jonesboro sealed the fate of Atlanta. Hood ordered Lee's corps to retrace its steps southward and link up with Hardee, while Stewart's corps pulled out of the city's defenses and also struck south to Lovejoy's Station. In the early morning hours of September 2, factories, mills, and supply depots were put to the torch to prevent their falling into Yankee hands. When trainloads of ammunition were detonated by the flames, one citizen thought "the very earth trembled as if in the throes of a mighty earthquake."

By late morning the only Confederate soldiers remaining in Atlanta were those too severely wounded to be evacuated. As a pall of smoke hung low over the rubble-strewn streets, the vanguard of Sherman's victorious armies entered unopposed, and to the stirring accompaniment of regimental bands, raised the Stars and Stripes over city hall. "So Atlanta is ours," Sherman wired Washington, "and fairly won."

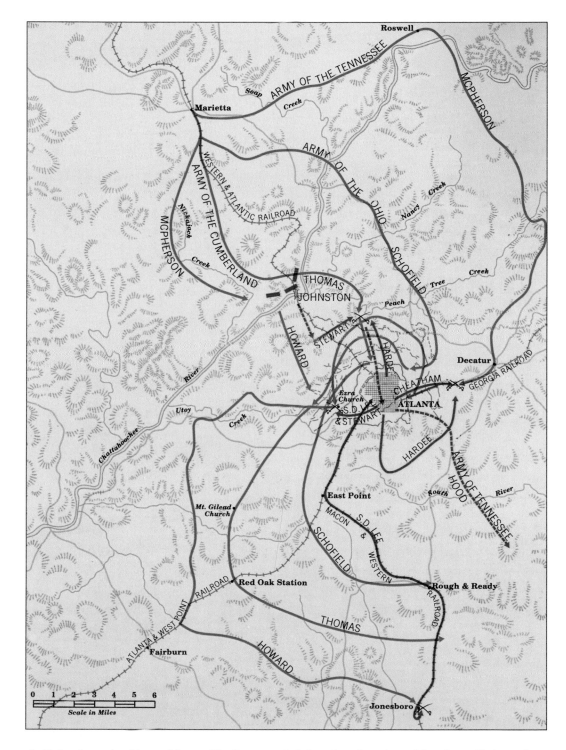

As Union forces closed in on Atlanta, Hood's army tried three times in vain to drive them off. A month-long siege ensued until Sherman completed the encirclement of the city and forced the Rebels to evacuate.

PRIVATE SAMUEL A. MCNEIL

31ST OHIO INFANTRY, TURCHIN'S BRIGADE

Turchin's brigade was one of the first Federal units to take up position near the Chattahoochee River. While the generals planned the next moves, McNeil and his comrades and the Rebel troops on the opposite shore declared an informal truce and spent the next few days fraternizing. A farm boy from Union County, Ohio, McNeil enlisted in 1861 at the age of 18. He served until July 20, 1865.

While occupying the same position on the Chattahoochie river, the officer in command of the Confederate outposts requested the officer in charge of our line to ask our brigade band, which we could hear as they played every evening, to come down to the river. The band responded and was accompanied by a number of officers and soldiers. It was the old regimental band of the 19th Illinois Infantry, which General Turchin had retained for his brigade band. They were a good bunch of musicians. I recall that scene. A band of musicians in their blue uniforms, standing out on the captured pontoon bridge, playing to an audience on each side of the river—on one side the blue, on the other side the gray. We cheered "The Red, White and Blue," and other old national airs. They yelled when the band struck up "Dixie" and "The Bonnie Blue Flag." Both sides applauded "Annie Laurie" and "The Campbells are Coming," but no demonstration followed "Home, Sweet Home," which closed the concert. . . .

That night, "Billy" Williams, Jerome Oatley and the writer entertained the men in gray until our entire stock of war songs and home songs were used up. "Yanks, that's all right, give us another," was the frequent call from the other side of the river. We finally gave them "John Brown," including the verse "We'll hang Jeff Davis to a Sour Apple Tree." That song went without any demonstration of approval from the men in gray. . . .

. . . a few days after the "band concert," we were on outpost duty at the river, and noticed an unusual commotion among the boys in gray on the other side. They were packing up their cooking utensils and camp equipage and hastily forming in line. On our side everybody seemed to take notice, and one of our fellows inquired the cause of their hurried movements. A Confederate replied: "Oh, nothin, only you all are coming down the river on our side," and our foes marched rapidly back from the river. A few minutes later some one called attention to something up the river. Imagine our surprise when looking to the left we saw a heavy skirmish line of blue coming down the south side of the Chattahoochee, at quick time and with their guns at "trail arms." Not a shot was heard from the retreating Johnnies, or from the advancing Yankees. It was a new phase of war, and we, who had been so chummy with the Alabama boys, almost regreted their sudden departure. They were jolly good fellows and we had carried on quite a business in trading coffee for tobacco, and some of our boys had swapped pocket knives with them.

The point for the exchange of goods was a rock near the middle of the stream. One morning a Confederate came across and ate breakfast with members of Company F, after which he returned to his own side of the river. The temporary truce on the skirmish lines was a matter which was arranged by the enlisted men of both sides. Our officers never objected to such a compact with the enemy, and the Confederate officers seldom interfered. It seems to me, now, that it was a sensible plan and doubtless saved many lives, and did not injure the cause for which we were fighting, namely: to crush the Southern rebellion and restore the Union.

SURGEON GEORGE W. PEDDY

56TH GEORGIA INFANTRY, CUMMING'S BRIGADE

A graduate of the New Orleans School of Medicine, Peddy was serving at a field hospital outside Atlanta when he wrote this letter to his wife, Kate (shown above with their daughter, Laura), advising her what to do should Federal troops approach their family home in Heard County, Georgia.

Honey, I scarcely know what to do about your leaving home. I do not know wheather we will give up Atlanta or not. I hope not without a fight. Your Pa can do as he thinks

"Honey, you must hide my uniform and all the cloth you have made for me in case you hear of them coming."

best. I trust to his judgment. He must be shure not to let the enemy get hold of him. The enemy are not interupting Ladies alone through the country they have passed, as letters received here from them to soldiers abundantly show. I do not think they will get to our place. They may pass down the river on the other side if we hold Atlanta. If we donot, you may look out for a raid in our town some day. Honey, you must hide my uniform and all the cloth you have made for me in case you hear of them coming, for they will be shure to take them from you. You must not let any of the negroes know whare you put them. . . . Your Pa must send the negro men or at least Lin, Lee and also Mary of[f], for should the enemy come, they will have you robed & whiped if they could. . . . If you want to go, I would, if I was your Pa, have some boats built and go down the river in them to get out of the way.

Honey, if you pretend to stay at home, stay their, donot run to the woods should the enemy come, but stay at the house. Honey, I think we will whip the enemy should they cross the river here. I think Gen. [Johnston] intends having a gen[eral] engagement here. . . .

Honey, my sweet one, I can see your lovely form in my imagination sitting in your rocking chair and hear your sweet talk to your little boy which so compleetly enraptures him as it does me. I almost envy the little fellow in the enjoyment of that bliss which is bliss indeed to me. Bless your sweet voice, which is so joyfully tuned for my ear. . . .

I am glad that you and Laura think so much of your little treasure. I am proud he is fattening. Hope Ma is too. Honey, never in life did I want to see you so much as now. Evry moment that I am away from you seems like years. I am glad, honey, to read that portion of your last letter in which you state you will allow no one to usurp in your affections myself. . . . Kiss Laura and the boy for Pappie. What are you going to name him, my love? Give my love to all.

Be sure to have the negroes sent off—those that I have spoken of. Be shure to have my clothes out of the way should the enemy get there. Do not put them in any trunk or any thing about the house, for they will look in evry box & trunk.

LOUISE WIGFALL
Daughter of Senator Louis T. Wigfall

Louise Wigfall, shown here wearing a star from General Johnston's collar, and her sister were placed in the care of Johnston's wife during the summer of 1862 when their parents were called away to Texas. Driven from Atlanta by the Federals' imminent arrival, Louise writes of the unforgettable trip to Macon they were forced to take.

Macon, July 11th, 1864

You see by the heading of my letter that already we have been forced to leave Atlanta—not that it has fallen, but Mrs. Johnston received a letter from the General in which he advised her to send us off at once—to remain until the fate of the city was decided either one way or the other. . . .

I shall never forget the horrors of the journey from Atlanta to Macon. We left in a hospital train, filled with wounded, sick and dying soldiers, in all imaginable stages of disease and suffering. My little sister and myself and one other lady were the only other passengers on the train, except the officer put in charge of us to see us safe to our journey's end. I never imagined what a hideous, cruel thing War was until I was brought into direct contact with these poor victims of "Man's inhumanity to man." For this was no modern hospital train with scientific arrangements for hygiene and the relief of suffering. There was scant supply of the common comforts, and even decencies of life—no cushions nor air pillows for weary heads; no ice to cool the fevered thirst;

no diet kitchen for broths and delicate food for these half starved sufferers; no wine or brandy to revive the failing pulse and stimulate the weakened vitality; not even medicine enough to check the ravages of disease; nor anaesthetics nor anodynes to ease their agonies—for the supply of medicines and anodynes was daily diminishing, and they could not be replaced, as our foes had declared them "contraband of war!" There was not even a place in that crowded car where the sick could lie down; but, packed in as close as possible on the hard uncomfortable seats, they made that journey, as best they might, in uncomplaining martyrdom. I reached Macon sick at heart over the suffering I had witnessed and was so powerless to avert.

CAPTAIN SAMUEL T. FOSTER
24TH TEXAS CAVALRY (DISMOUNTED), GRANBURY'S BRIGADE

After the Confederate Army of Tennessee fell back across the Chattahoochee River, President Jefferson Davis relieved General Johnston of command and replaced him with the younger, less experienced John Bell Hood. The ouster of the popular Johnston infuriated Confederate officers and enlisted men alike. According to Captain Foster, "If Jeff Davis had made his appearance in this army during the excitement, he would not have lived an hour."

No move today—A circular from Genl Johnson announces that he has been removed from the command of this Army, and that Gen Hood succeeds him.

In less than an hour after this fact becomes known, groups of three, five, seven, ten or fifteen men could be seen all over camp discussing the situation—Gen. Johnson has so endeared himself to his soldiers, that no man can take his place. We have never made a fight under him that we did not get the best of it. And the whole army has become so attached to him, and to put such implicit faith in him, that whenever he said for us to fight at any particular place, we went in feeling like Gen Johnson knew all about it and we were certain to whip.

He never deceived us once. It is true we have had hard fighting and hard marching, but we always had something to eat, and in bad weather, or after an extra hard march we would have a little whiskey issued.

Gen Johnson could not have issued an order that these men would not have undertaken to accomplish—

For the first time, we hear men openly talk about going home, by

Johnston received this telegram ordering his removal at 10:00 on the night of July 17 while he was conferring with his chief engineer about strengthening Atlanta's fortifications. On Davis' instructions, it was sent by the Confederate army's adjutant and inspector general, Samuel Cooper.

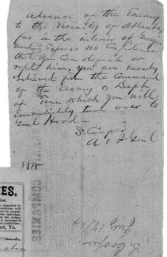

tens (10) and by fifties (50). They refuse to stand guard, or do any other camp duty, and talk open rebellion against all Military authority—All over camp, (not only among Texas troops) can be seen this demoralization—and at all hours in the afternoon can be heard Hurrah for Joe Johnson and God D——n Jeff Davis.

LOUISE WIGFALL
DAUGHTER OF SENATOR LOUIS T. WIGFALL

Johnston's removal from command stirred indignation among the civilians, who did all they could to show him their sympathy and respect. Reunited with the Johnstons in Macon, Wigfall witnessed a special tribute paid the general.

I shall never forget a scene which occurred at the church door on General Johnston's first appearance at service after his removal. Mrs. Clement Clay, wife of the former United States Senator from Alabama, had, with her husband, the warmest admiration and affectionate friendship for General Johnston. She was as impulsive and demonstrative, as he was shy and reserved. Her feelings of indignation at his removal were at a white heat. She not only felt incensed, but she wanted everyone to know that fact and the depth of her sympathy. They had not met since his arrival in Macon, and, catching sight of the old hero, as with reverent mien and modest air he moved with the crowd through the church door, she rushed up to him with hands outstretched, and rising on tip toe imprinted on his bronzed cheek a warm kiss of love and sympathy, in the face of the whole congregation. The effect was magical. A low murmur went around among the people, tears sprung into many eyes, as they saw the blush mount to his brow at this spontaneous tribute to the love which we bore him. Mrs. Clay had only expressed our feelings, and, surrounded by a half laughing, half tearful crowd, the old General made his way down the church steps and hurried homewards.

SERGEANT FENWICK Y. HEDLEY
32D ILLINOIS INFANTRY, ROGERS' BRIGADE

Once the Federals got word that Hood had replaced Johnston (Sherman learned of it from a newspaper smuggled out of Atlanta), they knew that the nature of the fighting was about to change. Whereas Johnston was respected as a shrewd defensive strategist, Hood had a well-earned reputation for aggressiveness.

There was a camp story to the effect that, on receiving the news of Hood superseding Johnston, General Sherman called a council of officers, who had known the new Confederate commander personally, in order to learn something of his character. Several officers, who had been classmates with General Hood at West Point, expressed themselves in various ways, pertinent and otherwise; but the climax was reached when an old Kentucky colonel remarked that he "Seed Hood bet twenty-five hundred dollars, with nary a p'ar in his hand!" This anecdote convinced all that such an exhibition of nerve was good evidence of the fighting qualities of the new commander. However this may be, General Sherman was satisfied that the change of commanders betokened more vigorous measures, and made his dispositions accordingly, sending notice of the fact to every part of the army, and notifying his subordinates to be prepared, at all times, for sharp and unexpected battle. The troops grasped the import of Hood's appointment with as quick intelligence as the officers, and expressed great satisfaction with the assignment, regarding Hood as a hot-headed fellow, who would butt his brains out against their entrenchments, thus shortening the campaign and the war.

"At all hours in the afternoon can be heard Hurrah for Joe Johnson and God D——n Jeff Davis."

Although his own clandestine reports to Richmond in the spring of 1864 had helped to undermine Jefferson Davis' confidence in Johnston, the ambitious Hood (above) expressed reluctance to replace his old commander. He begged Johnston to "pocket" Davis' dispatch until the fight for Atlanta was over.

Peachtree Creek

Once the retreating Joseph Johnston had settled into the earthworks that guarded the northern outskirts of Atlanta, he made plans to strike back. He would attack the leading Federal column—Thomas' Army of the Cumberland—as it made its way across Peachtree Creek. Stewart's and Hardee's corps would hit Thomas and drive the Yankees into the angle formed by the stream's confluence with the Chattahoochee. Trapped with their backs to the river, the Army of the Cumberland might well be forced to surrender en masse.

General Johnston never had the chance to execute his daring strategy, however, because on the evening of July 17 he was relieved of command of the Army of Tennessee. Johnston's successor, the fiery, one-legged John B. Hood, approved of Johnston's counterattack but made a number of fateful modifications to the plan.

Johnston originally intended to attack on July 19, but Hood pushed the launch date back to 1:00 p.m. of the following day. Concerned about the security of his right flank, Hood decided to shift his assault formations to the east, with the result that the attack was further delayed until 4:00 p.m. on July 20. By the time Hood was ready to strike, most of Thomas' units had crossed Peachtree Creek and were positioned along the high ground south of the stream. Only Daniel Butterfield's division of Hooker's XX Corps, now led by William Ward, had not yet come up. With Palmer's XIV Corps on the right, Hooker in the center, and Howard's IV Corps on the left, the Army of the Cumberland was well situated to meet any Rebel attempt to drive them back into the creek.

The Confederate onslaught began at 4:00 p.m. with Hardee's corps, on the Southern right, bearing down upon Howard's position. While the divisions of Cheatham, temporarily commanded by George Maney, and William Walker struck Howard head-on, Bate's division began working its way around the far Union left, where Newton's division angled back to Peachtree Creek. But heavy underbrush slowed Bate's advance, and when Brigadier General Luther P. Bradley swung his brigade into position to enfilade Bate's troops, the flank attack was fended off.

Walker's and Maney's divisions initially gained some ground along the center of Howard's position, where Ward's division had yet to come into line on Newton's right. But the Federals put up a stiff resistance, and Confederate losses mounted. Clement H. Stevens, a brigade commander in Walker's division, was struck from his horse by an artillery shell and fatally wounded.

Attacking on Hardee's left, Alexander Stewart's corps moved forward at 4:30 p.m. and also made some initial headway by taking advantage of gaps in the Federal line. Brigadier General Winfield Scott Featherston's brigade of Major General William W. Loring's division splashed across Tanyard Branch, pushed over the Collier road, and threatened to drive a wedge between Howard's and Hooker's corps. But the timely arrival of Ward's Federal division plugged the gap, and Featherston was forced to draw back with heavy loss.

Another of Loring's brigades, led by Brigadier General Thomas M. Scott, managed to inflict even greater damage to the center of the Yankee defenses. After overrunning the 33d New Jersey—the forwardmost regiment of Geary's division of the XX Corps—they surged on for the Collier road and the left flank of Geary's line. But the Federals rallied and caught Scott's Alabama and Louisiana regiments in a deadly cross fire. With his troops scattered and no support forthcoming, Scott had to withdraw from his hard-won ground.

On Loring's left, the division of Major General Edward C. Walthall advanced from a staging area near Mount Zion Church and soon gained the Collier road. Colonel Edward A. O'Neal's brigade threatened the right flank of Geary's Federal division, but Geary countered the move by turning his line to face the attackers. O'Neal's men soon found themselves trapped in a ravine between the fire of Geary's troops to their right and Brigadier General Alpheus S. Williams' division to their left, and they were forced to retreat.

On Walthall's left, Brigadier General Daniel H. Reynolds' Arkansas brigade also crossed the Collier road and began to lap around the flank of Brigadier General Joseph F. Knipe's brigade. But both of Reynolds' own flanks came under heavy fire, and when McCook's and Brigadier General Thomas H. Ruger's brigades came to Knipe's assistance, Reynolds was forced to extricate his troops in order to prevent them from being enveloped by the numerically superior Yankees. The failure of the Confederate assaults elsewhere on the line prevented Stewart's leftmost division, commanded by Samuel French, from engaging in anything more than long-range skirmishing.

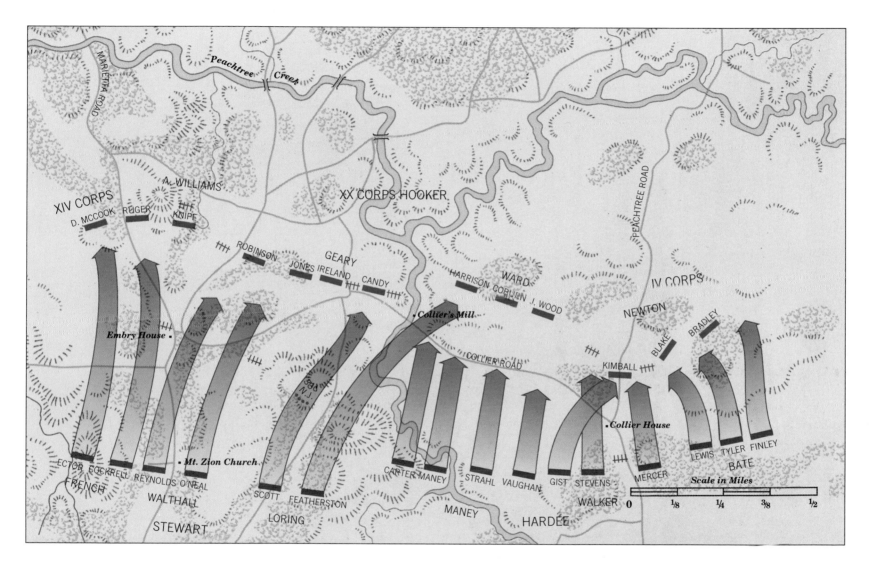

Around dusk, Hardee was preparing to launch another attack on the Federal left with Cleburne's division, which was held in reserve to the rear of Walker's troops. But Hood ordered Hardee to detach Cleburne's troops and send them to block McPherson's Federal army, which was approaching with alarming speed from the east. This move—and darkness—ended the fighting. The Battle of Peachtree Creek cost Thomas' Army of the Cumberland 1,900 casualties—1 out of every 10 Federals engaged. But Confederate losses were even greater—some 2,500—and Hood had signally failed to strike the crippling blow that he had envisaged. With Sherman tightening his grip on Atlanta, the Southern commander sought a new opportunity to catch the confident Yankees off guard.

Hood struck first on July 20 against Thomas' army just south of Peachtree Creek. The Rebels staged a furious assault, but faulty planning and selection of terrain, a late start, and a resilient foe forced them to withdraw with heavy losses.

SERGEANT RICE C. BULL
123D NEW YORK INFANTRY, KNIPE'S BRIGADE

Having crossed Peachtree Creek on the morning of July 20, Knipe's brigade faced a surprise attack that afternoon by Walthall's division. A farm boy from New York, Bull enlisted in 1862. Asked in later years why he and his friends had volunteered, he replied, "We felt that if our country was to endure as a way of life as planned by our fathers, it rested with us children to finish the work they had begun."

By this time it was noon and we were notified that we would halt long enough for our dinner. The Generals had their lunch prepared under the trees nearby. We made our little fires, fried our pork, boiled our coffee, and ate our hardtack. It was a bright day, though hot; after we had our meal we made ourselves as comfortable as we could. Some were soon sleeping, others reading books or papers, a good many were having a friendly game of cards using the greasy pack that always was handy when we halted. Thus things went on until three in the afternoon.

There had been so far no sign of the enemy, not a warlike sound broke the stillness; and were it not for the distant sound of cannonading far to our left, we might have felt we were on a pleasure trip in the most peaceful of lands. While we were resting the rumor spread that the enemy was on the retreat, and we were marking time and in all probability would enter Atlanta the next day. The attitude of our Generals, who were near us, would seem to confirm this opinion. . . .

We were congratulating ourselves on this unexpected good luck when suddenly, about three-fifteen that afternoon, there was a rifle shot on our front. It was as unexpected as would be thunder from out of a clear sky. A look of surprise and almost consternation came to every face; we knew the critical position our mass formation put us in; but the

feeling was only for the moment. The first shot was followed by others in quick succession, then came the rattle of musketry, and with it the familiar "Rebel Yell." We knew then for a certainty that serious work was ahead of us. . . .

On the sound of the first shot every man jumped to his feet and into line. There was no waiting for orders, the men knew what was required to get where they could make a defense. It was but the work of a moment to sling knapsacks and take guns from the stacks; in far less time than it takes to tell it we were ready to march. Meanwhile the musketry firing was coming closer and closer, the yells of the enemy louder and louder, and the bullets began to sing and whistle around us and through the trees over our heads.

LIEUTENANT ROBERT M. COLLINS
15TH TEXAS CAVALRY (DISMOUNTED), GRANBURY'S BRIGADE

Although Cleburne's division had been designated as a reserve for the July 20 attack, some of his units, including Collins', were briefly in the fight. Wounded, Collins was evacuated to nearby Atlanta, where doctors removed the ball that had just missed his femoral artery. During his convalescence in Forsyth and Americus, Georgia, Collins was administered morphine for 18 straight days to kill the pain in his thigh. He returned to active duty in November.

In front of our brigade was an open field about 400 yards across. About 4:30 o'clock the command was given, "Forward, march!" We quit the works and moved out into the field. The Federals greeted us with terrific fire of shot and shells, but as we were moving down the hill they passed over our heads, doing no damage except that of making a fellow feel like he was very small game to be shot with such guns.

On we go, now the lines come to the fence of a farm, the line halts and the men take hold of it and just bodily lift it and throw it down. Just at this moment a blinding flash right in our front and a shell explodes. It seemed to be filled with powder and ounce balls. It laid a good many of the boys out, and among the number was Capt. Ben Tyus and myself.

Capt. Tyus was wounded in the ankle while I received an ounce ball in the upper third of my left thigh. As I fell I noticed that about two inches square of my gray Georgia jeans pants had gone in with the shot; this was conclusive that a piece of shell had passed through my thigh and had necessarily cut the femoral artery, and that therefore I would be a dead Confederate in just three minutes, as my understanding was that the femoral artery cut would let all the blood in a man out in that time.

However, I made a grip on the wound with my right hand, intending to stop the blood as much as possible, and thereby hold on to life long enough to give my past history a hasty going over and to repeat all the

prayers I knew. Four big stout fellows picked me up on a litter and started back to the line of breastworks. We had to pass through a galling fire of minies, shot and shell; I was not alarmed at all at this, because my mind was made up to quit the earth and I was now only waiting, as the saying goes, for death to strike me square in the face.

I finally ventured to inquire of one of the men carrying me if I were bleeding much. He was a witty Irishman, and replied, "Not a drap of

Broken fence rails mark the graves of the dead at Peachtree Creek. Although Hood essentially followed Johnston's battle plan, he attacked across terrain that was much more rugged than the site where Johnston had chosen to fight. One Confederate officer described the heavily wooded hills and ravines as "almost an abatis by nature."

"Maybe this wound will win a good furlough, and if it does won't I have fun with those Georgia girls."

the rudy current to be seen, Lieutenant."

These words brought back my hope that had already gone over the hills out of sight, and made me remark that an improvement in gait would soon land us out of reach of these Yankee bullets. Then I chuckled in my sleeve when the thought occurred that maybe this wound will win a good furlough, and if it does won't I have fun with those Georgia girls. This may all sound like a strange line of thoughts to run through one's mind in so short a time and under such circumstances, but all this is sound common sense compared to some things we are guilty of doing during our natural lives.

LIEUTENANT STEPHEN PIERSON
33D NEW JERSEY INFANTRY, BUSCHBECK'S BRIGADE

Shortly after General Geary ordered the 33d New Jersey to fortify a hill 500 yards in advance of the 2d Division's line, Pierson and his comrades were overrun by Thomas M. Scott's Confederate brigade. At age 19, Pierson was the youngest officer in the regiment. One month earlier, he had been wounded in the chest at Pine Knob.

A bout noon of the next day, July 20th, the 33rd was ordered out to some high ground in our front to prepare a place for a battery. Gen. Geary went with us. We had just received a mail, the first for some weeks, and I remember, as we passed through the lines in front, I had opened a letter from my father and was reading it. The woods were ominously still; even the birds seemed to have

The 33d New Jersey's flag (above) was lost to the Rebels at Peachtree Creek. "No regiment was more proud of their blue banner," wrote Lieutenant Colonel Enos Fourat, the commanding officer, "and none ever fought better to preserve it."

stopped singing. Col. Jackson of the 134th New York rode up alongside of me, put out his hand and said: "Good-bye, Adjutant." I laughed at him, but he said: "There'll be trouble out there." He was right. There was to be trouble and plenty of it.

With no opposition we advanced to the knoll and were about to stack arms preparatory to making a place ready for the battery. The woods were dense; our skirmishers in front had made but small progress. Suddenly and unexpectedly a volley was fired at them and, so close were they to us, that the bullets came on over into our line. Evidently they had not expected our presence at that particular point any more than we had expected theirs, for the firing ceased for a moment. Col. Fourat ordered me to ride out to the open on our left. And there I saw a beautiful sight. Down through the great, open fields they were coming, thousands of them, men in gray, by brigade front, flags flying. Hood was making his first general assault, and it was against Thomas that he was making it. I stopped but a few moments to take it all in, and then rode back to report. Meantime, the force in the woods in our immediate front had sized us up as to numbers and on they came. How the bullets did come in from the front! Our reply was vigorous, too.

And for a time we held them. Every moment they could be held was of importance, giving our main line time to be more ready.

But very soon they were wrapping around both our flanks and getting into our rear. The firing was fearfully hot. Our isolated position was no longer tenable and the order to retire was given.

At first it was orderly enough, but, almost surrounded as we were, our line was soon broken and in confusion. I have an indistinct recollection of crossing a little brook and wondering at the splashes made by the rebel bullets as they struck the water. I remember, too, stopping for a rest a moment behind the little line we had left. I suppose I was still somewhat weak from my wound of a month before; anyway I could not keep up with the others. As I lay there to get breath, the rebel advance came up, and a long, lank Johnny, seeing me said: "Get out of that, you Yankee son of a gun." I got out. Whether he fired at me or not I do not know. Perhaps he had a momentary spasm of pity, the mark was so easy. Perhaps he did fire and missed. Going back further I met the same New York colonel who had bidden me good-bye. He was coming up by the flank. "Where are they, Adjutant?"

"Deploy quickly, Colonel, they are right here," was my answer. Before he could give his order he was wounded, and still further back we were all driven in great confusion and disorder.

CORPORAL EDMUND R. BROWN
27TH INDIANA INFANTRY, RUGER'S BRIGADE

Corporal Brown and his comrades dashed across an open field of about 70 yards to get into position to repel the attack by D. H. Reynolds' brigade against the Federal right. The 27th Indiana formed up along the edge of a ravine near a jungle of trees and bushes. The space was too cramped to allow everyone to form a line, so the soldiers in back handed their loaded muskets to the men in front, some of whom fired more than 100 rounds.

While we were lying in reserve, with our brigade, not long after we had seen General Knipe's riderless horse and heard the report that the general had been killed, the general himself came hurrying back from the front. He was a mercurial, demonstrative little man always; but now he was wrought up more than common. He was frantic. Without appearing to address himself to any one in particular, he inquired for General Williams, and added that he wanted a regiment to support his right flank. His line was in danger of being turned,

Brigadier General Joseph F. Knipe rose from humble beginnings. A shoemaker by trade, Knipe enlisted as a private in the Regular Army in 1842 and fought in the Mexican War. In 1861, after 13 years of employment with the Pennsylvania Railroad, he heeded Lincoln's call for 75,000 volunteers and was commissioned colonel of the 46th Pennsylvania Infantry.

Although respected by the men of his hard-fighting XX Corps, Major General Joseph Hooker was no favorite of Sherman's. After the death of General McPherson on July 22, Sherman bypassed the ranking Hooker in favor of Oliver Howard as commander of the Army of the Tennessee, prompting Hooker to ask to be relieved. Sherman swiftly obliged him.

and his own Forty-sixth Pennsylvania was suffering badly. These facts were stated in loud, impassioned tones, and with many vigorous gesticulations. General Hooker was sitting on his horse so near the Twenty-seventh that his voice could be easily heard, without his speaking loud. Shells were whistling and screaming everywhere, and minie balls frequently found their way over to us, but he was as calm and self-poised as if he had been resting in the shade, bordering a Northern harvest field.

When he found what Knipe wanted he turned and pointed to a regiment near by and said, "There, General Knipe, take that one." "No-o, no-o, I don't want that one," Knipe fairly screamed, with long drawn emphasis on the noes. In the meantime he had not stopped, but had hurried by, still calling for General Williams. Hooker called, "Here, General Knipe, General Knipe! come here!" Knipe did not hear, or affect to hear, at first, and one of Hooker's staff started after him, calling him to come back. Knipe finally turned and came back a few steps. Hooker this time pointed to the Twenty-seventh and said laconically, "Take that one." "All right!" said Knipe, "I'll take that one," still speaking in high tones and drawing out his words. Then, coming up to the regiment, as the men had fallen in ranks, he shrieked, "Twenty-seventh Indiana, I want you. This old brigade never has been whipped, and it never will be whipped.". . .

. . . He passed in rear of the Twenty-seventh while we were hotly

Private Benjamin Franklin Stone of the 3d Mississippi Infantry, Featherston's brigade, was killed in action at Peachtree Creek, July 20, 1864. Of all the Confederate units, Featherston's troops made the deepest penetration into the Federal lines before being driven back with heavy losses.

Attached to the staff of Colonel James S. Robinson's brigade, Lieutenant George Young was shot just below the knee while riding across the battlefield as a courier. His bullet-torn trousers are shown above. Despite several operations to remove diseased bone tissue, Young suffered from chronic pain until he died in 1909.

engaged. He was still afoot and carrying his sword in his hand, unsheathed, as it had been before. He was also in his high state of excitement and was urging and encouraging the men, with all his former demonstrativeness and energy. A sergeant of the Twenty-seventh said in very bland tones, "General, have you any chewing tobacco?" "Yes, I have some tobacco," the general replied, in the same high-keyed, long-drawn tone. And, jabbing his sword in the ground, with great energy, he produced from his breeches pocket a small piece of "plug," and handed it to the sergeant. The latter began turning it over and "sizing it up," as the boys now say, trying to decide whether or not there was too much of it for one good chew. When the general saw what the sergeant was about he said in a perfectly natural, though, plaintive, tone,—all of his strained, keyed-up condition entirely gone,—*"That's all I've got."* All the boys in hearing laughed heartily, the sergeant took out his knife, cut the tobacco in two parts, put one in his mouth and handed the other back to the general, who thereupon pulled his sword out of the ground and went on his way.

"I dislike to communicate such heartrendering news, but I feel that it is my duty as a relative to do so."

SERGEANT JOEL D. MURPHREE
57TH ALABAMA INFANTRY, SCOTT'S BRIGADE

Murphree was a 37-year-old merchant from Troy, Alabama, when he joined the Confederate service in April 1864. He served as a quartermaster and cook. Murphree had delayed his enlistment at the request of his nine brothers and brothers-in-law, who had volunteered earlier and wanted him to remain at home to look after their families. In this letter to his wife, Ursula, Murphree describes the death of Captain Baily Talbot, a brother-in-law.

Dear Sula

I wrote to you last Thursday from Atlanta in which I had to chronicle the sad news of the death of Baily. Letters misscarry sometimes, and for fear you have not received that letter I write again. I dislike to communicate such heartrendering news, but I feel that it is my duty as a relative to do so. Brother James returned from the Hospital yesterday, and he took down the names of 80 persons of the 57th Regiment that were killed wounded and missing, and a good many had been sent to other Hospitals whose names he never got. There is a faint hope that Baily has only been captured, perhaps wounded. No one knows positively that he was killed. James questioned the wounded of his company and he could learn nothing more than I wrote in my last concerning him, only that he acted imprudently, in the charge.

He was in advance of all the troops, in the face of the fire of the enemy from a battery and small arms, and in retreating was the last to leave the battery they had captured, hence he was in the rear returning when they were ordered to fall back. The charge was made through an open field & of course had to retreat over the same ground. The last that was seen of him he was coming through the field, had nearly reached the draw bars. The Soldier that saw him last, says after walking a few steps he looked back again but could see nothing of him. He thinks he was wounded which caused him to be so far in the rear. If Baily acted prudently he laid down, perhaps behind something that would protect him, and may yet be alive in the hands of the enemy. I am truly sorry for poor Mollie. I have thought of nothing else hardly since the sad

affair, but, Baily, Mollie & his other relatives. Maj. Arnold was killed in trying to save Lt. [Col] Bethune. Col. Bethune was wounded severely and Maj. Arnold went to him, and pulled him into a gully and when he steped out of the gully was shot dead. I learned that Henry Darby is missing. Jo. Whaley was slightly wounded, also Wm Motes, Lt. Colbert St. John, M. Hammel, Capt. Woodward and Capt Lane, Lt. Walter Wiley wound is worse than I first learned. He is wounded in the leg severely. Those are the only persons of your acquaintance that I have heard of though I expect there are others.

Private John E. Johnston of the 29th Alabama, O'Neal's brigade, was wearing this jean-cloth coat when he was killed at Peachtree Creek. The Minié ball struck his chest just below the left collarbone. Johnston's mother, on her way to bring her son additional homespun clothing, discovered his body on the battlefield.

Battle of Atlanta

Even as Hood was being repulsed at Peachtree Creek, Sherman was drawing the Federal forces closer to Atlanta. On July 20, while Thomas and Schofield held their ground north of the city, McPherson's Army of the Tennessee was marching from Decatur, six miles to the east. By the next day, Federal troops had driven the Confederates from Bald Hill, a commanding elevation that overlooked Atlanta's eastern defenses and brought much of the city within range of enemy guns.

Hood saw no option but to risk a daring flank assault on McPherson's troops while the Yankees were still taking up their new line, and on the night of July 21 Hardee's corps moved to within striking distance of McPherson's left flank. If all went according to plan, Cheatham would sally forth from the eastern defenses and pin the Federals in place while Hardee rolled up McPherson's left.

The left flank of the Army of the Tennessee, held by only two brigades, was indeed vulnerable. But while Hardee's tired soldiers tramped on through the night, McPherson had begun to shift troops from Brigadier General Grenville M. Dodge's XVI Corps to bolster his open left flank.

Delayed by the inevitable confusion of a night march, Hardee was not ready to launch his assault until midday of July 22. By that time most of Dodge's troops were already coming into line directly in the face of the imminent Rebel onslaught.

Originally intended to fall upon the Yankee rear, Hardee's right-hand divisions of Walker and Bate instead found themselves charging into a withering fire from two Federal brigades and a battery of artillery. Despite

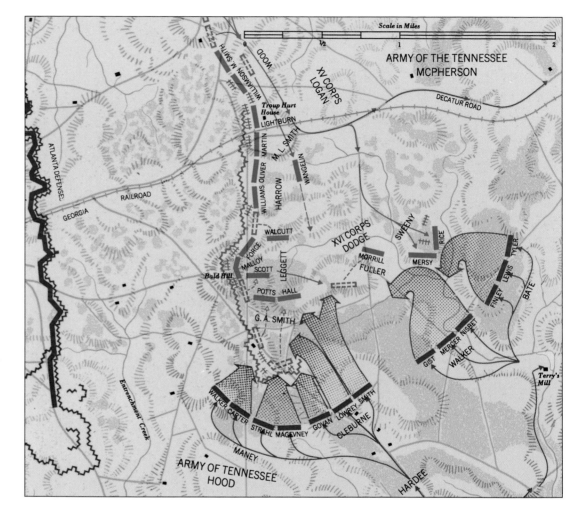

Hood's next target was McPherson's army, closing in on Atlanta from the east. The Federals were hit hard on their left flank around midday on July 22 but refused to break even after a Rebel bullet killed their commander.

a numerical advantage, the Rebels were held at bay, and casualties mounted.

At 12:45 p.m., about half an hour after Hardee commenced his attack, Cleburne's division surged forward. With Maney's division advancing in support, Cleburne gained the first Southern success of the day, slashing through Giles Smith's division and driving

the shattered Yankee regiments northward to the slopes of Bald Hill. The 16th Iowa Infantry was cut off and surrendered, and eight cannon were overrun by Cleburne's brigades. An even greater loss for the Union came just after 2:00 p.m., when General McPherson was fatally shot as he rode into the widening gap between the Federal corps.

Though his attack had not gone according to plan, at 3:00 p.m. Hood took advantage of Cleburne's success by ordering Cheatham to lash out at the Federal center. By 4:00 p.m. all of Hardee's and Cheatham's troops were committed to the massive assault.

The eight brigades of Maney's and Stevenson's Rebel divisions stormed the angle in the Federal line at Bald Hill from front and flank. But the stalwart defenders of Brigadier General Mortimer D. Leggett's division maintained their hold on the crucial high ground, which became a rallying point for the scattered Federal units. While Bald Hill continued to defy capture, the divisions on the left of Cheatham's line gained ground against the right flank of Logan's XV Corps.

With Manigault's brigade in the vanguard, the Southern troops charged eastward, astride the tracks of the Georgia Railroad, and penetrated the line of Brigadier General Morgan L. Smith's division near the Troup Hurt house. Manigault's regiments overran an Illinois battery, then swung north and rolled up the line of Lightburn's brigade. Pressing on, Manigault's men then captured the Troup Hurt house and the four guns of Francis De-Gress' battery. Meanwhile, Colonel Jacob H. Sharp's Mississippi brigade had widened the gap in the Yankee line still further, capturing two more cannon and routing Colonel James S. Martin's Federal brigade.

But the Confederate success proved to be short-lived. While the northernmost portion of the XV Corps held its ground, and Leggett's troops continued to stave off the Rebel assaults on Bald Hill, McPherson's successor in command of the Army of the Tennessee—

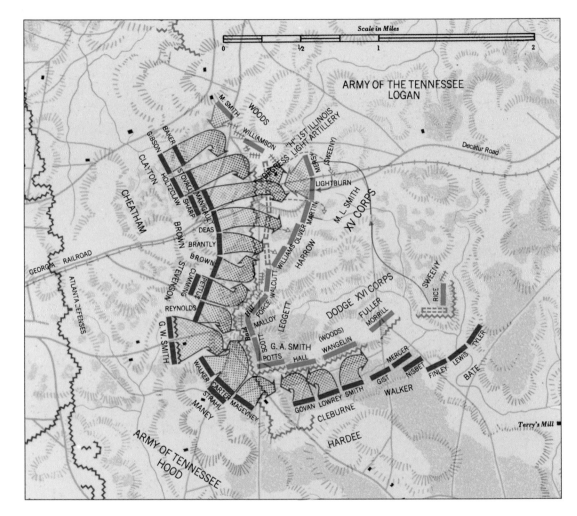

The Confederates continued the attack on the afternoon of July 22, when they hurled themselves against the Union center. The Federal line briefly gave way, only to stiffen and finally stall the Rebel onslaught.

Black Jack Logan—rushed reinforcements to plug the gap. Much to his chagrin, Manigault was ordered to abandon his hard-won ground. Colonel August Mersy's Federal brigade, along with the re-formed remnants of Lightburn's and Martin's brigades, soon recaptured the lost guns and restored the Union position at the Troup Hurt house.

By nightfall of July 22 the opposing forces were back where they started. Hood's gamble failed, with 5,000 Confederate casualties set against a Federal loss of some 4,000 men. While Sherman professed not to have been unduly concerned for the outcome, many in his army who fought that day felt they had come precariously close to disaster.

LIEUTENANT EDMUND E. NUTT
20TH OHIO INFANTRY, SCOTT'S BRIGADE

On July 21, 1864, the day after the Battle of Peachtree Creek, Scott's Federal brigade was in the center of the Army of the Tennessee's line east of Atlanta. Beginning in the late morning and continuing on into the next day, the men were busy modifying and expanding the line of entrenchments captured from the Confederates. The city was within sight and all seemed secure when Hood launched his surprise attack early in the afternoon of July 22. Lieutenant Nutt and his comrades suddenly found themselves fighting for their lives.

During the morning we discovered Johnnies passing southward about a mile in our front. They seemed to be on the run the short distance we could see them between patches of timber, and wondered where they were going. Some said to a picnic, some said they were evacuating Atlanta. As usual, many rumors were afloat.

It was a hot day. The men were playing cards and lounging in the shade, and the camp was quiet as the calm before a storm when "Whang!" went a musket shot, apparently about a quarter of a mile south and east to the left flank and rear. The sound was caught by hundreds of alert ears, and all sprang to their feet and faced in that direction. The shot was instantly followed by others and in less than a minute it was a rapid skirmish fire, and seeming to come nearer and nearer.

"Fall in! Fall in!" was the order. The men rushed to and fro, putting on accoutrements, grasping muskets and forming in the line of works with attention directed toward the advancing music, from whence were now coming the well known ping! whing! thud! from left and rear, striking our line on the end. The smoke and roar and roll of musketry proceeding from the plainly defined line of gray and butternut was preceded by our pickets and some of the 4th Division, which had been struck on the flank and run over. Those not killed or wounded were falling back, loading and firing in retreat. Their position between us and the advancing foe prevented us from firing until they arrived, so we were compelled to stand and wait the coming storm.

SERGEANT JOHN W. GREEN
9TH KENTUCKY (C.S.) INFANTRY, LEWIS' BRIGADE

Born on a plantation in Henderson County, Kentucky, Green had relatives on both sides of the conflict: His father was from Virginia, his mother from Massachusetts. On the night of July 21, Lewis' brigade, along with the other units of Bate's and Walker's divisions, made a grueling march to get into position to make the assault against McPherson's left.

Finally . . . the order for attack is given. It is supposed we have gone far enough to our right to over lap the left of the ennemy & thus turn his flank. Soon our skirmish line has found the enemy. We drive in their skirmishers & our line of battle comes up with our skirmishers. They fall into their position . . . & all push forward.

We now discover that the yanks have two lines of battle in front of us, both strongly entrenched. They pour their lead into us [and] their three batteries open on us slaying our men right & left. We give them a volley & push forward through an open woods. We are halted by a staked & ridered fence. The comma[n]d is, "Load boys, then go over the fence & rush on them; when in close range give them a volley & then charge & give them the bayonet."

In some places where the fence is not too strong to be thrown a number of the men take hold of it and throw it down. Just where I was, it was too strongly built to yield to our efforts to throw it, so we climbed over. Unfortunately for me when I got over the top rail my canteen, which was full of water & swung around my neck, stayed on the other side of the fence while I was held on the yankie's side suspended to the top rail by the strap of my canteen. I could not disentangle it & my feet could not reach the ground. Minnie balls & grape shot were splintering that rail & there I was held a fair mark for the yanks. I was making desperate efforts to free myself when much to my delight a yankee bullet that stung me on the shoulder cut that canteen strap & left me free to join the other boys in our rush upon the enemies works. . . .

We drove the enemy out of the first line of their works in our front

Hurling shells like the one at left, Captain Francis DeGress of Battery H, 1st Illinois Light Artillery, fired the first shots into the city of Atlanta with his 20-pounder Parrott guns at 1:00 p.m., July 20, 1864.

Major General William H. T. Walker, commander of a division in Hardee's corps, was killed by a Federal sharpshooter in the opening stages of the Battle of Atlanta. A West Point graduate with a distinguished career in the Regular Army, Walker suffered from bad health and slept in a sitting position as a result of wounds he sustained fighting the Seminoles and Mexicans two decades earlier.

COLONEL JAMES COOPER NISBET
66TH GEORGIA INFANTRY, STEVENS' BRIGADE

After General Clement Stevens was killed at Peachtree Creek, Nisbet took charge of the brigade and led it into the fight on July 22. One Federal soldier remembered Nisbet's men and the rest of Walker's division "tearing wildly through the woods with the yells of demons." But many of the Rebels, including Nisbet, were so determined that they rushed right into the Federal lines and captivity. Nisbet spent the remainder of the war in a prison camp for Confederate officers on Johnson's Island in Lake Erie.

I thought the enemy's advanced line was up on the hill, but as I emerged from the thicket, I was greeted by a volley from the 39th Ohio Regiment which was lying down—their left not more than forty yards away. Some ten men of my left company came out into the field with me. The shots passed over our heads but we were surrounded in an instant by a great number, all exclaiming: "You are my prisoner!"

I was in full uniform. They thought from the stars on my collar that I was a general. Seeing that the jig was up with us, at least for a while, I stood still and said nothing. The battle was roaring all around. There was a contention among my captors as to who had captured me and as to my rank.

As I stood watching the battle surge around us, a young lieutenant took hold of my arm to attract my attention and said: "I say, you are my prisoner, ain't you?"

I said: "It looks that way."

He said: "Well you don't seem *skeered* about it!"

I said: "I have captured thousands of your men, since the war commenced, and always treated them right."

"I'll treat you that way," said he.

No one had asked me for my sword and pistol, but my men had dropped their rifles. In the meantime, having detailed the young lieutenant and a guard to take charge of us, the Federal brigade moved forward. Just then a rear skirmish line came along driving up stragglers. They were Germans. One fellow spied me standing there. Leveling his gun at a charge-bayonet, he said: "Oh! by-tam, youse jest the feller I'se been looking for."

His eyes were fiercely gleaming. I drew my pistol and said: "You

but they fell back upon the second line & rallied in those works & our General, finding that the line on our left could not come up to our support, ordered us to fall back. This was really attended with more danger than to advance if it had not been for the fact that by this time the yanks had brought up so many reenforcements that to advance would have meant certain capture. But so soon as we turned our backs upon them they poured the shot into us & caused many of our dear boys to bite the dust. We fell back over the brow of a hill and reformed and laid down to rest after putting out a line of pickets.

As we were hurrying back with grape & canister & minnie balls pouring in on us & getting some of our men every second I passed by Capt Hewett standing by his dead horse apparently trying to get his saddle off the dead animal & I thought it was the most foolish thing I ever saw for a man to take all that risk for a saddle. That night when we were sitting around Head Qr's I asked Capt Hewett why he took such a risk for a saddle, [for] I expected every minute to see him fall.

He said, "No indeed I would never have stopped there for my saddle but as we were going into the fight one of the boys was about to throw his blanket away saying it was too hot to go into a fight a day like this with a blanket over your shoulder. I told him I would carry it on my horse. I had it tied to my saddle & as we were falling back I did not want him to lose his blanket. I brought it out & gave it to him & he will need it before this campaign is over." Such thoughtful kindness at such a moment shows the coolness & kindness of this dear officer & caused all the men to love him.

stop right there. I will blow your damn head off, if you attempt to bayonet me!"

This attracted the attention of my little lieutenant captor, who was watching his brigade advance. He turned and said, "What's the matter?"

I said, "He wants to bayonet me."

Seeing the German, he ran up to him and said: "You stick my prisoner and I will chop your damn Dutch head off."

Then came up the German's fat captain puffing and blowing, who recognizing his man said: "Vat for you stop here?"

The lieutenant said: "He wants to stick my prisoner."

The German soldier said: "He ish no prisoner, he vants to shoot me mit his pistol."

His captain said: "Say, you vants to keep out of de fight; go on!" and he struck the man on the back with the flat of his sword.

BRIGADIER GENERAL JOHN W. FULLER
DIVISION COMMANDER, XVI CORPS

A native of England, Fuller was one of a handful of foreign-born officers to attain the rank of general. When the Confederates tried to envelop the flank of one of his brigades, Fuller ordered two regiments to change front and rallied the men by plunging the national colors of the 27th Ohio into the ground directly in front of the charging Rebels.

oon the enemy appeared, and before he was in good musket range our battery opened fire. This seemed a surprise, for he halted and then retired into the woods to reform his line. Very soon, however, he marched out from the forest and moved in good order toward us.

He had come not more than a quarter of the way across the field when the 81st Ohio, across the ravine to our left and in plain sight, charged against a rebel regiment which was threatening our battery. The cheer of this regiment and its gallant charge was so contagious that the men of the 39th Ohio rose to their feet, fired a volley and went for the Johnnies on the double-quick. The 27th, next on the right, seeing the 39th charging the enemy, arose also and the rebels were still so near the woods they could quickly reach shelter. The 39th, however, was in time to capture the colonel, adjutant, a captain and all who did not run of the 66th Georgia, a regiment in Walker's division.

But that part of the rebel line which was not struck by the two Ohio

These soldiers from the 66th Illinois fought the Battle of Atlanta with 16-shot Henry repeating rifles like the one shown here. "I stood and fired 90 rounds without stopping," wrote Private Prosper Bowe (far left) in a letter to his sister. "My gun barrel was so hot that I could not touch it. Spit on it & it would siz."

" 'Sir, it is General McPherson. You have killed the best man in our army.' "

regiments continued marching toward the west, and the extraordinary spectacle presented itself of our men rushing across the field in one direction, while the rebels on their right were marching steadily the opposite way. It is true the enemy kept pretty close to the line of woods to the south, but as they approached the western side they began to widen out into the field.

Directly, the 64th Illinois, partly hidden by a piece of fence and by the bushes which lined the rivulet, opened fire at close range. This regiment was armed with the Henry repeating rifle and could fire 15 volleys without stopping to reload. They demoralized the rebel line in short order so that it began to waver and break.

Just then a fine-looking officer brought another regiment out of the woods. He rode forward, hat in hand, to rally his men; but by this time Col. Sheldon had moved up the 18th Missouri so as to get a flank fire on the rebels, and this proved more than they could stand. The officer who was so conspicuous was immediately shot down, and the whole mass swayed back into the forest. As the last of them were retiring, voices were heard shouting, "Bring off the general!" Some prisoners told us that "the general" was Gen. Walker, the commander of their division.

CAPTAIN RICHARD BEARD
5TH CONFEDERATE INFANTRY, L. E. POLK'S BRIGADE

Beard's regiment, reduced by casualties to fewer than 100 men, formed up with Brigadier General James A. Smith, in command of Granbury's Texans for the day, on Cleburne's right during the attack of July 22. Pushing into a gap in the Federal line, they caught General McPherson riding across their front. Beard was captured shortly afterward and spent the rest of the war as a prisoner.

We commenced a double-quick through a forest covered with dense underbrush. Here we ran through a line of skirmishers, and took them in, without the firing of a gun, and suddenly came up to the edge of a little wagon-road running parallel with our line of march, and down which General McPherson came thundering at the head of his staff, and, according to my best recollection, his body-guard.

He was certainly surprised to find himself suddenly face to face with the Rebel line. My own company and possibly others of the regiment had reached the verge of the road when he discovered, for the first time, that he was within a few feet of where we stood. I threw up my sword to him as a signal to surrender. Not a word was spoken. He checked his horse slightly, raised his hat as politely as if he was saluting a lady, wheeled his horse's head directly to the right, and dashed off to the rear in full gallop. Young Corporal Coleman, who was standing near me, was ordered to fire upon him. He did so, and it was his ball that brought General McPherson down. He was shot while passing under the thick branches of a tree, and as he was bending over his horse's neck, either to avoid coming into contact with the limbs or, more probably, to escape the death-dealing bullet that he knew was sure to follow him. He was shot in the back . . . the ball ranged upward across the body and passed near the heart. A number of shots were also fired into his retreating staff.

I ran immediately up to where the dead General lay, just as he had fallen, upon his knees and face. There was not a quiver of his body to be seen, not a sign of life perceptible. The fatal bullet had done its work well; he had been killed instantly. Even as he lay there, dressed in his major-general's uniform, with his face in the dust, he was as magnificent a looking picture of manhood as I ever saw.

Right by his side lay a man who, if at all hurt, was but slightly wounded, but whose horse had been shot from under him. From his appearance, I took him to be the Adjutant or Inspector General of the staff. Pointing to the dead man, I asked him, "Who is this man lying here?" He answered with tears in his eyes, "Sir, it is General McPherson. You have killed the best man in our army."

PRIVATE ANDREW J. THOMPSON
4TH COMPANY OHIO CAVALRY, ESCORT, ARMY OF THE TENNESSEE

Thompson was riding as General McPherson's orderly when the general's party suddenly encountered a Confederate battle line. Thompson's account of McPherson's death is but one of many versions. Whereas Beard credited a Corporal Coleman with firing the fatal shot, others have claimed it was Private Robert D. Compton of Company I, 24th Texas Cavalry (dismounted).

All at once the Rebels rose up on our left, and cried "Halt! halt!" General McPherson turned quickly from them to the right, and I followed. Just as we turned, they fired a volley at us. I dodged down, and hung on to the side of my horse, and several balls came so close that they fairly blistered the back of my neck. They shot over me and killed the General. I saw him fall, and just as he fell, his horse ran between two saplings, and my horse after the General's. My head struck one of the saplings, knocking me off my horse, senseless. When I came to, McPherson was lying on his right side, with his

DEATH OF GEN. J. B. McPHERSON.
In Battle of Atlanta, July 22, 1864.

right hand pressed against his breast, and at every breath he drew, the blood flowed in streams between his fingers. I went up to him and said to him, "General, are you hurt?" He raised his left hand and brought it down upon his left leg and said: "Oh, orderly, I am," and immediately turned over on his face, straightened himself out, trembling like a leaf. I stooped to turn him over, when one of the Rebels who had come up caught hold of my revolver strap and jerked it until he broke the buckle, at the same time calling me rough names, and ordered me to go to the rear quick, or he would shoot me. I know nothing further.

SERGEANT FENWICK Y. HEDLEY
32D ILLINOIS INFANTRY, ROGERS' BRIGADE

At 12:45 p.m. on July 22, G. Smith's 4th Division, XVII Corps, faced a series of assaults by Cleburne's division. Hedley describes the desperate fighting that followed the charge of Mark P. Lowrey's Confederate brigade. "So rapid were the movements, and so much was crowded into a few hours," Hedley recalled, "that it is impossible to gain an entirely correct idea of the sequence of events."

Lowry's assault was courageous and persistent in the highest degree. His troops actually reached the works of the Iowans, but were unable to surmount them. The contending lines were only separated by thin earthworks, less than shoulder high, and the fighting became desperate and promiscuous. Musket clashed against musket, and color-bearers flaunted their standards in face of each other.

As the 15th Iowa Regiment, Colonel (afterward General) Belknap commanding, sprang to the reverse of their works, they were confronted by the 45th Alabama Regiment, whose commander, Colonel Lampley, waved his light felt hat, as he led the charge. Colonel Belknap, tak-

ing the act to be a signal of surrender, ordered his men to cease firing (a command heard only by few, owing to the tumult of battle), and, at the same time, beckoned the rebel officer to come in. A young soldier by Lampley's side, and by his direction, as was plainly to be seen, fired three shots at Belknap, but without effect. Meanwhile the Alabamians advanced nearer and nearer, and Belknap discovered that, instead of thinking of surrender, they meant fight in bitter earnest. Three color-bearers of this one rebel regiment were shot down in rapid succession. When the last fell, the contending lines were at such close quarters that the flag was torn from his dying grasp by a member of the 11th Iowa. . . . The Alabamians were now at the very foot of the Union works, and to deliver a fire upon them it was necessary for the Iowans to hold their muskets over the works, almost perpendicularly. Belknap jumped upon the parapet and again beckoned Lampley to come in. The latter shook his head, and urged his men to make a final dash. He came nearer, until he was fairly against the works. Then Belknap, watching his opportunity, leaned over the parapet, fastened his grasp upon Lampley's coat-collar, and, with the aid of a corporal near by, dragged him inside. Within a few minutes, every Alabamian who was not killed, or lying wounded upon the field, was a prisoner. Colonel Lampley was found to be wounded, but the injury was so slight that his own men ascribed his death, which occurred a few days later, to depression at the misfortune of being captured, rather than to the wound.

Major General James B. McPherson falls from his horse on a forest road outside Atlanta in this rendering of his death (left). The body was recovered by the 64th Illinois and carried to General Sherman, who wept at the sight of his protégé's corpse. Sherman had expected the promising 35-year-old general (inset) to take over the army should anything happen to him.

Colonel Harris D. Lampley (left), who led the heroic charge of the 45th Alabama Infantry against the 15th Iowa, suffered the ignominy of being pulled into the Federal works by his rival commander, Colonel William W. Belknap. The burly Belknap earned a brigadier's star for his bravery that day; Lampley died in Federal custody.

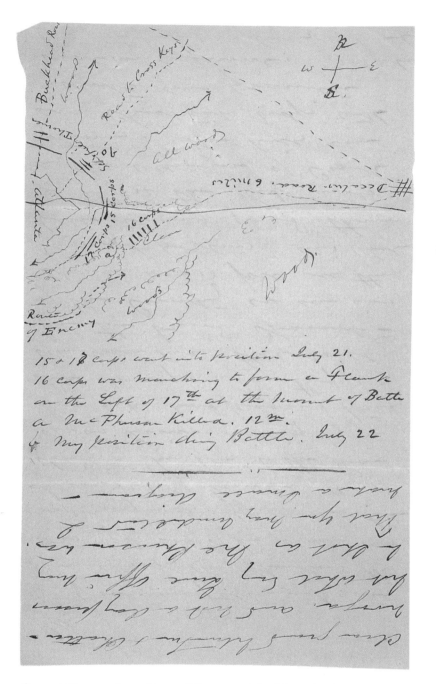

General Sherman drew this small diagram of the Atlanta battlefield and included it in a letter to his wife, Ellen. He marked the spot where McPherson was killed with the letter "a" and the site of his own headquarters with "b."

PRIVATE SAM R. WATKINS
1ST TENNESSEE (C.S.) INFANTRY, MANEY'S BRIGADE

Around 3:30 p.m. on July 22, Brigadier General George Maney, in temporary command of Cheatham's division, led his troops into action in support of Cleburne's assault that had earlier driven the Yankees back more than a quarter mile. But the Federals had quickly dug in around the treeless high ground known as Bald Hill. The Tennesseans repeatedly charged the enemy works from the southwest, but the Yankee line, now reinforced, held firm.

We advanced to the attack on Cleburne's immediate left. Cleburne himself was leading us in person, so that we would not fire upon his men, who were then inside the Yankee line. His sword was drawn. I heard him say, "Follow me, boys." He ran forward, and amid the blazing fires of the Yankee guns was soon on top of the enemy's works. He had on a bob-tail Confederate coat, which looked as if it had been cut out of a scrimp pattern. (You see I remember the little things.) We were but a few paces behind, following close upon him, and soon had captured their line of works. . . . The Yankee lines seemed routed. We followed in hot pursuit; but from their main line of entrenchment—which was diagonal to those that we had just captured, and also on which they had built forts and erected batteries—was their artillery, raking us fore and aft. We passed over a hill and down into a valley being under the muzzles of this rampart of death. We had been charging and running, and had stopped to catch our breath right under their reserve and main line of battle. When General George Maney said, "Soldiers, you are ordered to go forward and charge that battery. When you start upon the charge I want you to go, as it were, upon the wings of the wind. Shoot down and bayonet the cannoneers, and take their guns at all hazards." Old Pat Cleburne thought he had better put in a word to his soldiers. He says, "You hear what General Maney says, boys. If they don't take it, by the eternal God, you have got to take it!" . . .

We rushed forward up the steep hill sides, the seething fires from ten thousand muskets and small arms, and forty pieces of cannon hurled right into our faces, scorching and burning our clothes, and hands, and faces from their rapid discharges, and piling the ground with our dead and wounded almost in heaps. It seemed that the hot flames of hell were turned loose in all their fury, while the demons of damnation were laughing in the flames, like seething serpents hissing out their

"It seemed that the hot flames of hell were turned loose in all their fury, while the demons of damnation were laughing in the flames."

rage. We gave one long, loud cheer, and commenced the charge. . . .

On the final charge that was made, I was shot in the ankle and heel of my foot. I crawled into their abandoned ditch, which then seemed full and running over with our wounded soldiers. I dodged behind the embankment to get out of the raking fire that was ripping through the bushes, and tearing up the ground. Here I felt safe. The firing raged in front; we could hear the shout of the charge and the clash of battle. While I was sitting here, a cannon ball came tearing down the works, cutting a soldier's head off, spattering his brains all over my face and bosom, and mangling and tearing four or five others to shreds. As a wounded horse was being led off, a cannon ball struck him, and he was literally ripped open, falling in the very place I had just moved from.

Private Malcolm M. Hornsby of Company B, 18th Texas Cavalry (dismounted), fell into Federal hands when Cleburne's attack faltered. He had been captured once before—at Arkansas Post in January of 1863—but was soon exchanged. This time he was shipped to a prison camp in Ohio, where he spent the remainder of the war. Hornsby's grandnephew, Rogers Hornsby, grew up to become a legendary baseball star.

LIEUTENANT EDMUND E. NUTT
20TH OHIO INFANTRY, SCOTT'S BRIGADE

After Cleburne's Confederates shoved back the Yankee line, Scott's brigade became locked in a hand-to-hand struggle defending its earthworks. Nutt led two successful counterattacks and organized the defense of Bald Hill, the key position in the Union center. The Federals later renamed the prominence Leggett's Hill in honor of Nutt's divisional commander, Brigadier General Mortimer D. Leggett.

Some of our boys became panic-stricken and rushed to the rear and reported down the line that the command had all fallen back "cut to pieces"—the old straggler's story. But most "stood the storm." As the Johnnies came to the southeast broad side to our left flank extending to the rear, we climbed our works and faced the rear.

Their line struck the left of the 20th's works, and was received with shot, bayonet thrust, clubbed musket and crash, which for the moment checked that part of their line. . . .

This done, we saw another line following the first, which received our full fire as it advanced. But on it came, closing gaps as they were made by our close-range fire. They, too, struck our line as the first did, and were received in like manner—both parts of the line, and so with a third line. Having use of both sides of our works for each line, we were back and forth six times, each time our numbers growing less and less.

When the third line had passed and the bulk of the rebel army had swept our rear and were heard roaring far down the lines to the north, we were in for it. There was no rear to go to; our supplies were in their hands and reinforcements could not reach us. Every big tree in sight had a Johnny who was loading and firing at us as rapidly as possible. Those we had cut off from their line remained apparently disorganized but full of fight each for himself. They occupied every available spot, were in our trenches and in about half of the works we had dug and made ready for our own use. They brought their flag down one trench within a few feet of our 20th Ohio banner. Crouched down to load, they would rise and fire in our faces, to receive in turn a bayonet or clubbed musket. . . .

The muskets became hot with rapid firing, but there were plenty lying around cooling with comrades who could use them no more. The tree protection gave the Johnnies the advantage of the trench side of our works, and we have to take the other side.

"The sons of bitches are rifling our knapsacks, boys! Let's jump over and go for them! Up and at 'em, boys!"

Over we went, jumping down on them and mingling with slash and clash. With yells we rushed along the line, taking them in and ordering them over on our side and to pass down the line; recapturing our own

For his heroism during the Battle of Atlanta, Lieutenant Edmund E. Nutt received a Medal of Honor like the one above. He was one of no fewer than 13 men in the XVII Corps to be so honored for service during the fight on July 22.

Piled earth and a few palisade supports mark a line of abandoned breastworks on the Atlanta battle-field. The entrenchments were thrown up by the Rebels, then captured on July 21 by Blair's corps, who hurriedly modified the works to face west in time to defend against the next day's onslaught.

boys whom they were holding as prisoners, and thus passing through and among them, neither daring to fire as we were all mixed together. It was a question of audacity how far we could go and be obeyed. Several of these raids were made during the afternoon, and the intermediate time was occupied in crouching to load and reaching over to fire.

BRIGADIER GENERAL ARTHUR M. MANIGAULT
BRIGADE COMMANDER, HINDMAN'S DIVISION

With Hardee's corps stalled to the south, Hood hurled Cheatham's corps, spearheaded by Manigault's brigade, against Logan's XV Corps. The Rebels broke through the Yankee lines, but after two hours of hard fighting they were ordered to retreat. A native of Charleston, South Carolina, Manigault served on the staff of General P. G. T. Beauregard when South Carolina militiamen fired the first shot of the war at Fort Sumter in April 1861.

*S*eeing at last that the other brigade on my right appeared to be in readiness, the order to move forward was given, and on clearing the brow of the hill, there stood the enemy in their breastworks, not over two hundred and fifty yards from us. Their flags fluttering lazily in the breeze indicated the length of line occupied by each regiment, and the numbers opposed to us. I saw and noticed all this only for a moment, and thought it looked very pretty, but in the next instant the whole scene was shut out, everything enveloped in smoke. A deafening roar smote upon the ear, and a storm of bullets and cannister tore through our ranks and around us. The men by this time were well under way, and altho the line staggered and reeled for a moment, it quickly recovered and went forward. The space that separated us being half cleared, or perhaps as much as two-thirds of it cleared, the fire became more deadly and alarming. The pace at which the men were moving slackened; large gaps were visible here and there. The line had lost its regularity, warbling like the movements of a serpent, and things looked ugly, but our supports were coming up in capital style, not more than one hundred yards in rear. The men saw them, and gathered confidence. All the field and most of the line officers played their part well at this crisis. . . . The gallant examples set by so many overcame all hesitation, excepting in small portions of two regi-

ments, and the brigade nearly as a whole, dashed forward and over the works, rifles and artillery flashing in their faces.

At the last rush, most of the enemy broke and fled. Still a goodly number fought on, until they saw that further resistance was useless or were killed or overpowered. Many of our men were killed or wounded in the work itself, amongst the latter, Colonel Pressley, shot through the shoulder with a rifle ball, fighting hand to hand with several Federal soldiers.

CAPTURE OF DE GRESS'S BATTERY BY THE CONFEDERATES.
A single line of Confederates (of Hardee's corps), with no support, stormed the works and captured this magnificent battery.
July 22, 1864.

GEN. JNO. B. HOOD,
Commanding Confederate Army.

GEN. W. T. SHERMAN,
Commanding United States Army.

PRIVATE JOHN HENRY PUCK
37TH OHIO INFANTRY, LIGHTBURN'S BRIGADE

When Manigault's brigade broke through the Federal lines, Puck was with a squad of sharpshooters in the Troup Hurt house, a two-story brick structure just behind the Federal breastworks. The Confederates who nearly took him prisoner were probably from the 10th South Carolina led by Colonel James F. Pressley.

It must have been near 2 p.m. when we could see that the rebels were making active preparations for an attack. Major Hipp asked for volunteers to go into the brick house as sharpshooters. Some 12 or 15 of our boys responded, mostly from Companies C and G, I being among the number. Upon reaching the upper story of the house we immediately distributed ourselves in the different rooms and began to break holes through the walls to enable us to fire upon the rebels as they advanced. And none too soon, for we had hardly made our portholes of sufficient size to enable us to see and fire through when the rebels advanced in solid columns. But by the steady fire poured into them they were forced to retreat.

. . . It seems that the rebels only retreated far enough to come under shelter of the houses aforementioned, and from there marched onto the railroad track and a wagon road running parallel with it. There being a deep cut in both we could not see or hurt them. . . .

. . . we in the house were in blissful ignorance of what was going on below. We had been ordered to keep a sharp lookout in our front, and the house not having any openings in the sides toward the railroad we could not see what was going on on our left. I presume those of the regiment below were too busy just then to pay any attention to us; in fact, they might not have known that we were in the house. But we were there, and as we thought we were doing our duty in watching our front we were ready to fire on the first rebel who would dare to show himself. Of course, we expected that if they would make another attack it would come from the same direction as the first one. But as 15 or 20 minutes

This engraving depicts Manigault's brigade (erroneously assigned to Hardee's corps in the original caption) overrunning DeGress' battery late on the afternoon of July 22. Shortly afterward, however, General Hood ordered Manigault to fall back, allowing the Federals to retake their four 20-pounder Parrott guns. "There was nothing left for us to do but obey," Manigault angrily recalled. "I never saw men obey an order so unwillingly."

went by and no rebels came into sight we supposed the fight was over. All at once we heard firing on our left but it lasted only a few minutes.

We paid very little attention to this noise, never dreaming that we were in danger or that our line could be broken. But after several minutes we became uneasy. We wanted to see what our boys below were doing, so one of the boys in the room I was in leaned out of the window in order to see the works below. To his horror he discovered that our boys were gone and the works full of rebels. Upon learning this fact we hurried downstairs as fast as we could, but upon reaching the second floor we found that rebel soldiers were already in the house and some of them had started to come upstairs.

. . . If we were going to try to escape we must act at once. So I, with perhaps a half dozen others, made a break from the window and jumped down. The house had five windows on the side we jumped out, and I chose the center window followed by two more boys of my company.

I should mention here that when we had gone to work in the morning to change front to the rebel works our regiment unslung knapsacks and piled them up in the rear of the house. As I jumped out of the window I came down upon this large pile of knapsacks, which, of course, broke my fall but sent me sprawling on the ground. As I rose to my feet there were several rebels standing at the corner of the house to my right who commanded me to halt. But without taking a second thought I started on a dead run. Better time was never made than I made in that run of perhaps 400 to 500 yards!

LIEUTENANT COLONEL ROBERT N. ADAMS
81ST OHIO INFANTRY, BURKE'S BRIGADE

In May Colonel Mersy replaced the wounded Patrick E. Burke as brigade commander. After Mersy fell wounded during the counterattack that recovered De-Gress' battery, Adams assumed command. An Ohio native, Adams enlisted as a private but earned the rank of brevet brigadier general by war's end. After the war he attended theological school and was ordained as a Presbyterian minister.

The charge of this brigade that followed, was quickly and handsomely made, and on reaching the works it poured a deadly fire into the ranks of the retreating enemy. It also turned the recovered guns upon the enemy and succeeded in cracking one of them in the operation. After the firing ceased, we found fifty Rebels crouching behind the works, who preferred Northern prisons to the risk of an attempted retreat. Among these prisoners was a darkey, and

Confederate dead lie in tangled heaps in front of a line of Federal fieldworks on the morning after the Battle of Atlanta. "This war has demonstrated that earthworks can be rendered nearly impregnable on either side against direct assault," wrote Lieutenant Henry O. Dwight of the 20th Ohio, who sketched the grisly scene. "An attack on fortified lines must cost a fearful price and should be well weighed whether the cost exceed the gain."

the only darkey I saw during the war firing the wrong way. Captain DeGress, who sat upon his horse near General Logan while the charge was being made, came hurriedly to the front when he witnessed the result and coming in sight of his battery, wept like a child as he saw not only the dead horses but several of his brave men who had fallen at their post when the guns were captured. The captain grasped my hand and said, so that the men as well as myself could hear, "I want to thank you and your brigade for what you have done."

"Ominous black-covered ambulances . . . made their slow, pain-laden way up Decatur Street."

This image of Captain Francis DeGress, commander of Battery H, 1st Illinois Light Artillery, was taken early in the war when he was a lieutenant. DeGress, who carried the cavalry saber shown below into the battle, recovered all four of his guns. One of them, however, burst from a double charge loaded by its overzealous liberators as they fired on the retreating Rebels.

SARAH HUFF
RESIDENT OF ATLANTA

Forced from their home on the Marietta road when the fighting drew danger-ously near in late July, eight-year-old Sarah Huff and her family sought safety in the heart of Atlanta. But the city's fortifications offered little surcease from war's cruelty. As the battle for Atlanta raged, the Huffs witnessed a seemingly endless procession of carnage as the wounded were brought into the city.

*I*t was on July the 22, the day after we left home because the fighting was so near, that my younger brother John's keen ears caught the sound of distant firing.

Before that fiery July sun had set, thousands of as brave men as ever joined battle, were numbered among the dead. And I saw thousands more brought into the city in ominous black-covered ambulances which made their slow, pain-laden way up Decatur Street to several improvised hospitals where Dr. Noe D'Alvigny and Dr. Logan, as well as many of Atlanta's most prominent ladies, waited to try to ease their suffering.

As the battle, raging to the east and southeast of us, grew more fierce, the line of ambulances creeping up Decatur street increased. The dismal-looking vehicles had their side curtains lifted to let in the air, for the heat was intense.

We could see from our viewpoint, in front of the old-time residence of Charles Shearer, Sr., the blood trickling down from the wounds of the poor helpless victims of one of the war's most terrible battles.

Men were clinging to sides of the hospital vans trying to fan away the terrible swarms of flies which hovered over the wounded. My young brother John went into action, as he usually did when he saw a chance to be helpful. Noticing that a fly brush had just fallen from the hands of a man on one of the ambulances, and had been crushed by the heavy wheels, he grabbed the slit-paper fly brush that mother handed him, and leaping to the side of the slow-moving ambulance, became one of the most efficient fly-fanners in the procession. He was less than 12 years of age.

Ezra Church

Four days after the Battle of Atlanta, Sherman decided to execute another wide flanking maneuver, one he had discussed before the battle with General McPherson. Sherman designated the commander of the IV Corps—Oliver Howard—as McPherson's successor in command of the Army of the Tennessee, preferring a West Pointer to the politically appointed general, John Logan, who had been exercising temporary command since McPherson's death. The ambitious Logan was not pleased, but he dutifully reverted to command of the XV Corps. Joseph Hooker, who was senior in rank to Howard, was not as accommodating and tendered his resignation. Alpheus Williams assumed temporary command of Hooker's XX Corps, and Howard prepared to carry out Sherman's plan.

On July 27 the Army of the Tennessee moved out of its entrenchments east of Atlanta on a counterclockwise march that took Howard's force around the northern edge of the city, then south, threatening to sever the last major Confederate line of supply. At East Point, about six miles southwest of the city's defenses, the Macon & Western and Atlanta & West Point Railroads met to form a single rail line leading into Atlanta. If Howard could seize and destroy the railroad, Sherman believed, Hood's army would have to abandon Atlanta or be forced to give battle in order to retake the vital artery.

In order to keep the Rebels off balance while Howard made his move, Sherman dispatched the bulk of his cavalry forces on far-reaching raids intended to spread destruction along the enemy transportation routes. Major General George Stoneman would ride southeast, join with Garrard's mounted division, and ravage the line of the Macon & Western all the way to the defenses of Macon, 70 miles from Atlanta. If possible, Stoneman would free the Union prisoners confined at Macon, then ride on 50 more miles to liberate the inmates of the notorious Rebel stockade at Andersonville. Meanwhile Brigadier General Edward S. McCook would lead the troopers of his division southwest of Atlanta, destroying the Atlanta & West Point Railroad at Palmetto, then cutting east to link up with Stoneman and Garrard at Lovejoy's Station.

Hood quickly became aware that something was up, and on July 27 he moved to protect the vulnerable rail lines that fed Atlanta's defenders. Stephen D. Lee, who had recently arrived in the city and taken command of Hood's old corps, was sent west on the Lickskillet road with Brigadier General John C. Brown's and Brigadier General Henry D. Clayton's divisions to intercept Howard's army before it could get astride the railroad. Lee's force was augmented by two divisions of Stewart's corps, with two additional divisions to follow the next day. If all went well, by July 29 Hood hoped to be able to strike Howard's exposed right flank the same way that Hardee struck at McPherson five days earlier.

But increased Confederate cavalry activity alerted General Howard that his march was discovered. He decided to halt and dig in on the best defensive position he could find —a line of ridges near a Methodist meeting house known as Ezra Church. In order to safeguard his flanks, Howard positioned his troops in a horseshoe-shaped line with Logan's XV Corps on the right, facing south, and Major General Francis P. Blair's XVII Corps on the left, facing east.

By noon on July 28, Lee's corps had arrived at a point just south of Howard's position at Ezra Church. According to Hood's plan, Lee would pin Howard in place with his two divisions, while Stewart—coming up behind Lee—would continue marching west, then turn on the Yankee right flank and rear. But Stewart had not yet arrived when, at about 12:30 p.m., the impetuous Lee sent his men forward to the attack. Brown's division, on the Confederate left, commenced the assault; Clayton was instructed to continue the charge on the right once Brown struck the Yankee line.

Rough ground hampered Brown's advance, and once his troops neared the enemy breastworks they were staggered by a hail of bullets from the well-concealed Yankees of Morgan Smith's division. Only one of Brown's brigades was able to make any headway—Brigadier General William F. Brantley's Mississippians, who briefly broke Lightburn's brigade on the far right of the Federal line. But the gap was soon closed, and Brown's entire division began to retreat in disorder. Furious at what he considered a half-hearted effort on the part of the Southern fighting men, S. D. Lee sent Manigault's brigade against the Federal strongpoint, but this assault also failed.

Clayton started his division forward 10 minutes after Brown's men stepped off, but by the time Clayton's three brigades became engaged, most of Brown's troops were already falling back. Clayton's leftmost brigade, the

Louisianans led by Brigadier General Randall L. Gibson, became separated from the rest of the line and charged the apex of the Federal position near Ezra Church. Before Gibson's men could reach the enemy lines, Colonel Hugo Wangelin's Missouri brigade emerged from the defenses and spearheaded a counterattack that drove the Louisianans from their front. Realizing the futility of continuing the one-sided engagement, Clayton called off the attack and put his division on the defensive.

The first of Stewart's corps—Walthall's division—arrived on the field at 2:00 p.m. and was immediately ordered into action on Clayton's left, to relieve Brown's shattered troops. But Walthall's charge was no more successful than Brown's had been, and again the Southern lines fell back. Before Loring's division could be deployed on Walthall's right, both Loring and his corps commander, Stewart, were wounded. Walthall took command, and at his urging, Lee called off the fruitless assaults.

With only 632 casualties, Howard inflicted five times as great a loss on his opponents and might well have launched a counterattack. But the newly appointed commander of the Army of the Tennessee preferred to rest on his laurels, while the bloodied Rebels drew back closer to Atlanta. Neither Howard's thrust to the southwest nor Stoneman's and McCook's cavalry raids succeeded in accomplishing all that Sherman desired. But Federal morale was high, and Sherman saw the victory at Ezra Church as one more sign that it was only a matter of time before Atlanta would fall.

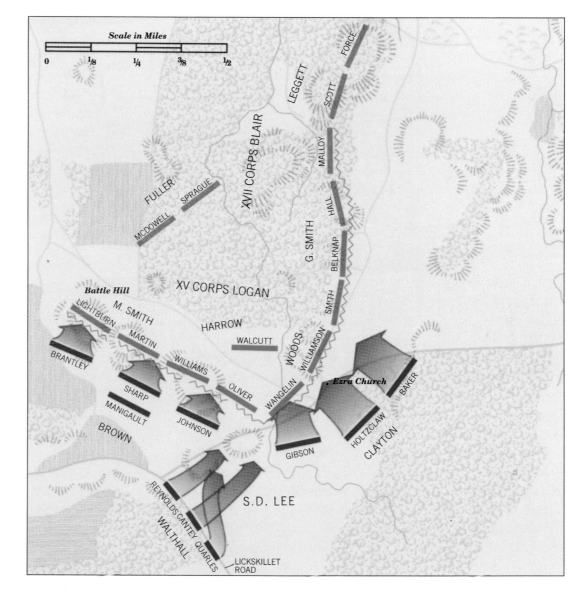

On July 28 Hood sought to intercept a Federal encircling movement around the western side of the city. Near Ezra Church the Rebels again struck a well-prepared enemy, suffered heavy casualties, and had to withdraw.

PRIVATE EDWIN W. SMITH
54TH OHIO INFANTRY, LIGHTBURN'S BRIGADE

Lightburn's brigade, positioned in the far right of the XV Corps in the early afternoon of July 28, was the first target of S. D. Lee's corps, coming up west around Ezra Church. A schoolteacher by profession, Smith enlisted in the 49th Ohio in August 1861 but was discharged for medical reasons the following October. He reenlisted in February 1864, joining the 54th Ohio.

In one of our gallant charges on hen-roosts and kitchens, my mess had gobbled a coffee-boiler large enough to hold more of that soldiers' precious tonic than Bragg and Warner could both drink in a week, though I would not vouch for it if filled with the genuine old "commissary." We coffee-coolers took turns to carry this huge coffee-boiler, and the day of the battle it happened to be my turn to tote it, which I did, fastened on my gum blanket and swung around on the middle of my back.

Gen. Lightburn had but recently taken command of our squad, and perhaps thinking us somewhat awkward, he thought it best to put us through a little drill. So early in the morning he marched us quite a way through the woods and underbrush in line of battle. Then commenced a series of the most wonderful evolutions on record. We marched straight to the front, right-about to the rear, filed to the right, then to the left, left-oblique, right-oblique, left flanked, right flanked; in short, having exhausted Hardee's tactics and his own, too, for that matter, as well as our patience, he halted us somewhere in the Southern Confederacy. I have often thought since that the Johnnies and Yanks were playing the game of hide and seek that morning, or perhaps both parties were trying to find Ezra Church and got lost in the brush.

All this time the coffee-boiler clung tenaciously to my back, catching in the brush and briars, which made me think none the more of Lightburn's drill. The 54th Ohio was deployed on the right as skirmishers. We had advanced but a short distance when Major Moore wanted some of the boys to climb some tall trees and look for Johnnies on the other side of a hill in our front. Another fellow and myself threw off our traps and skinned up the trees. We had just gotten comfortably seated for observation when "zip-zip, ping-ping" told us plainly the rebels could see us, if we could not see them, and that we were a little too high for health.

We hustled down as lively as we could, donned our accoutrements, not forgetting the coffee-pot, and joined our comrades who had found the rebel skirmishers posted behind some stone piles, log house, blacksmith shop, corn-crib and rail fence. Talk about your officers leading and encouraging their men in time of battle. We most generally fought on our own hook, at least we did on this occasion.

Some of us moved to the right and others to the left of the stone piles and buildings, pouring in a close, well-directed fire, cheering and encouraging each other at the same time. Comrades fell badly wounded around us, but still we pressed on.

The rebels, finding themselves flanked, slowly fell back, disputing every foot of the ground. As we took possession of their line we cast our eyes to the front, and there a sight met our gaze that I shall never forget.

At the edge of the woods about 300 yards distant it looked to me as though the whole Southern Confederacy stood in compact line of battle. As far as the eye could reach to the right and left stood a mingled line of yellow and gray in all the pomp, splendor and circumstance of glorious war. Hood was about to make another mighty effort to crush Sherman, and this was the living cyclone that he was in the act of hurling against him. . . .

We fell back as rapidly as our war harness would permit. I never did such poor running in my life; and that coffee-boiler! How I wished it was a shield or bullet proof. Every moment I expected to get a bullet into it. How it retarded my locomotion! I was tempted a dozen times to throw it, my gun traps and everything else to the Johnnies. They came so close that they called us pet names and ordered us to halt, but we were under Sherman's orders and did not obey Hood worth a cent.

On nearing our lines we were obliged to fall down and crawl on our hands and knees, our men firing over our heads. We were badly scattered; some of the boys and myself fell in with an Illinois regiment. Their volleys checked the exultant foe and gave us a little breathing spell, which was improved by the ordnance boxes being brought to the front at full gallop, knocked to pieces and the cartridges strewed along on the ground.

Charge after charge was made by the massed rebel forces on our single line, but were met and repulsed by the undaunted coffee-coolers with a fearful slaughter. Our guns would get so hot that we could not hold them. Three times when the rebels were driven back we let them cool, and twice poured water in them to clean them out.

At one time when the rebels had met with a bloody repulse, we were letting our guns cool and peering intently into the dense smoke. Dur-

"The slaughter was terrible. They seemed to melt like wax figures in the flame."

ing this short cessation they had massed their forces in a deep, heavily timbered ravine in our front, and under cover of the smoke had silently moved up close to our line. An ominous stillness like that which precedes the dreadful storm prevailed, and as the battle curtain rolled slowly up it showed their compact lines of yellow and gray standing at right-shoulder shift, coolly taking in the situation and mentally calculating how long it would take to gobble us up.

Our front rank was kneeling, the rear rank standing. The front rank fired just as they were taking aim. The slaughter was terrible. They seemed to melt like wax figures in the flame. Still they rallied, closed up their bleeding, shattered ranks and rushed forward with a dreadful yell, only to meet a withering volley from the rear rank. This swept through their dense lines like a sword blade, causing them to stagger and fall in all directions. Human valor could stand it no longer; they became completely demoralized and amidst the confusion the coffee-coolers pushed out among them, capturing quite a number and several battle flags.

A disproportionately high number of Confederate officers were killed or wounded at Ezra Church, among them Captain James B. Howard of the 49th Tennessee Infantry (above). He died leading a charge along the Lickskillet road.

CAPTAIN JOHN W. LAVENDER
4TH ARKANSAS INFANTRY, D. H. REYNOLDS' BRIGADE

When D. H. Reynolds' brigade went into action at about 2:00 p.m. with the rest of Walthall's division, Howard's well-positioned Federals had already exacted a terrible toll. One of the few Confederate regimental officers to come out of the Battle of Ezra Church unscathed, Captain Lavender was captured five months later outside of Nashville, Tennessee.

On the afternoon of July the 28th our Brigade was ordered to advance on the Enemys Brest works on our Extream left near Ezra Church. It was Extreamly warm and we had to advance some Distance through an open Field The Federal Brest works being in the Edge of the Woods Just out side the Field. When our lines Entered the open Field some three Hundred yards From their works they opened a terific Fire of Shells & Small arms on our line.

We held our fire and advanced rapedly as Possable. When aboute half way we opened fire and advanced in Double Quick time. We got near the works but our Fire done Them but Little Damage as they was Protected by Splendid Earth works and was literally mowing our men Down. So our lines was Forced to fall back or all be killed. We fell Back with fearful loss, the worst we had in any one Battle During the war for the number of men ingaged in it. The report was that we went into that Charge with 2600 Guns and lost aboute 1300 Killed and wounded including our Col. H. G. Bunn and nearly all the Field oficers of the Brigade and a great Many company officers. Col. Bunn had his Right arm Broken and wounds in Both Thighs but afterward got well.

This Battle Discouraged our men Badly as they could never understand why they Should have been Sent in to such a Death Trap to be Butchered up with no hope of gaining any thing. If we had suceeded in takeing that one Point we never could have held it but Such is War. We Fell Back to our line in a teriable shattered and Demoralized Condition.

piece of oak rail fence and part of a stone wall. In one length of that fence behind which the rebels were concealed, I count 100 bullet holes. And along that field, and within the distance of 80 rods, we count 1,600 dead rebels, most of them lying on their backs, eyes open, faces black, hands folded on their breasts.

Here lies one upon his side, eyes closed, feet slightly drawn up, his head resting easily upon his knapsack. He looks a weary soldier, sound asleep. I speak to him, he stirs not; put my hand upon him, he will not wake. Dead.

Here is a soldier, a rebel captain, sitting against this tree. His limbs are crossed, and his cap hangs naturally upon his knee. One hand in the breast of his coat, the other hangs by his side. Dead.

Here, leaning against this wall, is a rebel soldier with his leg broken below the knee, and a Union surgeon lying dead across his feet. They are both dead. The surgeon was evidently dressing his wound when he received his death shot, for there is the bandage wound twice around the limb, the other end of which is still in the dead surgeon's hand. The rebel soldier evidently bled to death.

CHAPLAIN GEORGE W. PEPPER
80TH OHIO INFANTRY, RAUM'S BRIGADE

Detached from his unit, which had been left behind to guard the rear areas, Pepper camped on the Ezra Church battlefield. Pepper, shown above with his fellow officers (seated, center), was haunted by images of war. "Sometimes I think I have seen too intensely," he wrote. "Sleeping or waking, its pools of blood, its ghastly forms, its staring eyes, its heaps of dead, are before my mind. Its groans and horrid cries, and howling shells, smite ever on my ears."

Here in these woods where Logan's corps was first engaged (on the 28th), there is not a rock or tree, or log, or leaf, but shows the desperate strife. One section of woods is literally cut off, torn down, scattered. Acres of this forest are topped by canister and grape-shot and shell almost as completely as our farmers top their cornfields with a sickle.

At the corner of the cornfield where the corps was engaged, there is a

Newly arrived from Mississippi, 30-year-old Stephen D. Lee replaced General Cheatham as commander of Hood's old corps for the Battle of Ezra Church. Lee was the youngest lieutenant general in the Confederate army. One observer described him during the fighting as looking like "the God of War, positively radiant."

GENERAL SHERMAN'S CAMPAIGN—EZRA'S CHURCH, July 28, 1864.—[Sketched by T. R. Davis.]

DEAD BROOK—BATTLE OF EZRA'S CHURCH.—[Sketched by T. R. Davis.]

GENERAL SHERMAN'S CAMPAIGN—SHERMAN'S HEAD-QUARTERS, NEAR DECATUR, July 19, 1864.—Sketched by T. R. Davis.—[See Next Page.]

PARIS FASHIONS FOR AUGUST, 1864.—[See Next Page.]

One month after the Battle of Ezra Church, Harper's Weekly featured the latest hoop skirt fashions from Paris juxtaposed with scenes from the Georgia battlefield, including the stiffened dead lying along a narrow brook, the wounded being treated outside Sherman's headquarters, and the small Methodist chapel that lent its name to the fight.

"I put the cup to his lips, but he could not swallow, and reluctantly I left him to die."

A feeding cup (above) was an indispensable item carried by nurses in Atlanta area hospitals to aid patients unable to eat or drink on their own.

with blood. The edge of my dress was red, my feet were wet with it. As we drew near the suffering men, piteous glances met our own. "Water! water!" was the cry.

Dr. McAllister had previously discovered in one of these the son of an old friend, and although he was apparently wounded unto death, he hoped, when the ambulances returned with the stretchers sent for, to move him into town to the hospital. He now proceeded with the aid of the instruments, bandages, lint, etc., I had brought to prepare him for removal. Meantime, taking from my pocket a small feeding-cup, which I always carried for use in the wards, I mixed some brandy and water, and, kneeling by one of the poor fellows who seemed worse than the others, tried to raise his head. But he was already dying. As soon as he was moved the blood ran in a little stream from his mouth. Wiping it off, I put the cup to his lips, but he could not swallow, and reluctantly I left him to die. He wore the blue uniform and stripes of a Federal sergeant of cavalry, and had a German face.

FANNIE A. BEERS
CONFEDERATE NURSE

Fannie Beers ran the Buckner Hospital at Newnan, 35 miles southwest of Atlanta, during some of the heaviest fighting of the campaign. In the aftermath of the fighting at Ezra Church, Beers' duties took her to the battlefield.

The battle-field was not three miles away. I was soon tearing along the road at breakneck speed. At an improvised field-hospital I met the doctor, who vainly tried to prepare me for the horrid spectacle I was about to witness.

From the hospital-tent distressing groans and screams came forth. The surgeons, both Confederate and Federal, were busy, with coats off, sleeves rolled up, shirtfronts and hands bloody. But our work lay not here.

Dr. McAllister silently handed me two canteens of water, which I threw over my shoulder, receiving also a bottle of peach brandy. We then turned into a ploughed field, thickly strewn with men and horses, many stone dead, some struggling in the agonies of death. . . .

Several badly wounded men had been laid under the shade of some bushes a little farther on; our mission lay here. The portion of the field we crossed to reach this spot was in many places slippery

BRIGADIER GENERAL WILLIAM W. BELKNAP
BRIGADE COMMANDER, XVII CORPS

Belknap, just promoted to general, wrote this letter of condolence to the mother of Second Lieutenant Emmanuel M. Gebhart on August 2, 11 days after the young officer lost his life in the Battle of Atlanta. In his official report, Belknap was equally laudatory, declaring that the army had in its ranks "no braver man" than Gebhart.

Madam: I take the earliest occasion in my power to address you on the subject of the sad death of your gallant son, 2d Lt. E. M. Gebhart of D. Co. 15th Iowa not for the purpose of opening afresh your wounded heart, but to assure you of the sincere sympathy of his late Commander. On July 22d I, as Colonel, commanded the 15th. On the 21st the Regt. had made a charge on Rebel works in which attack your son acted with conspicuous bravery. On that after-

Lieutenant Emmanuel M. Gebhart of the 15th Iowa, killed on July 22, took part in the fighting that day even though he had been wounded the day before. Severely wounded and captured at the Battle of Shiloh in April 1862, Gebhart was paroled after several months. After regaining his health, he rejoined his old regiment.

LIEUTENANT LAURENS W. WOLCOTT
52D ILLINOIS INFANTRY, RICE'S BRIGADE

Lieutenant Wolcott wrote this tongue-in-cheek letter comparing his life in the field with his sister's activities back home in Illinois. Five days earlier, on August 9, the Federals had bombarded the city of Atlanta, which still housed about 10,000 civilians, with more than 5,000 shells.

noon we moved to the left and on the 22d when the enemy attacked us, the Regt. was on the extreme left of the 17th Army Corps. They came upon us in such force as to turn our unsupported flank and the Regt. with the whole line of our Division fell back. We formed soon after however in a cornfield, but our right was again flanked when we retired to the line of breastworks and here received the charges of the enemy & defeated them with great loss on their side. It was while the 15th was falling back from the cornfield that I last saw your lamented son. We were together and my attention was attracted by his heroism and utter want of all idea of danger. I missed him however when we formed the next line but I understand from Sergeant Major Safely of the 11th Iowa that Lieut. G. remained on the right of the line—charged with many others a body of Rebels who had taken possession of a part of our own works—routed them, captured several prisoners and while falling back with them was shot in the back of the head and instantly killed. His bravery was the cause of his death. I hardly know what to say, my dear Madam, to lessen the grief that must overwhelm you. Loving your son as I did and appreciating his soldierly qualities—his energy & his devotion to his work I cannot help feeling that his loss is a great one. You have my condolence and sympathy & can rest assured that I will never forget the manly qualities & gallant deeds of Emanuel M. Gebhart— Lt. Col. Hedrick will show you a copy of my report in which I refer to your son's conduct.

*A*ug 14th, 1864
Dear Sister Mary
Yours of the 4th inst. came safely to hand two or three days ago. Am very much obliged for the graphic account of your doings. Think I can very well imagine just what sort of a time you had. If I wasn't afraid it might make me homesick afterward, I should have liked it amazingly to have been there and helped you enjoy yourselves. But we have gay times too. We have had 109 days of continual pic-nic, we feast upon "hard tack" and "sowbelly," and have our pleasure excursions on (or in) the southern rivers though they differ from ordinary water excursions in generally being across the streams instead of up or down them; we have beside this *plenty* of music, in fact there is no time of the day or night that one may not hear it such as it is, viz minnie balls for soprano, round shot, shells, "camp-kettles" & "threshing machines" (otherwise known as rifled shell) furnish what may pass for alto, while field and siege guns afford a powerful tenor and *thundering* bass, and we have "fourth of July" and fireworks, gratis, continually—more than all

we have the promise of fireworks extraordinary one of these days; furnaces are building for heating shot to burn the town which is in full view from our batteries and not over a mile distant.

It seems almost too bad, as you stand on the hill overlooking the town, taking care to keep your head under cover, however, for if you expose it ever so little "whiz" goes a ball from the rifle of some sharpshooting individual of rebellious proclivities so close to your ears that you involuntarily duck though you know the ball passed by the time you hear it. Everything looks so cool and comfortable in the shady streets and the white houses look out so invitingly from among the trees that you almost envy the inhabitants till the boom of a heavy gun and the little cloud of white smoke rising in the midst of the houses remind you that even *that* place, nice and clean and cool as it looks, has its drawbacks.

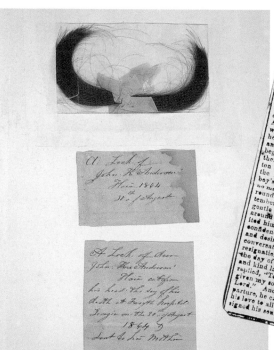

The Army of Tennessee lost more than one-third of its men defending Atlanta, among them 18-year-old John K. Anderson, who died on August 30 of complications from a leg wound inflicted by a Federal sniper. Anderson's obituary is shown above, along with a lock of his hair snipped by a nurse on the day he died.

This view of the Confederate works ringing Atlanta was taken fr

...e northwest corner of the defense line looking east from Fort Hood. It was not far from this spot that Mayor James M. Calhoun surrendered the city on September 2, 1864.

"Great volumes of sulphurous smoke rolled over the town, trailing down to the ground, and through this stifling gloom the sun glared down like a red eye peering through a bronze colored cloud."

WALLACE P. REED
RESIDENT OF ATLANTA

Although he was only 14 years old during the summer of 1864, Wallace Reed, who would later become an editorial writer and a reporter for the Atlanta Constitution and publish a history of Atlanta, recorded the scenes of devastation he witnessed during the weeks-long siege of the city. Recalling the day of the heaviest shelling, Reed wrote of the stiff price Atlanta paid in civilian lives.

The famous artillery duel! If any one day of the siege was worse than all the others, it was that red day in August, when all the fires of hell, and all the thunders of the universe seemed to be blazing and roaring over Atlanta. It was about the middle of the month, and everything had been comparatively quiet for a few days, when one fine morning, about breakfast time, a big siege gun belched forth a sheet of flame with a sullen boom from a Federal battery on the north side of the city. The Confederates had an immense gun on Peachtree street, one so large and heavy that it had taken three days to drag it to its position. This monster engine of destruction lost no time in replying to its noisy challenger, and then the duel opened all along the lines on the east, north, and west. Ten Confederate and eleven Federal batteries took part in the engagement. On Peachtree, just where Kimball street intersects, the big gun of the Confederates put in its best work, but only to draw a hot fire from the enemy. Shot and shell rained in every direction. Great volumes of sulphurous smoke rolled over the town, trailing down to the ground, and through this stifling gloom the sun glared down like a red eye peering through a bronze colored cloud. It was on this day of horrors that the destruction of human life was greatest among the citizens. A shell crashed into a house on the corner of Elliott and Rhodes street, and exploded, killing Mr. Warner, the superintendent of the gas company and his little six year old girl. . . . A lady who was ironing some clothes in a house on North Pryor, between the Methodist Church and Wheat street, was struck by a shell and killed. Sol Luckie, a well-known barber, was standing on the James's Bank corner, on Whitehall and Alabama, when a shell struck a lamp-post, ricocheted, and exploded. A fragment struck Luckie and knocked him down. Mr. Tom Crusselle and one or two other citizens picked up the unfortunate man and carried him into a store. He was then taken to the Atlanta Medical College, where Dr. D'Alvigney amputated his leg. The poor fellow was put under the influence of morphine, but he never rallied from the shock, and died in a few hours. A young lady who was on her way to the car shed was

A free black man, Solomon Luckie, a popular Atlanta barber at the Barber Shop and Bathing Salon on Decatur Street, died of wounds suffered when he was struck by shell fragments while standing at a street corner in mid-August.

struck in the back and fatally wounded. On Forsyth street a Confederate officer was standing in the front yard, taking leave of the lady of the house, when a bursting shell mortally wounded him and the lady's little boy. The two victims were laid side by side on the grass under the trees, and in a few minutes they both bled to death. The sun was sinking behind the western hills when the great artillery duel ended, and the exhausted gunners threw themselves on the ground. From a military standpoint there were no results worthy of mention. Nothing was gained by either side.

PRIVATE SAMUEL K. VANN

19TH ALABAMA INFANTRY, DEAS' BRIGADE

Private Vann wrote the letter below to his 14-year-old sweetheart, Nancy Elizabeth "Lizzie" Neel, during the siege of Atlanta. The young soldier survived the war and fulfilled his dream of marrying Lizzie—only to die prematurely in 1870 at the age of 24.

Line of Battle Near Atlanta, Ga.
August 25, '64
Miss N.E. Neel.

Most lovely Lizzie, I again seat myself behind the breastworks in the ditches for the purpose of trying to write you a few lines, as the railroad was torn up about the time I wrote before and I thought perhaps you would not get the other and therefore I thought it prudent to drop you another short note, as I am anxious to get a letter from you, and I fear that you have quit writing to me, though I hope not—for I would not know what to do if you were to fail writing, though I have a far better opinion of you than that. I do not think that you would try me thus. . . .

There are not many of us dirty Rebs here but what few of us are here are in fine spirits and can whip many a Yank yet.

Well Lizzie, if you could have seen me night before last when I came off picket, you would have thought that I was a . . . well I don't know what you would have thought for I was a sight sure, for we had to lie in the ditches in the mud, and water, over knee-deep for 24 hours, and you know that was awful sure, but we took it all fair and easy for we were obliged to do it. I have never seen the like before and I hope that I never will again, lying there in the mud and fighting all the time at that. We get somebody hurt every day in our Regt. and we lose one man from our "Co." every time we go on picket, which is every three days, and tonight is our time again and who will get wounded this time or killed. . . .

If you cannot read this I hope you will please excuse me for I cannot half write for the canon balls are flying thickly around me all the time, so you of course know that I am so scarry that I can't write as I should. I often think of you indeed when I retrospect—the many happy hours that we have spent together. I then think of my perilous residence at present and think perhaps I may never see your sweet smiling face again, I can hardly refrain from indulging floods of tears. O! may God speed the time when this unholy war shall cease so that we can return to those whom we have so long battled for. I will have to stop writing and go to work on the breast-works. I want you to write again and if you knew how well I like to read letters from you, you would certainly write. So write often and tell me all about the meeting at Killoughs as I recon you was there—whether you had a good meeting or not and how you enjoyed yourself there. I recon you think I am scarce of paper. Well I am. So I must close for the present. I remain yours as ever.

SKV

Jonesboro

On August 25, 1864, Sherman sent most of his troops on a march to seize control of Atlanta's remaining rail lines. By threatening the Macon & Western and Atlanta & West Point Railroads with so large a force, Sherman hoped that Hood could be drawn from the security of his defenses into a decisive engagement.

By August 30 Howard's Army of the Tennessee had severed the Atlanta & West Point Railroad and was headed east for the Macon & Western. Hood was alarmed to learn that Howard was approaching the Macon & Western near the town of Jonesboro, about 15 miles south of Atlanta, and dispatched Hardee, followed by S. D. Lee's corps, to intercept the Yankee column.

Skirting the Federal forces in the early morning of August 31, Hardee marched his weary men by a circuitous route, arriving at Jonesboro that afternoon. Several more hours elapsed before the entire Confederate force was in place. In the meantime Howard had reached the Flint River, a mile west of Jonesboro. Logan's XV Corps crossed the river and deployed on a ridge facing the Rebel position.

With no time to rest his tired soldiers, at 3:00 p.m. Hardee ordered an attack on the Yankee troops west of Jonesboro. Cleburne, commanding Hardee's old corps, moved forward on the Confederate left, wheeling to strike the right flank of the Federal line. S. D. Lee's divisions, led by Major Generals Carter Stevenson and Patton Anderson, were to wait until Cleburne was engaged before joining the assault on the Federal center and left.

Brigadier General Mark P. Lowrey, who temporarily commanded Cleburne's division, rushed upon Brigadier General Judson Kil-patrick's Yankee troopers and drove them across the Flint River. But Bate's division—commanded by General John C. Brown—was unable to break the entrenched Federal line. By the time Cleburne got Cheatham's division, now commanded by George Maney, forward from their position in reserve, Brown had been repulsed.

Unaware that Cleburne's intended flanking maneuver had failed, at the first sound of gunfire Lee launched his troops in a headlong charge on Logan's XV Corps. But the attack fell apart in the withering fire from Logan's battle line. When Lee sent his second wave forward, Stevenson's and Anderson's divisions were caught in the hail of bullets and fell back in disorder.

For a loss of 172 men, Howard's Federals had inflicted 2,200 casualties on Hardee's troops. That night orders came from General Hood, calling for Lee's corps to be withdrawn to the north to reinforce Atlanta. Hood, poorly informed, was convinced that the Union presence at Jonesboro was a diversion and Lee's corps was needed to help defend the city against a Federal assault. With Lee's sleepless soldiers tramping northward, Hardee was left with only a single corps to counter the inevitable Federal assault on September 1. Woefully outnumbered, Hardee's three divisions would be facing not only Howard's army to the west but three additional Union corps closing in on Jonesboro from the north.

Pulling back to a position just west of the Macon & Western, Hardee stretched his thin line over a mile-wide front and dug in. Maney's division held the left, Brown's the center, and Cleburne's the right, where the Confederate line angled east across the railroad tracks. Concerned for his vulnerable right, at 1:00 p.m. Hardee shifted most of Maney's command to extend Cleburne's line southeastward to block any Federal move on his flank and rear.

Sherman, who arrived to take personal charge of the operation, had just such a flanking maneuver in mind. Taking advantage of his superiority in numbers, Sherman instructed Logan to assault the front of the Rebel line with the XV Corps, while Jefferson C. Davis' XIV Corps struck at the angle held by Cleburne's troops. Meanwhile, Major General David S. Stanley's IV Corps would advance south down the Macon & Western and come into action against the vulnerable Confederate right and rear.

At 4:00 p.m. the Yankee juggernaut rolled forward. Despite the odds, Hardee's troops put up a stout defense. But they were unable to hold back the massed ranks of Davis' XIV Corps. The Confederate line was breached, eight pieces of artillery overrun, and Brigadier General Daniel C. Govan forced to surrender with 600 men of his brigade. As Hardee's embattled line bent back like a jackknife, Stanley's IV Corps made a belated appearance on the Confederate rear. But the Union formations came under heavy fire and were unable to force their way through what Stanley described as a "perfect entanglement" of felled trees and brush. This abatis, erected by the soldiers of Colonel Ellison Capers' brigade, bought Hardee enough time to extricate his beleaguered corps from the jaws of Sherman's trap.

That night Hardee marched his beaten force south to Lovejoy's Station, and dispatched a message to Hood informing him of the catastrophe. With his army scattered and not enough troops remaining to safeguard Atlanta's defenses, Hood saw no alternative but to abandon the city to General Sherman's victorious Yankees.

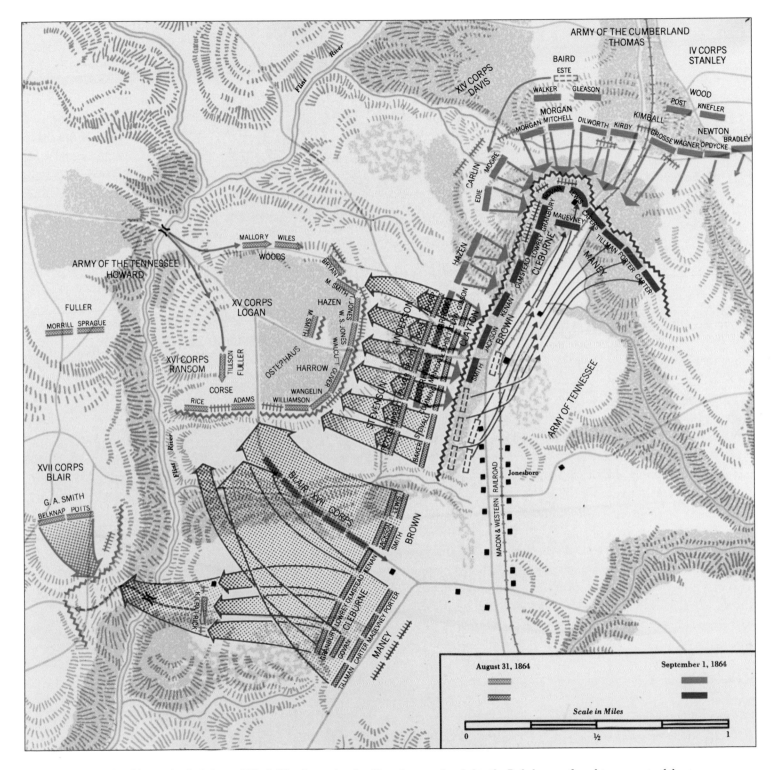

ARMY OF THE CUMBERLAND
THOMAS

IV CORPS
STANLEY

BAIRD
ESTE

WALKER   GLEASON

WOOD

XIV CORPS
DAVIS

MORGAN

POST
KNEFLER

MORGAN MITCHELL   DILWORTH   KIRBY   KIMBALL

NEWTON

GROSSE WAGNER OPDYCKE   BRADLEY

CARLIN
MOORE

EDIE

HAZEN

ARMY OF THE TENNESSEE
HOWARD

MALLORY   WILES

WOODS

CLEBURNE

MANEY

BRYANT

FULLER

M. SMITH

MORRILL   SPRAGUE

XV CORPS
LOGAN

HAZEN

M. SMITH

J. JONES

ANDERSON

CLAYTON

BROWN

ARMY OF TENNESSEE

XVI CORPS
RANSOM

TILLSON

FULLER

W. S. JONES

WALCUTT OLIVER

OSTERHAUS

HARROW

SMITH

KENAN

CORSE

JACKSON

RICE   ADAMS

WANGELIN
WILLIAMSON

Jonesboro

XVII CORPS
BLAIR

BLAIR XVII CORPS

LEWIS

JACKSON
SMITH

BROWN

G. A. SMITH

BELKNAP POTTS

MACON & WESTERN RAILROAD

KILPATRICK

CLEBURNE

JACKSON SMITH

KENAN

GRANBURY GOVAN CARTER MAGEVNEY PORTER

TILLMAN LOWREY OLMSTEAD

MANEY

August 31, 1864	September 1, 1864

Scale in Miles

0   ½   1

When Sherman closed in on the city's last rail link, Hood gave battle. After the two-day fight, the Rebels were forced to evacuate Atlanta.

COLONEL CHARLES H. OLMSTEAD

1ST GEORGIA INFANTRY, MERCER'S BRIGADE

So weakened was Hood's Army of Tennessee by the end of August that at Jonesboro more than a dozen of its units were led by replacement officers who had never handled such large commands. Among them was Olmstead, who led Mercer's brigade; General Mark Lowrey in turn led Cleburne's division, while Cleburne led Hardee's corps.

All that morning we waited, most of the time in line of battle, doing nothing save the shifting of position, sometimes a little to the right and then to the left, while every now and then a man would fall under the fire of the enemy's sharpshooters. It was very trying, much more so than positive action would have been, even though it brought us into greater danger. At last the order to advance was given and on we went; the pace gradually quickening almost to a run. The ground before us was a gentle slope down to where the Flint River wound its way through the lowlands—then upward to the works of the enemy.

As the men went forward cheering, a battery of light artillery commanded by Capt. Beauregard (a son of the general) followed, the guns leaping and bounding over the uneven surface of the ground, drivers whipping and spurring, horses wild with excitement, cannoneers clinging for dear life to their seats on the caissons and ammunition boxes—as fine an exhibition of warlike power as could be imagined. Again and again at the order *"Action front!"* the teams were brought around in sweeping curves in the full run, the men leaped to their places, the guns were unlimbered and bang!! bang!! went the shells hurtling over our heads. It fascinated me to watch them.

Nearing the river I happened to strike a boggy place in which my mare sank to the saddle flaps, and every struggle seemed to sink her deeper. Meanwhile, the line was advancing, leaving me, the brigade command-er, stuck in the mud. It was an unendurable plight in which to remain for a minute under the circumstances, so I climbed over the mare's head and pushed forward on foot, hoping that Linsky, my orderly, would find Lady Gray and rescue her, which very fortunately he did. . . .

I spoke of the passage of the Flint as having been made without difficulty, and so it was for all excepting Capt. Charlie Russell of the 54th. As that regiment got to the bank and looked at the yellow water of unknown depth, the men hesitated a little before entering the stream. Noticing this, Russell, who was always inclined to be melodramatic, waved his sword and shouted, "Don't be afraid of a little water, men; it's only knee deep. Follow me!" Then he stepped in *up to his neck,* having unfortunately found a place where the current had washed a hole under the bank. Of course, there was a great shout of laughter as the men went by on either side of him through the shallow water.

SERGEANT JOHN W. GREEN

9TH KENTUCKY (C.S.) INFANTRY, LEWIS' BRIGADE

On September 1 Lewis' troops rushed to the right of the Confederate line to meet the onslaught of General Thomas' Army of the Cumberland. Part of the brigade was overrun, and Green, who had been wounded, was among those captured. He was transported to Nashville but released when Sherman and Hood agreed to exchange prisoners.

We hurried to the position shown us & could see myriads of the enemy concentrated in our front already advancing against us. A few picks & spades & axes were given us with instructions to work for dear life to erect some defence to enable us to keep the yanks at bay until night for the remnant of the army had not yet been rescued from Atlanta. . . .

We have done but little in the way of digging rifle pits before the enemy's first line charges upon us. We drop the entrenching tools & seize our guns, fire a volley into them & go at them with charged bayonets. They fall back hurriedly & we as quickly return to our entrenching because we see four solid lines of battle advancing across a wide field against us. . . .

A second charge is now made upon us. Two lines coming in Solid phalanx determined to overrun our thin gray line, our men being two yards apart. But with steadiness & deadly fire we meet them. They

Federal artillerymen soften up Confederate positions near Jonesboro as a line of XIV Corps infantry (upper left) begins the assault that culminated with the capture of Govan's Arkansas brigade and part of Lewis' Orphan Brigade. The sketch was drawn by Lieutenant Henry Dwight of the 20th Ohio.

stagger; they waver. Our fire is so sure [and] so steady we have covered the ground in our front with their dead & dying. They fall back out of this withering fire but a third line advancing to their support presses them on with them. Surely with five times our numbers there is but little chance for us to withstand them. They come as a death wave. Their fire is thinning our slender ranks & surely I never saw men brave death more defiantly than they. . . .

But our men were surely falling like leaves in wintry weather. Fourqueran of our regiment, who had been on the picket line under command of Lieut' Jas McAllen & was now fighting on the left of the regiment, cried out, "Oh I am killed! what shall I do?"

I looked at him & he was sitting down in the trenches trying to pull a bullit out of his forehead. I said, "Fourquin (for that is what we called him) I will pull it out & you then run to the rear & go to the hospital."

Just then he got it out & said, "Never mind now, I have it out."

I just then saw Sam Boutcher fall dead from a ball which killed J. E. Adams at the same time. The shot came from a gun poked through the crack between the end of our front trenches & the transverse. Jim

McAllen saw it at the same instant & grabbed the muzzel of the gun which a yank had poked through there, fired it off & killed those two men at one shot. Jim McAllen [had] some one else to help him bend the gun barrel in there so that Mr Yank could not get it out & no other gun could be poked in there to do such murderous work. . . .

Their fourth line has now come up to their assistance; they have pressed on regardless of our death dealing fire until they are lying down flat just on the other side of our works. One great big Yank jumped up on our works & called to Booker Reed, "Surrender, you dam rebels."

Booker said to him, "The H——l you say," & shot him dead on the works.

I had my gun loaded, for notwithstanding I as Sergeant Major carried ordinarily only a sword, I always carried a gun into a fight with me. I rose from a stooping posture in the trenches to shoot but just as I looked over our trenc[h]es a yankee with the muzzle of his gun not six inches from my face shot me in the [face] & neck but fortunately it was only a flesh wound. It stung my face about as a bee sting feels but in my knees I felt it so that it knocked me to a sitting posture. But my gun was loaded and the other fellow had had his shot. I rose & put my gun against his side & shot a hole through him big enough to have run my fist through.

With bayonets fixed, Federal troops of Brigadier General Jefferson C. Davis' XIV Corps make the decisive charge at Jonesboro. The attack was directed at the angle in the Confederate works held by Hardee's depleted corps. Earlier that day, the Confederate corps commanded by General S. D. Lee had departed Jonesboro, leaving only 13,000 men to defend against a Federal phalanx of three corps, nearly half of Sherman's command.

SERGEANT LEE H. RUDISILLE
38TH OHIO INFANTRY, ESTE'S BRIGADE

Colonel George P. Este's troops formed part of the spearhead of the XIV Corps' assault against the Confederates at 4:00 p.m. on September 1. The 38th Ohio sustained the highest number of casualties of any Federal regiment at Jonesboro. Of 360 officers and men, 72 were killed or mortally wounded and 78 wounded—a toll so devastating that in the days to come Rudisille's company had to be led by an orderly sergeant.

At the command the brigade went forward at the double-quick up a slight grade, the rebels reserving their fire until the front line of the charging column reached the edge of the timber, and then delivered a volley straight into our faces. But their aim being too high, it did comparatively little execution. The works no doubt would have been reached before they could reload if it had not been for the scraggy, tangled brush the line here encountered. As it was, before the advance had forced its way more than half the distance through, it received a withering fire from the works that thinned the ranks frightfully and staggered it for a moment. But the second line soon came up and joined the remnant of the first, and together they fought their way through to the rebel works amid a very hell of carnage. The battle smoke had become so thick that one could scarcely see anything but the flash of the guns.

The color-bearer of the 38th Ohio was killed while clambering over the brush, well in advance of the line. One of the [color] guards picked up the flag and he, too, went down a moment later. Then another took it, only to leave the impression of his death-grasp upon its staff and moisten its folds with his warm life-blood. Then another and still another of the dauntless and devoted color guard raised the old flag to its place in the hot breath of the battle front, and the fifth man took it onto the works and kept it there until the fight was won. This man was Charlie Donze.

There were two guns of a rebel battery near the right of our regiment, with others still farther to the right. It was near this that the Confederate line was first broken. A portion of our line then swinging to the left took that of the Confederates in the flank and rear, and by this means they were about all gobbled in—the smoke be-

652

HARPER'S

CHARGE OF THE FEDERAL TROOPS ON THE REBEL WORKS AT JONESBOROUGH.—[See next page.]

ing so thick they could not see that their line had been broken.

Well to their right they were found steadily firing to the front and looked somewhat disgusted when the order to surrender was backed up by a nearness and a rear-ness of Federal bayonets. Even after they had been picked out of their works in this manner and gathered together, one regiment would curse the other for allowing the line to be broken, so much at a loss were they to know how and where it had occurred. They were especially indignant when they saw the weakness of our own line. They comprised Govan's entire brigade, one of the best in the Confederate army, which greatly outnumbered our own after the battle as we had lost over one-third of our number before we reached the works.

A 20-year-old farm boy from Erie, Ohio, Private Gurden R. B. Dunbar (right) of Company K, 38th Ohio, lost his life attacking the Confederate breastworks at Jonesboro on September 1, 1864. His older brother, William, also in the 38th Ohio, had died of disease at Chattanooga the previous winter.

MARY RAWSON
RESIDENT OF ATLANTA

Daughter of a prominent Atlanta family, Rawson, along with countless other citizens, spent a sleepless night on September 1, dreading the arrival of the Yankees and listening to exploding munitions stores put to the torch by the fleeing Confederates. She wrote in her diary, "The memory of the incident of this night is indelibly fixed in my mind."

This day witnesses the downfall of the hopes of the citizens of Atlanta. Today Gen. Hood commenced his evacuation of our city. The gentlemen who did not wish to fall into the hands of the federals might have been seen in the afternoon of this day in company of the last of the soldiers, wending their way slowly out of the now desolate Atlanta as night threw around our home its sable shadows, silence reigned broken only by pleasant converse with our now absent friends, how different from the few last nights preceeding; the pleasure and repose of these evenings was disturbed by the noise of exploding shells and the sharp crack of the death dealing musketry. Oh! how much more pleasure there would have been had it not been for the expectation of the scene of the coming tomorrow. Nine oclock comes and we retire for the night, but sleep and dreams were soon interrupted by rapid and loud explosions. On arising a most beautiful spectacle greeted our sight. The Heavens were in a perfect glow while the atmosphere seemed full of flaming rockets crash follows crash and the swift moving locomotives were sent in pieces and the never tiring metalic horse lay powerless while the sparks filled the air with innumeral spangles. This grand exhibition was occassioned by the burning of the military stores which could not be removed with the soldiers.

COLONEL GEORGE W. ADAIR
STAFF, LIEUTENANT GENERAL JOHN B. HOOD

As a wealthy Atlanta businessman, Adair had originally opposed the idea of secession. Following the final surrender of the Confederacy in the spring of 1865, he returned to Atlanta and played a key role in rebuilding the city. During the last months of fighting, Adair served as an aide to cavalry leader Nathan B. Forrest.

I shall never forget the night we left Atlanta. The old rolling-mills were on fire, and four hundred bales of cotton belonging to old man Wells were burning. On going up a big hill below Atlanta the fire was blazing so brightly I could count the hairs in the horse's tail by its light. Gen. Hood had placed me in charge of the headquarters wagons. I had a wagon of my own, an old-fashioned North Carolina tobacco-pedler's. Just as we were pulling out, Henry Watterson, the Louisville editor, who had refugeed here and had been conducting his paper from this point, and "John Happy," of the Nashville paper, came up and climbed into my wagon. Gov. Harris, his body-servant, Ran, myself, and my "nigger," Wash, Watterson, and "Happy" made up the party. We drove all night. It was a sick crowd, sick in heart and mind. Atlanta had fallen; Hood was pushing on toward the sea, and the relentless Sherman was following. There seemed nothing left but to surrender. Harris, proud, defiant man that he was, was the sickest man I have ever seen. He sat there, gloomy and quiet, but without a thought of surrender. I had old Wash to make some coffee for us, which he could do better than any human I have ever seen before or since, and this somewhat revived our drooping spirits.

Atlanta was the second Southern state capital from which Isham G. Harris (left), the governor of Tennessee, was forced to flee. In 1862 he had escaped from Nashville, the first capital to fall to the Federals. During the Battle of Shiloh, Harris served on the staff of Confederate major general Albert S. Johnston.

"The Heavens were in a perfect glow while the atmosphere seemed full of flaming rockets."

Severed tracks and scattered axles testify to the force of the explosion that ripped through a Confederate ordnance train on the night of September 1, leveling the walls of the rolling mill in the background. Hood's troops touched off the blast as they prepared to abandon Atlanta to the Federals.

Defeat and Desolation

As his weary troops regrouped at Lovejoy's Station, General Hood wired news of the disaster to Jefferson Davis and the Confederate cabinet. Rather than accept any personal responsibility for the tragic course of events, the embittered commander of the Army of Tennessee blamed the defeat on his soldiers' lack of spirit. "According to all human calculations we should have saved Atlanta," the general stated, "had the officers and men of this army done what was expected of them." Hood alleged that Hardee's troops could have overrun the Federals at Jonesboro on August 31, but the men "had been taught to believe that entrenchments cannot be taken," and "would not attack breastworks." Hood demanded that Hardee be relieved of command, and Davis duly transferred the senior corps commander to a new assignment in Charleston, South Carolina.

While Hood licked his wounds at Lovejoy's Station, Sherman was savoring the fruits of his successful campaign. More than 30,000 Union troops had been killed, wounded, or captured in the four months of fighting, but Sherman knew his foes had sustained a comparable loss—one their smaller army could ill afford. "You have accomplished the most

gigantic undertaking given to any general in this war," Grant wrote his old friend, "and with a skill and ability that will be acknowledged in history as unsurpassed if not unequaled." President Lincoln issued a proclamation declaring a day of thanksgiving in honor of the victory, and cannons boomed in celebration throughout the North.

Having secured his prize, Sherman decided not to seek a decisive engagement with the battered but still formidable Rebel army; he informed his superiors in Washington, "I will move to Atlanta and give my men some rest."

When Sherman and his staff entered Atlanta on September 7 most of the Federal troops were already encamped on the outskirts of the city, while three regiments patrolled the desolate streets. After instructing his chief engineer, Captain Orlando Poe, to rebuild and strengthen the old Rebel earthworks in order to forestall any counterattack

Federal officers strike a pose in front of the Windsor Smith house, near the southwest edge of Atlanta. Formerly Hood's headquarters, the house was taken over by the staff of the Federal XX Corps, whose star insignia flies at the right side of the building.

on Hood's part, Sherman made a controversial decision. All Southern citizens remaining in Atlanta would be expelled from the city. "I was resolved to make Atlanta a pure military garrison," Sherman recalled, "with no civilian population to influence military matters."

General Hood protested the action, calling it "studied and ingenious cruelty," and Mayor James M. Calhoun made a personal appeal to Sherman to spare the Atlantans from the "appalling and heart-rending" eviction. But the Union commander was adamant. "You might as well appeal against the thunderstorm," Sherman told the mayor, "as against these terrible hardships of war." Between September 12 and 21 some 1,600 people were loaded aboard wagons and escorted from the city. More than half of the refugees were children.

Once the inhabitants were gone, Federal troops set about demolishing war-ravaged dwellings, taking any salvageable materials for use in their encampments. Major James T. Holmes of the 52d Ohio wrote his family that "all around the city fine houses are leaving, by piece-meal, on the backs of soldiers." Surveying the once bustling city's destruction, a Yankee private noted, "I don't think any people will want to try and live there now."

While Sherman's troops rested on their laurels, on September 21 Hood began shifting his army to Palmetto, 20 miles west of Lovejoy's Station. Four days later Jefferson Davis arrived to assess the condition of the Confederate forces and to confer with Hood on his future intentions. During a review of the troops the Confederate president received a decidedly chilly reception. "Give us Johnston!" some soldiers shouted, "Give us our old commander!"

But Davis remained unwavering in his loyalty to Hood and was pleased to learn that despite his recent misfortunes the general was eager to resume the offensive. The president sanctioned the move, and on September 29 Hood led the Army of Tennessee, 40,000 strong, north across the Chattahoochee River to strike at Sherman's principal line of supply, the Western & Atlantic Railroad. By October 3 more than 15 miles of track had been demolished, and the Union garrisons at Acworth and Big Shanty had surrendered.

The enemy move caught Sherman off guard and left him little choice but to follow in the hope of bringing the Rebel force to battle. The Federal commander was uncertain whether Hood's continued march northward was merely a large-scale raid or portended an eventual assault on Chattanooga. "I cannot guess his movements as I could those of Joe Johnston, who was a sensible man and only did sensible things," Sherman complained in a letter to Brigadier General John M. Corse, whose successful defense of Allatoona Pass against Hood's raiders provided one of the few bright moments in an increasingly frustrating campaign.

By the end of October Hood was at Gadsden, Alabama, having laid waste to more than a dozen Federal supply depots, including Tunnel Hill, the starting point of Sherman's drive on Atlanta. Fired with confidence, Hood won approval for an audacious new campaign from General P. G. T. Beauregard, the recently appointed commander of the Military Division of the West. The army would cross the Tennessee border, capture Nashville, and free the state from Yankee occupation. If all went well, they would continue on into Kentucky and carry the war to the border of Ohio.

While Hood prepared to embark on his daring enterprise, Sherman made a fateful decision of his own. The Federal commander had lost interest in Hood: "If he will go to the Ohio River, I'll give him rations," Sherman declared; "my business is down south." Dispatching Thomas to Chattanooga, and bolstering the Tennessee defenses with two corps, Sherman retraced his steps to Atlanta.

Sherman had received permission from Grant and Lincoln to undertake a bold thrust at the very heart of the Southern Confederacy. The Gate City of the Deep South would become the launching point for a great march east, one that would take Sherman's armies across Georgia all the way to the Atlantic Ocean. "I can make this march," Sherman asserted, "and make Georgia howl!"

Before his 62,000 troops left Atlanta on November 15 Sherman ordered a final act of destruction. All structures of potential military value to the Confederacy were put to the torch, the city's railroad depot and roundhouse reduced to rubble, and miles of track demolished. At that point, Sherman noted, Atlanta "became a thing of the past."

For Southerners the fate of Atlanta seemed an ominous portent of still greater tragedy. The war had entered a grim phase in which the future of the Confederacy appeared more hopeless than ever before. Diarist Mary Chesnut expressed the fears of many when she wrote, "Since Atlanta I have felt as if all were dead within me, forever."

ATLANTA CAMPAIGN CASUALTIES

FEDERAL

Killed	4,423
Wounded	22,822
Missing	4,442
Total	31,687

CONFEDERATE

Casualties up to July 9 (Johnston commanding)	8,873
Estimated casualties July to September (Hood commanding)	22,103
Total	30,976

BRIGADIER GENERAL ALPHEUS S. WILLIAMS
Division Commander, XX Corps

In this letter of September 3 to his daughters, Williams first relates that "I have dated my letters so long from Near Atlanta that it is quite a change to write 'In Atlanta.'" During the Federal sweep to Jonesboro, the XX Corps was left behind to guard the Chattahoochee River crossings. Advance elements of the corps were nearest the city and thus the first to enter, taking the surrender from Mayor James M. Calhoun on the morning of September 2.

As I was marching at the head of my column last night through the dark streets, made intensely so by the heavy shade-trees, I heard a window shoved up and a female voice cry out, "Welcome!" I cried back, "Thank you, and the more so as it is a rare sound down here." It did, indeed, seem strange, that voice of welcome where we have met little but battle and carnage, coming so suddenly from the impenetrable darkness. For more than a month we have lain face to face with the heavy works thrown around this city, and day after day have I peered over our trenches to catch some new idea of the position of affairs. Three high, broad parapets seemed to bid defiance, and my curiosity was generally met with sharp efforts to plug my head. Week after week their heavy guns and ours have kept up a roaring, during which we have thrown thousands of projectiles from the twenty-pounder Parrott to the sixty-odd-weight ball into this city.

It seemed, therefore, very strange to march unopposed, as I did last night, through these same hostile works, and especially right alongside of one of those frowning fortresses that lay in my original front and which had killed or maimed hundreds of men of my division. I rode along full of queer sensations and exciting emotions. It was too dark to see much, but there was the principal battlement which had caused so much trouble and injury and not a sound came from it. I could hardly realize that its strong and defiant voice had really been silenced.

SERGEANT RICE C. BULL
123d New York Infantry, Knipe's Brigade

By noon on September 2 the Stars and Stripes flew over Atlanta's city hall. All through that day and into the next the regiments of the XX Corps poured into the city with their bands playing. The soldiers, elated with their triumph, joined in with their own choruses—patriotic airs and more caustic selections like the one performed by Bull and his mates, sung to the tune of "John Brown's Body."

Hurried orders were received on Friday, September 2nd, directing our Regiment to make preparations to make reconnaissance in the direction of the city. Only fifteen minutes were had for breakfast and we were only to take our guns, ammunition, and canteens. A guard was left behind to take charge of our knapsacks and any other belongings. Our breakfast consisted of hardtack and raw bacon; we had no time to make coffee. Within thirty minutes from the time we got the order, we were on the move with Colonel Rogers in command. . . .

With our faces toward the town, we covered the distance in record time. On the way all was quiet and peaceful. When we passed through the enemy's works we saw how formidable they were. They had no less than three lines, two of them protected by the strongest kind of abatis. I do not think it would have been possible to have taken them by assault. When we reached Atlanta, we were of course in the best of spirits and marched through with great cheering. Very few white people were in sight, but lots of Negroes watched us as we marched along. To the best of our ability we sang, "We will hang Jeff Davis on a sour apple tree."

Federal soldiers pose with a Rebel 24-pounder seacoast gun (foreground) and other large-caliber weapons, prizes that fell into their hands with the capture of Atlanta. These heavy guns had been brought up by rail from the Gulf Coast forts to augment the city's defenses; the Confederates were forced to abandon them when they hurriedly evacuated on September 1.

"To the best of our ability we sang,
'We will hang Jeff Davis on a sour apple tree.'"

S. P. RICHARDS
Atlanta Bookseller

English-born S. P. Richards had never carried a musket until he was ordered to guard duty in the Georgia militia. Fearing that his unit would be evacuated with the army when the Federals arrived, Richards resigned on September 1. His diary describes what the first few days of the Union occupation were like.

*F*riday 2. About noon today the Yankees came in sure enough a party of five or six came riding by our house. A committee of our citizens went out early and met *Gen Slocum* and got his word that private property should be respected, upon which the city was surrendered to them and in they came. The Stars and Stripes were soon floating aloft over the city. The private houses were not molested by the soldiers and I was therefore very much surprised when I went down town to see armsful and baskets full of books and wall-paper going up the street in a continuous stream from our store and when I reached the store, the scene would have required the pencil of Hogarth to portray. Yankees, men, women, children and niggers were crowded into the store each one scrambling to get something to carry away,

regardless, apparently, whether it was any thing they needed, and still more heedless of the fact that they were stealing! Such a state of utter confusion and disorder as presented itself to my eyes then, I little dreamed of two hours before when I left it all quiet and, as I thought, safe. The soldiers in their mad hunt for tobacco had probably broken open the door and the rabble had then "pitched in" thinking it a "free fight."—At first I was so dismayed that I almost resolved to let them finish it, but finally I got them out and stood guard until after dark when I left it to its chances until morning, as I was very sleepy. The night passed quietly and at day break I went to the store again to re-pack and prepare to move the balance of the books &c to the house. But a new difficulty soon arose; one of the mules was stolen from the stable and the hauling stopped as Joe said. I borrowed Mr Clarks one horse wagon and putting the mule that was left (a little one) before it we began to haul with the prospect of two days work before us, but with the aid of Mrs Holbrooks Cray in the afternoon we managed to get away the most of the goods. A number of books were *stolen* by the Yankees during the day before our eyes and that by men who *looked* like gentlemen! Of course their looks belied their character. Several took books and *paid* for them.

Sunday 4. It is strange to go about Atlanta now and see only Yankee uniforms. The City Hall is Head Quarters for the Provost Guard I guess. The enemy behave themselves pretty well except in the scramble for tobacco and liquor during which every store in town nearly was broken into yesterday. We heard the Church bells ring this morning and went to the Epis Church and heard Mr Freeman preach and a Fed. Chaplain read the prayers. When I got home Joe informed me that our *mule* had come back which I was glad to hear. This afternoon three soldiers asked for dinner saying their rations had not come and they would pay for their dinner, so Sallie had some cooked for them. They belonged to Co E 2nd Mass.Vols but the chief spokesman was a Scotchman. They think that McClellan will be next president as he has been nominated by the Chicago Convention. At Mrs Roots request I accompanied herself and Mrs West to our church this afternoon and we heard an *Abolition* preacher from Indiana preach on the "home of the blessed." Returning to our homes we heard that another big fight at Jonesboro had resulted disastrously to the Confederates, and in confirmation of this we saw 1800 "rebel prisoners" marched into town. They filled the street from the Baptist Church to Whitehall St. It was a sad sight but the Yankees *cheered* at it lustily of course.

SERGEANT FENWICK Y. HEDLEY
32D ILLINOIS INFANTRY, ROGERS' BRIGADE

The news of Atlanta's capture gave a much-needed lift to the soldiers of Grant's army stalled before Richmond and Petersburg. The victory also convinced a majority of the Northern public that the war could be won and helped ensure Lincoln's reelection in November. Sergeant Hedley recorded the thanks from Grant and Lincoln.

Immediately upon the occupation of Atlanta, General Sherman issued orders proclaiming the end of the campaign, and ordering the army into camp "for rest, and reorganization for a fine winter's campaign." . . . That evening, general orders were read to the troops, communicating the following historic papers:

Executive Mansion,
Washington, Sept. 3, 1864.
The national thanks are rendered by the President to Major General W. T. Sherman and the gallant officers and soldiers of his command, before Atlanta, for the distinguished ability and perseverance displayed in the campaign in Georgia, which, under Divine favor, has resulted in the capture of Atlanta. The marches, battles, sieges, and other military operations that have signalized the campaign, must render it famous in the annals of war, and have entitled those who have participated therein to the applause and thanks of the nation.
Abraham Lincoln,
President of the United States.

City Point, Va., Sept. 4.
Maj. Gen. Sherman: I have just received your dispatch announcing the capture of Atlanta. In honor of your great victory, I have ordered a salute to be fired, with shotted guns, from every battery bearing upon the enemy. The salute will be fired within an hour, amid great rejoicing.
U. S. Grant,
Lieutenant General.

And now that the troops fully recognized the import of their brilliant but wearisome and bloody three months' campaigning, and learned

"The brass and martial bands, which had been silent all the long way from Chattanooga to Atlanta, now played their most exultant airs."

with what joy the news was received at home, they gave way to a protracted jubilee. The brass and martial bands, which had been silent all the long way from Chattanooga to Atlanta, now played their most exultant airs; and the men vied with the instruments in making noise expressive of great joy. All were happy and smiling, from the commander-in-chief to the humblest private in the ranks, and even the bray of the half-starved government mule seemed mellow and melodious, as it added to the din.

SERGEANT JOHN W. GREEN
9TH KENTUCKY (C.S.) INFANTRY, LEWIS' BRIGADE

Green was among the hundreds of Rebels taken prisoner when the Federal tidal wave overran their line at Jonesboro on September 1. Slightly wounded himself, Green tended to some of his fellow captives and then tried but failed to slip away that night. Exchanged shortly afterward, he rejoined the 300 survivors of his brigade, all that remained of the 1,100 who had started out in May.

The next morning all those who were able to march were marched over to the head Quarters of the Union Genl Jefferson C. Davis. He ordered a tent fly pitched for us, directed that rations be issued to us and that wood & water & cooking utensils be brought to us. We had the best breakfast that morning we had eaten for many a day, good genuine coffee, hard tack & bacon. Before he sent us to our quarters he said to me, "My good fellow you seem to have been wounded. Has your wound received our Surgeons attention?"

I told him I had dressed it the best I could. He replied, "That wont do. Here orderly take this man to the surgeon & have his wounds dressed," & I was carefully & skilfully ministered to by their surgeon. . . .

GENERAL SHERMAN'S VICTORY—REBEL PRISONERS BEING CONDUCTED TO ATLANTA FROM JONESBOROUGH.—[SEE PAGE 638.]

A long line of Confederate prisoners taken at Jonesboro, mostly Arkansas and Kentucky men, trudge north to holding pens in Atlanta. All were spared the hardships of a Northern prison after Sherman and Hood brokered an exchange that returned all captives to their armies by September 19.

We remained here for three days. The next day they marched us up to Atlanta & put us in a prison pen which we had used to put Federal prisoners in. It had a large frame building in the centre but not large enough to shelter all of us from the rain or from the sun, both of which we had an abundance of. The rations of hard tack, bacon & coffee were so good that we felt we would soon be growing fat. Every day they sent emissaries in to ask if some did not want to take the oath of allegiance to the United States. They would stick hand bills all around offering amnesty & transportation home to any who would take the oath not to fight again in the confederate army but I rejoyce to say not a Kentuckian would listen to them.

comfort 'tis to me to know that he received Christian burial. You will see Father's letter & see by that all that John Stoney wrote me, he got a pass for Sergt Owens & himself to pass in front of our pickets. Sergt Owens said he could show the place where he fell, he showed a great deal of interest John Stoney says in trying to recover the body, having asked Gen M before John Stoney got there to let him go in search of it. John Stoney says they "could not identify his features, but could his clothes, pieces of which I send you, although the color is much changed I am sure they were his. The men of the co who were present all were of the same opinion" & I myself from the pieces am sure they were his. I send you some of the pieces. 'Tis a comfort to me to know that he could not have suffered. Sergt Owens said as soon as the line began to move forward under the heavy fire, Mr Palmer went ahead & said

ALICE A. PALMER

WIFE OF CAPTAIN JOHN S. PALMER, 10TH SOUTH CAROLINA INFANTRY

Even though the guns were silent around Atlanta, the tragic plight of the families who had lost loved ones was far from over. Alice Palmer's nightmare began when she received word that her husband, Captain John S. Palmer of the 10th South Carolina (seated with Alice, above), was missing and presumed dead after the fight at Ezra Church. Just after the fall of the city, her desperate hope that he might still be alive was shattered by a letter from one of Palmer's fellow officers informing her that her husband's body had been found.

Charleston Sept 7th 1864
    My Dear Mother,
    We got down safely this morning. On my arrival found a letter from John Stoney, telling me that they had recovered the body of my precious husband, & that Bishop Lay, at his request had performed the funeral service when they laid him in the cemetery at Atlanta & now Atlanta has gone, when will I ever be able to get my beloved one laid in our own state & where I can go sometimes? No one knows what a

Captain Palmer's regimental commander, Colonel James Pressley, who was himself wounded on July 22, sent Alice Palmer the first news of her husband in the telegram above. Swatches of cloth cut from his uniform (left) provided the grim confirmation of his death. About the pieces, Alice wrote John's sister, "Thank God he had on clothes that we knew otherwise we never would have felt sure that they were his precious remains."

"Come on boys" they were his last words. Oh my God, how hard it is to give him up, altho' I know he is so much happier now. I try to feel resigned, but at times my heart feels so rebellious. All this time I have allowed myself, altho' I felt it was wrong, to cling to the hope of his being alive. I could not help it try what I would. What a blank lies before me. When I think of all our bright hopes & anticipations of a happy life together, when this war was ended & remember that now they will never be realized! Oh! what anguish, my poor weary heart sighs for rest. All my hopes blasted & my young heart blighted forever, the prospects of a long, lonely, cheerless life ahead of me, when I have always looked forward to so much happiness. What a contrast! No one knows the intense love I bore for my precious husband, think sometimes that perhaps I loved him too much & that is the reason God has seen fit to afflict me thus, as a means of drawing me nearer to Him & to make me remember that we are not to look to earthly objects entirely for happiness. Oh may this [ ] blow be sanctified to me & may I soon be permitted to join my loved one in that happy world above. God knows how I have struggled to be able to say with patience and submission "Thy Will O Lord be done." I try to feel resigned & I trust I am, but oh how hard to give up one so very dear. I know there are many left who still love me, but he who was everything to me has gone, & I feel that there is no pleasure left in life for me now.

I will of course be happy to hear of peace being proclaimed but what a bitter moment it will be for us, when others are returning to gladden the hearts and homes of their dear ones ours will still be missing, then it is we will feel more keenly our heavy bereavement. Oh how I wish it were possible for those precious remains to be brought on now & placed at St Stephens, but who knows when that can be done since the enemy hold possession of Atlanta.

I cannot tell you Mother, what a comfort it was to me to be with you, for I know you could feel more with me than any one. . . .

Give my love to all the girls & accept the same from your affec. Daughter.

Alice A. Palmer

Near the end of August, one of John Palmer's fellow officers, J. Stoney Porcher, took a party of men out through the picket lines to recover the captain's body. After organizing a decent burial in the city for the remains, Porcher wrote Palmer's father about his son—the second of his sons to fall in the war. On the last page (above) Porcher included a map of the cemetery where he laid the body to rest "in a place not yet filled with graves."

PRIVATE JOHN F. BROBST
25TH WISCONSIN INFANTRY, SPRAGUE'S BRIGADE

Although most of the Yankee occupation troops treated Atlanta's residents with a measure of politeness, few saw any reason to suspend their foraging—or their abiding preoccupation with the opposite sex, as exhibited by Private Brobst.

Well, now for the news. I suppose you have heard that we have got the long sought-for prize, the city of Atlanta. Well, we have it at last, and lots of real nice things with it. We got large warehouses full of tobacco, plenty of dry goods, plenty of everything but money. But the greatest prizes that we had the good fortune to capture was a fine lot of secesh war widows and girls, and oh, lots of babies and little ones of all sizes and colors, ages and looks, fine looking things, resembling anything from a baboon up or down to a donkey. The fact of the business is they are a hard looking nation. They look worse than I used to look when I had been poorly stayed with when I was up north. But you had ought to see what fools our soldiers are. Those fairs of the south will tell a very pitiful and heartrending story and the boys must marry them to get them out of their misery. There have been more than fifty weddings now since we have got in here and how many more there will be is more than I can tell you. Perhaps you may get catched yourself, Mr. John, your affections are so easily ensnared, but rather think not. No ragamuffin gal can catch this chick. They want more hoops, because it is a Yankee invention, and the nicest fashion they have down here is that of snuff-dipping. The way that it is done, they take a small stick, such a one as they can get into their mouth, and wind a rag around the end of the stick, and wet the rag, then dip it in the snuff and chew it, spit and slobber around just like an old tobacco chewer, and you know how I am down on tobacco chewers.

Today all the women and children must leave Atlanta. All those who have husbands in the rebel army or brothers, fathers, or anyone that they depend on for maintenance, have to go south. It goes against the grain for some of them to go, but old Billy Sherman has said it and go they must, and all those that have got no one to depend on for support in the rebel army are to go north if they choose to go there. If not, south.

There are about twelve thousand women and children in Atlanta, drawing their supplies from the government and we have to be down here fighting their husbands, sons, brothers, and fathers who have run and left them behind for our government to support, but Sherman is bound to send them after their loved lords of southern soil and it is just right in my opinion.

THE REVEREND JOHN JONES
PRESBYTERIAN MINISTER

Although a resident of Liberty County in southeast Georgia and far removed from the fighting in Atlanta, Jones nevertheless keenly felt the loss of the Gate City to its Federal invaders. By the time he wrote his sister, Mrs. Mary Jones, Atlanta had been evacuated of all civilians—among them Mary Jones' daughter and her husband—none of them knowing if they would ever return.

Refuge, *Friday,* September 23rd, 1864
My dearest Sister,
The loss of Atlanta is the greatest blow of the war. Our prospects are exceedingly dark to me, and without special divine interposition we are a ruined people. The militia who have just returned home report much drunkenness among the higher officers of our army. Sad evil to exist when we are suffering from exhaustion of men, and need the best of officers to lead and husband our feeble armies! Oh, for a General Lee at the head of every *corps d'armée!* But regrets and reproaches are unavailing, and we must roll our great burden on our Heavenly Father and both hope and wait *for the salvation of the Lord....*

Your ever affectionate brother,
John Jones.

"And what has this helpless people done that they should be driven from their homes, to wander as strangers, outcasts and exiles, and to subsist on charity?"

JAMES M. CALHOUN
MAYOR OF ATLANTA

Atlanta's mayor since 1862, James Calhoun sought to have General Sherman rescind his order to expel the civilians from the city. In an impassioned letter penned at the eleventh hour, the mayor and two councilmen underscored the extraordinary hardships the Southern refugees would face.

Atlanta, Ga., Sept. 11, 1864.

Major-General W. T. Sherman—*Sir:* The undersigned, Mayor and two members of Council for the city of Atlanta, for the time being the only legal organ of the people of said city to express their wants and wishes, ask leave most earnestly but respectfully to petition you to reconsider the order requiring them to leave Atlanta. At first view, it struck us that the measure would involve extraordinary hardship and loss, but since we have seen the practical execution of it, so far as it has progressed, and the individual condition of many of the people, and heard the statements as to the inconvenience, loss and suffering attending it, we are satisfied that the amount of it will involve in the aggregate consequences appalling and heart-rending.

Many poor women are in an advanced state of pregnancy; others having young children, whose husbands, for the greater part, are either in the army, prisoners, or dead. Some say: "I have such a one sick at my house; who will wait on them when I am gone?" Others say: "what are we to do; we have no houses to go to, and no means to buy, build, or rent any; no parents, relatives or friends to go to.". . .

We only refer to a few facts to illustrate, in part, how this measure will operate in practice. As you advanced, the people north of us fell back, and before your arrival here a large portion of the people here had retired south; so that the country south of this is already crowded, and without sufficient houses to accommodate the people, and we are informed that many are now staying in churches and other outbuildings. This being so, how is it possible for the people still here (mostly women and children) to find shelter, and how can they live through the winter in the woods; no shelter or subsistence; in the midst of strangers who know them not, and without the power to assist them much if they were willing to do so?

This is but a feeble picture of the consequences of this measure. You know the woe, the horror, and the suffering cannot be described by words. Imagination can only conceive to it, and we ask you to take these things into consideration. We know your mind and time are continually occupied with the duties of your command, which almost deters us from asking your attention to the matter, but thought it might be that you had not considered the subject in all of its awful consequences, and that, on reflection, you, we hope, would not make this people an exception to all mankind, for we know of no such instance ever having occurred—surely not in the United States. And what has this helpless people done that they should be driven from their homes, to wander as strangers, outcasts and exiles, and to subsist on charity?

We do not know as yet the number of people still here. Of those who are here a respectable number, if allowed to remain at home, could subsist for several months without assistance; and a respectable number for a much longer time, and who might not need assistance at any time.

In conclusion, we most earnestly and solemnly petition you to reconsider this order, or modify it, and suffer this unfortunate people to remain at home and enjoy what little means they have.

Respectfully submitted,

James M. Calhoun, Mayor

E. E. Rawson, S. C. Wells, Councilmen.

MAJOR GENERAL WILLIAM T. SHERMAN

COMMANDER, MILITARY DIVISION OF THE MISSISSIPPI

A man of unyielding convictions, Sherman was steadfast in his mission—to win the war and reunite the nation. Hardened by three years of fighting and devastated by the death of his son, Willy, of typhoid fever in July 1863, Sherman saw little place for humanity in war making. In the letter below he refuses to revoke his orders despite heartfelt appeals from the people of Atlanta.

Hdqrs. Military Division of the Mississippi, in the Field, Atlanta, Ga., Sept. 12, 1864.
James M. Calhoun, *Mayor,* E. E. Rawson and S. C. Wells, *representing City Council of Atlanta.*

Gentlemen: I have your letter of the 11th, in the nature of a petition to revoke my orders removing all the inhabitants from Atlanta. I have read it carefully, and give full credit to your statements of the distress that will be occasioned by it, and yet shall not revoke my order, simply because my orders are not designed to meet the humanities of the case, but to prepare for the future struggles, in which millions, yea hundreds of millions of good people outside of Atlanta have a deep interest. We must have *Peace,* not only at Atlanta, but in all America. To secure this, we must stop the war that now desolates our once happy and favored country. To stop war we must defeat the Rebel armies that are arrayed against the laws and Constitution which all must respect and obey. To defeat these armies we must prepare the way to reach them in their recesses, provided with the arms and instruments which enable us to accomplish our purpose.

Now, I know the vindictive nature of our enemy, and that we may have many years of military operations from this quarter, and therefore deem it wise and prudent to prepare in time. The use of Atlanta for warlike purposes is inconsistent with its character as a home for families. There will be no manufactures, commerce or agriculture here for the maintenance of families, and sooner or later want will compel the inhabitants to go. Why not *go now,* when all the arrangements are completed for the transfer, instead of waiting till the plunging shot of contending armies will renew the scene of the past month? Of course I do not apprehend any such thing at this moment, but you do not suppose that this army will be here till the war is over. I cannot discuss this subject with you fairly, because I cannot impart to you what I propose to do, but I assert that my military plans make it necessary for the inhabitants to go away, and I can only renew my offer of services to make their exodus in any direction as easy and comfortable as possible. You cannot qualify war in harsher terms than I will.

War is cruelty, and you cannot refine it; and those who brought war on the country deserve all the curses and maledictions a people can pour out. I know I had no hand in making this war, and I know I will make more sacrifices to-day than any of you to secure peace. But you cannot have peace and a division of our country. If the United States submits to a division now, it will not stop, but will go on until we reap the fate of Mexico, which is eternal war. The United States does and must assert its authority wherever it has power; if it relaxes one bit to pressure it is gone, and I know that such is not the national feeling. This feeling assumes various shapes, but always comes back to that of *Union.* Once admit the Union, once more acknowledge the authority of the National Government, and instead of devoting your houses and streets and roads to the dread uses of war, I, and this army, become at once your protectors and supporters, shielding you from danger, let it come from what quarters it may. I know that a few individuals cannot resist a torrent of error and passion such as has swept the South into

The loss of Atlanta meant the elimination of one of the South's important centers for munitions production. This ammunition box, captured and put to use by the Atlanta Arsenal, once held a batch of rifle cartridges that had been turned out in June 1864, just before the factory was dismantled and evacuated.

"You might as well appeal against the thunderstorm as against these terrible hardships of war."

rebellion; but you can point out, so that we may know those who desire a Government and those who insist on war and its desolation.

You might as well appeal against the thunderstorm as against these terrible hardships of war. They are inevitable, and the only way the people of Atlanta can hope once more to live in peace and quiet at home is to stop this war which can alone be done by admitting that it began in error and is perpetuated in pride. We don't want your negroes or your horses, or your houses or your land, or anything you have; but we do want and will have a just obedience to the laws of the United States. That we will have, and if it involves the destruction of your improvements, we cannot help it. You have heretofore read public sentiment in your newspapers, that live by falsehood and excitement, and the quicker you seek for truth in other quarters the better for you.

I repeat, then, that, by the original compact of the government, the

The four-month-long campaign for Atlanta had taken a harsh toll on General Sherman's armies, and the occupation of the city afforded his troops a much-needed rest. Once a bustling hub of commerce, Atlanta was turned into a Union camp as the Federals settled in, officers taking residences and enlisted men erecting barracks and tent cities. In this photograph, men of the 2d Massachusetts bivouac in Atlanta's main square, directly in front of city hall. The planks and windows used to build their canvas-roofed huts were scavenged from nearby buildings.

United States had certain rights in Georgia which have never been relinquished, and never will be; that the South began war by seizing forts, arsenals, mints, custom-houses, etc., etc., long before Mr. Lincoln was installed, and before the South had one jot or tittle of provocation. I myself have seen in Missouri, Kentucky, Tennessee, and Mississippi, hundreds and thousands of women and children fleeing from your armies and desperadoes, hungry and with bleeding feet. In Memphis, Vicksburg, and Mississippi we fed thousands upon thousands of the families of rebel soldiers left on our hands, and whom we could not see starve. Now that war comes home to you, you feel very different—you deprecate its horrors, but did not feel them when you sent car-loads of soldiers and ammunition and molded shell and shot to carry war into Kentucky and Tennessee, and desolate the homes of hundreds and thousands of good people, who only asked to live in peace at their old homes, and under the government of their inheritance. But these comparisons are idle. I want peace, and believe it can only be reached through Union and war, and I will ever conduct war purely with a view to perfect and early success.

But, my dear sirs, when that peace does come, you may call on me for anything. Then will I share with you the last cracker, and watch with you to shield your homes and families against danger from every quarter. Now, you must go, and take with you the old and feeble; feed and nurse them, and build for them in more quiet places proper habitations to shield them against the weather, until the mad passions of men cool down, and allow the Union and peace once more to settle on your old homes at Atlanta.

Yours, in haste,

W. T. Sherman, Maj.-Gen.

A Federal supply convoy of covered wagons wends its way along Atlanta's Peachtree Street. In the weeks following the Federals' triumphant march into the city, the conquering armies enjoyed a period of relative comfort. "We felt perfectly at home," General Sherman later wrote; "the trains arrived with regularity and dispatch, and brought us ample supplies."

MARY RAWSON
Resident of Atlanta

General Sherman's order expelling all civilians from Atlanta was heartbreaking news to a citizenry who had endured weeks of privation and siege. Writing in her diary, Mary Rawson, daughter of city councilman E. E. Rawson, described what it felt like to be torn from one's home.

The order compelling all person to evacuate the city was today plainly written out; we could not misunderstand it. All those whose husbands were in the service were to leave on Monday, while the remainder were given fifteen days to pack and leave. Now comes a deliberation as to which home we should choose. My grand parents, aunt and cousins were to leave on Monday for the South; besides I had relations and friends down in South-western Georgia. This would have made it much more pleasant for us and in addition to this, the climate was much more congenial in the South. That that would have undoubtedly have been our choice had not one great barrier here presented itself. This was that all the men of the Confederacy were conscripted and were compelled to serve in the Army, this we knew Father could stand only a short time and he had no inclination to enter the Army. But a difficulty equally as great debarred us from entering a life in the "Yankee land of Canan," the difference in the currency occassioned this embarrassment. Fathers property mostly consisted in lands and Confederate money so we had not means enough to venture North; unless Pa could get something for his tobacco. So we were in a vassalating condition for several days.

. . . This morning Mother concluded that although we had not the slightest idea of our future home, we had better commence the task of packing. Scarcely was the work begun when we heard that all those who went South would have their trunks searched and all goods not ready made be removed. Now came the question as to how we could secrete them and so take them with us. We finally prepared two trunks to go either way by folding pieces of goods between ready made clothes and by tearing the cloth into pieces of sufficient length to make dress skirts and a great many other ways we found of hiding our goods. While we were in the midst of our work Aunt Charlotte came over from Grandmas and told us they had already opened Auntys trunks twice and came to perform the same detestable office again, when Aunty refused decidedly to open her baggage any more and Col. Beckworth coming in at that moment gave

him a sound cudgeling. Aunt Charlotte expressed her determination to follow her master and mistress wherever they go. Dear old Granny may you be well protected and carefully nursed during your old age and when life is over be laid gently to rest by those who can and do appreciate you. This afternoon on hearing martial music, we looked up from the front porch where we were sitting to see the street filled with cavalry and infantry pack mules, army wagons and cattle crowded promiscuously together, the cavalry and infantry ensigns floating in unison together. The musicians all riding on white horses. (I don't know whether with propriety they could be called charges or not.) After making the signal for the march to commence they rode silently along until they passed in front of Gen. Gearys headquarters when simultaneously they broke into the old soul stirring "Hail Columbia," the suddenness of the music startled me. They then, (after finishing this piece) slowly and silently marched through the city. A few minutes after this Mother went over to see my Grandparents and Aunty; and I went to have a little talk with Mattie, her father had determined to go to the North and so it seemed probable that the friends of seven years would be separated. We finally parted I with a beautiful sprig of honeysuckle in my hair, placed there by Mr. Andrews who remarked that this would be the last time he would deck my hair for me. Oh Southern climate with your roses and honeysuckle, roses and oleanders. May the time soon come when I shall again walk through bowers of yellow jasmine and gather boquets of scarlet verbena and tube-roses.

. . . Taking a sad farewell from servants and friends we seated ourselves in the ambulance which slowly moved out of the yard. In a few moments we found ourselves on the hill on which stood our school house and from which a fine view of our place could be obtained. Never never did this hill look so pleasant in the setting sun as it now did, and now as I look upon the groups of oaks and hedges of arbortia I for the first time could appreciate the words of the song which after such a beautiful sentiment "the dearest spot of earth to me is home sweet home." . . . Dear dear Atlanta! . . . When oh when shall I again tread your pavement and breathe your exhilerating atmosphere.

. . . The word was finally give for us to get on board and one by one we were placed in our rough temporary home. There were ten of *us* then came Mr. Andrew family of six and lastly a little pet dog, sixteen refugees in a box as Mr. Andrews said on getting in. We were scarcely seated when the shrill whistle of the engine told us we were about leaving. Then in a few seconds we received a sudden jerk that nearly seated us on the floor, then we went dashing and clattering along, and soon Atlanta and with it home was not distinguishable in the distance.

REBELS MOVING SOUTH FROM ATLANTA.—SKETCHED BY D. R. BROWN.—[SEE NEXT PAGE.]

Although hostilities had been temporarily suspended, the 10-day armistice brought little comfort to the civilian population of Atlanta. Complying with Sherman's evacuation order meant, for most, separation from family and friends as they prepared to seek refuge with relatives in the South and, for some, the uncertainty of building a new life up North. In this Harper's Weekly engraving by D. R. Brown dated October 15, 1864, refugees load their household goods and furniture onto covered wagons furnished by the Union army. Most were directed south to Rough and Ready, where they were turned over to Confederate authorities.

CHAPLAIN THOMAS H. DEAVENPORT

3D TENNESSEE (C.S.) INFANTRY, BROWN'S BRIGADE

For the Confederacy, the fall of the city seemed to signal the end to any prospects for a negotiated peace and the survival of their young nation. Chaplain Deavenport continued to be bouyed by his faith, but most in the Confederacy saw the signs of irreparable decay. The South Carolinian diarist Mary Chesnut spoke for many in the South when she wrote, "Atlanta is gone. That agony is over. There is no hope, but we will try to have no fear."

An armistice of ten days was agreed upon, that the citizens of Atlanta might be sent through the lines. Here was a piece of heartless cruelty. There seems to be no deed too base or cruel for a Yankee. *Gen. Sherman* had without warning shelled the city more than a month destroying a vast amount of property and many lives and when he gained possession of it immediately ordered every man woman and child to leave, and also all living in five miles of the R. R. in the rear, thus several thousand women and children were turned out of their homes, driven away from all the[y] possessed and cast upon the charities of the world. How shall that base man answer for all his dark deeds. The campaign just closed has been the most arduous of the war....

... I am not discouraged, though there is some discontent in the army. Oh God, how long will this cruel war last? My heart yearns for the society of home. I count each day and ask when will the last come? Poor weak human nature is ready to complain and say my burden is too heavy. Cease thy murmuring, God is wise and good. He doeth all things well. Health is yet mine. Through many dangers I have been led, have just escaped death time and again. It seems that I have led a charmed life. God be praised for his goodness. I see around me such distress and my heart sickens at the destruction of life and property on every hand, in the army and out of it. I see grey hairs and helpless infancy driven from home, penniless almost friendless. I see the strong man cut down without a moment's warning, or left a cripple for life. I see the poor soldier as he toils on, sustained by the hope of better days and by the love he bears to those far away. I saw but yesterday the Captain commanding this regiment barefoot. Such men will not be conquered. I cannot give the history of this campaign language to describe its suffering. It has been long and bloody, many of our noblest have fallen. "Requiescant in pace." They live in our hearts.

"I cannot give the history of this campaign language to describe its suffering. It has been long and bloody, many of our noblest have fallen. 'Requiescant in pace.' They live in our hearts."

In this George Barnard photograph of Atlanta's railroad yard, a covered military caravan rolls past wagons used by refugees to carry possessions to the station. For 10 days in September, civilians boarded trains that took them into exile. Only weeks later, the Federals would put to the torch anything deemed useful to the enemy; buildings were razed, and those too large to burn, such as the vaulted car shed in the background, were demolished. General Sherman's army would leave in its wake only a vestige of the city it fought so hard to capture.

GLOSSARY

abatis—A defensive barrier of fallen trees with branches pointed toward the enemy.

adjutant—A staff officer assisting the commanding officer, usually with correspondence.

ambrotype—A photograph produced with a wet, glass-plate process.

battery—The basic unit of artillery, consisting of four to six guns.

bivouac—A temporary encampment, or to camp out for the night.

breastwork—A temporary fortification, usually of earth and about chest high, over which a soldier can fire.

caisson—A cart with large chests for carrying artillery ammunition. It was connected to a horse-drawn limber when moved.

canister—A tin can containing lead or iron balls that scatter when fired from a cannon. Used primarily in defense of a position as an antipersonnel weapon.

carbine—A lightweight, short-barreled shoulder arm used especially by cavalry.

case shot—*Case shot* properly refers to shrapnel or spherical case. The term is often mistakenly to refer to any artillery projectile in which numerous metal balls or pieces were bound or encased together. See also *shrapnel*.

change front—To alter the direction troops face to deliver or defend against an attack.

clubbed musket—A musket swung like a club in hand-to-hand combat.

coffee cooler—A shirker or malingerer. One who will begin work "when the coffee cools."

"commissary"—A kind of whiskey issued by the army's commissary department.

double-shotted artillery—Artillery charged with two projectiles rather than the normal one.

Enfield rifle—The Enfield rifle musket was adopted by the British in 1853, and the North

and South imported nearly a million to augment their own production. Firing a .577-caliber projectile similar to the Minié ball, it was fairly accurate at 1,100 yards.

enfilade—Gunfire that rakes an enemy line lengthwise, or the position allowing such firing.

flank—The right or left end of a military formation. Therefore, to flank is to attack or go around the enemy's position on one end or the other.

fly tent—A shelter constructed out of a single, rectangular piece of canvas or other cloth.

forlorn hope—A last-ditch, desperately difficult or dangerous assignment, or the body of men given such a task.

furlough—A leave of absence from duty granted to a soldier.

grapeshot—Iron balls (usually nine) bound together and fired from a cannon. Resembling a cluster of grapes, the balls break apart and scatter on impact. Although references to grape or grapeshot are numerous in the literature, some experts claim that it was not used on Civil War battlefields.

guidon—A small flag used to identify a mounted military unit.

gum blanket—A waterproof blanket, treated with rubber, and often in poncho form.

Hardee's tactics—A reference work by William J. Hardee, who was commandant of cadets at West Point before the war. Entitled *Rifle and Light Infantry Tactics,* the two-volume, pocket-size textbook was the basic training manual for both the Confederate and Union armies. Hardee resigned his U.S. Army commission and joined the Confederate army when his native state of Georgia seceded.

haversack—A shoulder bag, usually strapped over the right shoulder to rest on the left hip,

for carrying personal items and rations.

Henry repeating rifle—Invented in 1860 by B. Tyler Henry of Oliver Winchester's New Haven Arms Company, this .44-caliber rifle had a tubular magazine that held 15 rimfire copper cartridges. Moving the trigger guard cocked the hammer, ejected the spent shell, and loaded a new round. It was the first magazine rifle used in quantity by the Union army.

limber—A two-wheeled, horse-drawn vehicle to which a gun carriage or a caisson is attached.

marquee—A large tent, usually without sides.

Minié ball—The standard bullet-shaped projectile fired from the rifled muskets of the time. Designed by French Army officers Henri-Gustave Delvigne and Claude-Etienne Minié, the bullet's hollow base expanded, forcing its sides into the grooves, or rifling, of the musket's barrel. This caused the bullet to spiral in flight, giving it greater range and accuracy. Appears as minie ball, minnie ball, Minnie ball, and minnie bullet.

musket—A smoothbore, muzzleloading shoulder arm.

Napoleon—A smoothbore, muzzleloading field artillery piece developed under the direction of Napoleon III. It fired a 12-pound projectile (and therefore was sometimes called a 12-pounder). The basic light artillery weapon of both sides, Napoleons were originally cast in bronze; when that material became scarce in the South, iron was used.

oblique—At an angle. Units would be ordered to fire or move in a direction other than straight ahead.

orderly—A soldier assigned to a superior officer for various duties, including carrying messages.

Parrott guns—Muzzleloading, rifled artillery pieces of various calibers made of cast iron with a unique wrought-iron reinforcing band around the breech. Patented in 1861 by Union officer Robert Parker Parrott, the guns were more accurate at longer range than their smoothbore predecessors.

picket—One or more soldiers on guard to protect the larger unit from surprise attack.

Pioneers—Construction engineers.

provost guard—A detail of soldiers acting as police under the supervision of an officer called a provost marshal.

redoubt—An enclosed, defensive stronghold, usually temporary.

rifle—Any weapon with spiral grooves cut into the bore, which give spin to the projectile, adding range and accuracy. Usually applied to cannon or weapons fired from the shoulder.

rifle pits—Holes or shallow trenches dug in the ground from which soldiers can fire weapons and avoid enemy fire. Foxholes.

right shoulder shift—A position for holding a musket in which the butt of the gun is held in the right hand at just below chest height, the breech area rests on the right shoulder, and the muzzle points skyward. The rough equivalent of the modern *shoulder arms.*

Rodman—An artillery piece manufactured through a process devised by Union brigadier general Thomas J. Rodman that allowed the tube to withstand more internal pressure than normally cast guns. These were primarily smoothbores.

salient—The part of a fortress, line of defense, or trench system that juts out toward the enemy position.

secesh—A slang term for secessionist.

section of artillery—Part of an artillery battery consisting of two guns, the soldiers who manned them, and their supporting horses and equipment.

shotted guns—Artillery pieces fully loaded with powder and shot, as opposed to those used for signal or celebratory firings, which contain powder only.

shrapnel—An artillery projectile in the form of a hollow sphere filled with metal balls packed around an explosive charge. Developed by British general Henry Shrapnel during the Napoleonic Wars, it was used as an antipersonnel weapon. A fuse ignited the charge at a set distance from the gun, raining the balls down on the enemy. Also called spherical case.

Sibley tent—Named for its inventor, Confederate general Henry Hopkins Sibley, this tent resembled the tipis of the Plains Indians. Conical, erected on a tripod, with a smoke hole at the top, it could easily accommodate a dozen men and their equipment.

skirmisher—A soldier sent out in advance of the main body of troops to scout out and probe the enemy's position. Also, one who participates in a skirmish, a small fight usually incidental to the main action.

Stars and Bars—The first national flag of the Confederacy. It had two broad, horizontal red stripes separated by one white stripe, and a dark blue field in the canton with from seven to 13 white stars representing the states of the Confederacy.

trail arms—To grasp a musket at about midpoint and carry it at one's side, roughly parallel to the ground.

ACKNOWLEDGMENTS

The editors wish to thank the following for their valuable assistance in the preparation of this volume:

John Anderson, Texas State Archives Prints and Photographs Collections, Austin; John C. Bernhardt; Elizabeth P. Bilderbach, South Caroliniana Library, University of South Carolina, Columbia; Robert B. Bradley, Alabama Department of Archives and History, Montgomery; Rickie Bruner, Alabama Department of Archives and History, Montgomery; Ellen R. Callahan, New Jersey State Archives, Trenton; Sara Clark, Mississippi Department of Archives and History, Jackson; DeGress family, Boulder, Colorado; Tammy H. Galloway, Atlanta History Center, Atlanta; Marcia M. Gilmore, Washington, D.C.; Kirk Henderson, Atlanta History Center, Atlanta; John Hightower, Berryville, Virginia; Steven W. Hill, Westwood, Massachusetts; William F. Hull, Atlanta History Center, Atlanta; Gordon L. Jones, Atlanta History Center, Atlanta; Lawrence T. Jones III, Confederate Calendar Works, Austin, Texas; Norwood Kerr, Alabama Department of Archives and History, Montgomery; Charles Lamb, Archives of the University of Notre Dame, Notre Dame, Indiana; Ronald A. Lee, Tennessee State Library and Archives, Nashville; Anne Lipscomb, Mississippi Department of Archives and History, Jackson; Peter J. Lysy, Archives of the University of Notre Dame, Notre Dame, Indiana; Howard Madaus, Cody Firearms Museum, Cody, Wyoming; Greg Mast, Durham, North Carolina; Helen Matthews, Atlanta History Center, Atlanta; Maurey Meador, Old State House, Little Rock, Arkansas; Luke Messinger, Dawes Arboretum, Newark, Ohio; Nelson W. Morgan, The Hargrett Rare Book and Manuscript Library, University of Georgia, Athens; Courtney Page, Special Collections Division, Howard-Tilton Library, Tulane University, New Orleans; Paul W. Romaine, Gilder Lehrman Collection, New York; Ted Ryan, Atlanta History Center, Atlanta; Locke W. Smith Jr., Lenoir, North Carolina; Jennifer Songster, Ohio Historical Society, Archives Library Division, Columbus; Cavett Taff, Mississippi State Historical Museum, Jackson; Ken Turner, Ellwood City, Pennsylvania; David Wynn Vaughan, Atlanta; David Vermilion, Dawes Arboretum, Newark, Ohio.

PICTURE CREDITS

The sources for the illustrations are listed below. Credits from left to right are separated by semicolons, from top to bottom by dashes. Dust jacket: Front, National Archives Neg. No. 165-SC-46, calligraphy by Mary Lou O'Brian/Inkwell, Inc.; rear, courtesy South Caroliniana Library, University of South Carolina. 6, 7: Map by Paul Salmon. 8: Special Collections (Orlando Poe Collection), U.S. Military Academy Library, West Point, N.Y., copied by Henry Groskinsky. 9: Calligraphy by Mary Lou O'Brian/Inkwell, Inc. 13: Map by Peter McGinn. 16: Massachusetts Commandery of the Military Order of the Loyal Legion of the United States and the U.S. Army Military History Institute (MASS-MOLLUS/USAMHI), Carlisle Barracks, Pa. 17: Painting by J. R. Walker, courtesy Confederate Memorial Hall Museum & Library, Washington, D.C., photographed by Larry Sherer; The Gilder Lehrman Collection on deposit at the Pierpont Morgan Library, New York, GLC 2703. 18: National Archives Neg. No. 111-BA-90. 19: Library of Congress Neg. No. 21314-6480; L. M. Strayer Collection—Ken Turner Collection, photographed by Buquo Studio (4). 20: From *The Rough Side of War*, edited and biographical sketch by Arnold Gates, The Basin Publishing Co., Garden City, N.Y., 1987; courtesy the DeGress family, Boulder, Colo., photographed by Carl Yarbrough (3). 21: From *Life in Dixie during the War,* by Mary A. H. Gay, The DeKalb Historical Society, Inc., 1979, copied by Philip Brandt George; The Jesse Dupont Library, The University of the South, Sewanee, Tenn. 22: From *Even More Confederate Faces,* by William A. Turner, Moss Publications, Orange, Va., 1983. 23: John C. Bernhardt (3)—Old State House, Little Rock, Ark. 24, 25: From *Life in Dixie during the War,* by Mary A. H. Gay, The DeKalb Historical Society, Inc., 1979, copied by Philip Brandt George; courtesy Atlanta History Center. 25-27: Courtesy Atlanta History Center. 28: From *Yours Till Death*, edited by Lucille Griffith, University of Alabama Press, Tuscaloosa, Ala., 1951; Charles Colcock Jones Papers, Special Collections, Howard-Tilton Memorial Library, Tulane University. 29: Courtesy John C. Culver. 30, 31: Frank & Marie-Thérèse Wood Print Collections, Alexandria, Va. 32: Library of Congress Neg. No. B8184-10401. 33: Calligraphy by Mary Lou O'Brian/Inkwell, Inc. 35: Map by Walter W. Roberts. 37, 38: Library of Congress. 39: U.S. Army Military History Institute (USAMHI), Carlisle Barracks, Pa., copied by A. Pierce Bounds; L. M. Strayer Collection. 40: Frank and Marie-Thérèse Wood Print Collections, Alexandria, Va. 41: From *Four Years on the Firing Line,* by James Cooper Nisbet, McCowat-Mercer Press, Inc., Jackson, Tenn., 1963, copied by Philip Brandt George. 43: Map by R. R. Donnelley & Sons Co., Carto-graphic Services, overlay by Time-Life Books. 44: Michael Welch, Atlanta; courtesy Blue Acorn Press. 45: Library of Congress. 47: From *A Yankee Private's Civil War,* by Robert Hale Strong, Henry Regnery Company, Chicago, 1961, copied by Philip Brandt George; David Wynn Vaughan Collection. 48: Alabama Department of Archives and History, Montgomery. 49: Library of Congress Neg. No. B8184-10010. 51: Courtesy Margaret Brobst Roth. 52, 53: Library of Congress Neg. No. 38184-10159-03; from *Gleanings from Southland*, by Kate Cumming, Roberts & Son, Birmingham, Ala., 1895. 55: Map by R. R. Donnelley & Sons Co., Cartographic Services, overlay by Time-Life Books. 56: USAMHI, Carlisle Barracks, Pa., copied by A. Pierce Bounds; from *The Twenty-Seventh Indiana Volunteer Infantry in the War of the Rebellion,* by a member of Company C., private printing, Monticello, Ind., 1899. 57: Library of Congress. 58: Alabama Department of Archives and History, Montgomery. 59: Library of Congress Neg. No. B8184-8126-03. 60: The family of Betty A. Foster Strauss. 61: Courtesy The Dubose Collection, photographed by William F. Hull. 62: Courtesy Marcelina Teveni, photographed by Peggy Tenison. 63: Courtesy The Dawes Arboretum (2); Ohio Historical Society, photographed by David R. Barker. 64: From *Reminiscences of a Mississippian in Peace and War,* by Frank A. Montgomery, Robert Clarke Company Press, Cincinnati, 1901, copied by Philip Brandt George. 65: Courtesy Atlanta History Center; from *The Church That Stayed,* by John Robert Smith, © The Atlanta History Center, Atlanta, 1979, copied by Philip Brandt George; Alabama Department of Archives and History, Montgomery. 66: Courtesy Southern Historical Collection, Library of the University of North Carolina at Chapel Hill. 67: The Jesse Dupont Library, The University of the South, Sewanee, Tenn.; from *Still More Confederate Faces,* by Domenick A. Serrano, Metropolitan Company, Bayside, N.Y., 1992, copied by Philip Brandt George. 68: Library of Congress. 70, 71: Herbert Peck Jr. and Lawrence T. Jones III; Atlanta History Center, photographed by Larry Sherer—Frank and Marie-Thérèse Wood Print Collections, Alexandria, Va. 73: Map by Walter W. Roberts. 74, 75: L. M. Strayer Collection—The Gilder Lehrman Collection on deposit at the Pierpont Morgan Library, New York, GLC 4610, No. 1 and No. 2. 76: L. M. Strayer Collection. 77: Library of Congress. 78: L. M. Strayer Collection. 79: L. M. Strayer Collection. 80: Library of Congress. 81: American Documentaries, Walpole, N.H. 82: Alabama Department of Archives and History, Montgomery; courtesy Blue Acorn Press. 83: Courtesy Atlanta Historical Society, photographed by Larry Sherer; cour-tesy Atlanta History Center, photographed by Larry Sherer. 84: Alabama Department of Archives and History, Montgomery; courtesy Blue Acorn Press. 85: Frank and Marie-Thérèse Wood Print Collections, Alexandria, Va. 86: USAMHI, Carlisle Barracks, Pa., copied by A. Pierce Bounds. 87: Courtesy the Illinois State Historical Library. 88: Library of Congress Neg. No. B8184-10410. 89: Calligraphy by Mary Lou O'Brian/Inkwell, Inc. 91: Map by R. R. Donnelley & Sons Co., Cartographic Services. 92: Library of Congress Neg. Nos. B8184-10403; B8184-10404. 93: From *A Southern Girl in '61,* by Mrs. D. Giraud Wright, Doubleday, Page & Co., New York, 1905. 94: Courtesy the Huntington Library, San Marino, Calif. 95: Museum of the Confederacy, Richmond. 97: Map by R. R. Donnelley & Sons Co., Cartographic Services, overlay by Time-Life Books. 98: Courtesy Rensselaer County Historical Society, Troy, N.Y. 99: Library of Congress Neg. No. B8184-10009. 100: New Jersey Historical Society, Newark, courtesy Roger D. Hunt; New Jersey State Archives, Department of State. 101: USAMHI, Carlisle Barracks, Pa., copied by A. Pierce Bounds—National Archives Neg. No. 111-B-3320. 102: Courtesy Atlanta Historical Society, photographed by Henry Groskinsky (2); courtesy Grayson R. Worthington and H. Grady Howell Jr. 103: Courtesy Atlanta Historical Society, photographed by Larry Sherer. 104, 105: Maps by Walter W. Roberts. 106: Courtesy Atlanta History Center. 107: From *The Confederate General, Vol. 6.*, edited by William C. Davis, National Historical Society, Harrisburg, Pa., 1991. 108: L. M. Strayer Collection—Lonn Ashbrook, courtesy Blue Acorn Press—inset, Smithsonian Institution, National Museum of American History, photographed by Larry Sherer. 110: USAMHI, Carlisle Barracks, Pa., copied by A. Pierce Bounds; Library of Congress. 111: Alabama Department of Archives and History, Montgomery. 112: The Archives of the University of Notre Dame. 113: Archives Division, Texas State Library, Austin. 114, 115: Courtesy Stamatelos Brothers collection, Cambridge, Mass., photographed by Larry Sherer; Library of Congress Neg. No. B816-8103; from *A Carolinian Goes to War: The Civil War Narrative of Arthur Middleton Manigault, Brigadier General, C.S.A.,* edited by R. Lockwood Tower, University of South Carolina Press, Columbia, 1983. 116: Library of Congress. 118, 119: The Ohio Historical Society; the DeGress family, Boulder, Colo. (2). 121: Map by R. R. Donnelley & Sons Co., Cartographic Services, overlay by Time-Life Books. 123: Confederate Calendar Works, Austin, Tex. 124: L. M. Strayer Collection; Library of Congress. 125: Frank and Marie-Thérèse Wood Print Collections, Alexandria, Va. 126, 127: Museum of the Confederacy, photographed by

BIBLIOGRAPHY

BOOKS

Adams, Robert N. "The Battle and Capture of Atlanta." In *Glimpses of the Nation's Struggle: Papers Read before the Minnesota Commandery of the Military Order of the Loyal Legion of the United States, 1892-1897*. Fourth series. Wilmington, N.C.: Broadfoot, 1992 (reprint of 1898 edition).

Beers, Fannie A. *Memories: A Record of Personal Experience and Adventure during Four Years of War*. Philadelphia: Press of J. B. Lippincott, 1891.

Benton, Charles E. *As Seen from the Ranks: A Boy in the Civil War*. New York: G. P. Putnam's Sons, 1902.

Bierce, Ambrose. *Ambrose Bierce's Civil War*. Ed. by William McCann. Chicago: Gateway Editions, 1956.

Boatner, Mark Mayo, III. *The Civil War Dictionary*. New York: David McKay, 1959.

Brown, Edmund R. *The Twenty-Seventh Indiana Volunteer Infantry in the War of the Rebellion, 1861-1865, First Division 12th and 20th Corps*. Monticello, Ind.: private printing, 1899.

Brown, Joseph M. *The Mountain Campaigns in Georgia, or War Scenes on the W. & A.* Buffalo: Matthews-Northrup, 1895.

Bull, Rice C. *Soldiering: The Civil War Diary of Rice C. Bull, 123rd New York Volunteer Infantry*. Ed. by K. Jack Bauer. San Rafael, Calif.: Presidio Press, 1977.

Carter, Samuel, III. *The Siege of Atlanta, 1864*. New York: Ballantine Books, 1973.

Carter, W. R. *History of the First Regiment of Tennessee Volunteer Cavalry in the Great War of the Rebellion*. Johnson City, Tenn.: Overmountain Press, 1992 (reprint of 1896 edition).

Castel, Albert. *Decision in the West: The Atlanta Campaign of 1864*. Lawrence: University Press of Kansas, 1992.

Clark, Walter A. *Under the Stars and Bars, or Memories of Four Years Service with the Oglethorpes, of Augusta, Georgia*. Jonesboro, Ga.: Freedom Hill Press, 1987 (reprint of 1900 edition).

Compton, James. "The Second Division of the 16th Army Corps, in the Atlanta Campaign." In *Glimpses of the Nation's Struggle: Papers Read before the Minnesota Commandery of the Military Order of the Loyal Legion of the United States, 1897-1902*. Fifth series. Wilmington, N.C.: Broadfoot, 1992 (reprint of a 1903 edition).

The Confederate General. Vol. 1. Ed. by William C. Davis. Harrisburg, Pa.: National Historical Society, 1991.

Connolly, James A. *Three Years in the Army of the Cumberland*. Ed. by Paul M. Angle. Bloomington: Indiana University Press, 1959.

Conyngham, David P. *Sherman's March through the South*. New York: Sheldon, 1865.

Cotton, John W. *Yours till Death: Civil War Letters of John W. Cotton*. Ed. by Lucille Griffith. Tuscaloosa: University of Alabama Press, 1951.

Culver, J. F. *"Your Affectionate Husband, J. F. Culver": Letters Written during the Civil War*. Ed. by Leslie W. Dunlap. Iowa City: Friends of the University of Iowa Libraries, 1978.

Cumming, Kate. *Kate: The Journal of a Confederate Nurse*. Ed. by Richard Barksdale Harwell. Baton Rouge: Louisiana State University Press, 1959.

Foster, Samuel T. *One of Cleburne's Command*. Ed. by Norman D. Brown. Austin: University of Texas Press, 1980.

Gay, Mary A. H. *Life in Dixie during the War*. Atlanta: DeKalb Historical Society, 1979.

Glimpses of the Nation's Struggle: Papers Read before the Minnesota Commandery of the Military Order of the Loyal Legion of the United States, 1892-1897. Fourth series. Wilmington, N.C.: Broadfoot, 1992 (reprint of 1898 edition).

Green, Johnny. *Johnny Green of the Orphan Brigade: The Journal of a Confederate Soldier*. Ed. by A. D. Kirwan. Lexington: University of Kentucky Press, 1956.

Harwell, Richard B., ed. *The Union Reader*. New York: Longmans, Green, 1958.

Hedley, F. Y. *Marching through Georgia: Pen-Pictures of Every-Day Life*. Chicago: Donohue, Henneberry, 1890.

Hoehling, A. A. *Last Train from Atlanta*. Harrisburg, Pa.: Stackpole Books, 1958.

Howell, H. Grady. *To Live and Die in Dixie: A History of the Third Regiment Mississippi Infantry, CSA*. Madison, Miss.: Chickasaw Bayou Press, 1991.

Huff, Sarah. *My 80 Years in Atlanta*. Private printing, 1937.

McGee, B. F. *History of the 72d Indiana Volunteer Infantry of the Mounted Lightning Brigade*. LaFayette, Ind.: S. Vater, 1882.

McNeil, S. A. *Personal Recollections of Service in the Army of the Cumberland and Sherman's Army: From August 17, 1861 to July 20, 1865*. [Richwood, Ohio: private printing, 1910.]

Madaus, Howard Michael. *The Battle Flags of the Confederate Army of Tennessee*. Milwaukee: Milwaukee Public Museum, 1976.

Manigault, Arthur Middleton. *A Carolinian Goes to War: The Civil War Narrative of Arthur Middleton Manigault, Brigadier General, C.S.A.* Ed. by R. Lockwood Tower. Columbia: University of South Carolina Press, 1983.

Military Essays and Recollections. Vols. 1 and 2. Wilmington: N.C.: Broadfoot, 1992 (reprints of 1891 and 1894 editions).

Montgomery, Frank A. *Reminiscences of a Mississippian in Peace and War.* Cincinnati: Robert Clarke Company Press, 1901.

Mosman, Chesley A. *The Rough Side of War.* Ed. by Arnold Gates. Garden City, N.Y.: Basin, 1987.

Myers, Robert Manson, ed. *The Children of Pride: A True Story of Georgia and the Civil War.* New Haven, Conn.: Yale University Press, 1972.

Nisbet, James Cooper. *Four Years on the Firing Line.* Ed. by Bell Irvin Wiley. Jackson, Tenn.: McCowat-Mercer Press, 1963.

Peddy, George W., and Kate Featherston Peddy. *Saddle Bag and Spinning Wheel.* Ed. by George Peddy Cuttino. Macon, Ga.: Mercer University Press, 1981.

Pepper, George W. *Personal Recollections of Sherman's Campaigns in Georgia and the Carolinas.* Zanesville, Ohio: Hugh Dunne, 1866.

Polk, William M. *Leonidas Polk: Bishop and General.* Vol. 2. New York: Longmans, Green, 1915.

Quintard, C. T. *Doctor Quintard: Chaplain C.S.A. and Second Bishop of Tennessee.* Ed. by Arthur Howard Noll. Sewanee, Tenn.: University Press, 1905.

Reed, Wallace P., ed. *History of Atlanta, Georgia: With Illustrations and Biographical Sketches of Some of Its Prominent Men and Pioneers.* Syracuse, N.Y.: D. Mason, 1889.

Rice, Ralsa C. *Yankee Tigers: Through the Civil War with the 125th Ohio.* Ed. by Richard A. Baumgartner and Larry M. Strayer. Huntington, W.Va.: Blue Acorn Press, 1992.

Roth, Margaret Brobst. *Well Mary: Civil War Letters of a Wisconsin Volunteer.* Madison: University of Wisconsin Press, 1960.

Scaife, William R. *The Campaign for Atlanta.* Saline, Mich.: McNaughton & Gunn, 1993.

Sherman, William Tecumseh:

Home Letters of General Sherman. Ed. by M. A. DeWolfe Howe. New York: Charles Scribner's Sons, 1909.

Memoirs of General William T. Sherman. Westport, Conn.: Greenwood Press, 1957.

The Sherman Letters: Correspondence between General and Senator Sherman from 1837 to 1891. Ed. by Rachel Sherman Thorndike. New York: AMS Press, 1971 (reprint of 1894 edition).

Sifakis, Stewart, ed. *Who Was Who in the Confederacy.* New York: Facts On File, 1989.

Simpson, Richard Wright, and Tally Simpson. *"Far, Far from Home": The Wartime Letters of Dick and Tally Simpson, Third South Carolina Volunteers.* Ed. by Guy R. Everson and Edward W. Simpson Jr. New York: Oxford University Press, 1994.

Smith, John Robert. *The Church That Stayed.* Atlanta: Atlanta Historical Society, 1979.

Strayer, Larry M., and Richard A. Baumgartner, eds. *Echoes of Battle: The Atlanta Campaign.* Huntington, W.Va.: Blue Acorn Press, 1991.

Strong, Robert Hale. *A Yankee Private's Civil War.* Ed. by Ashley Halsey. Chicago: Henry Regnery, 1961.

Strong, William E. "The Death of General James B. McPherson." In *Military Essays and Recollections.* Vol. 1. Wilmington: N.C.: Broadfoot, 1992 (reprint of 1891 edition).

United States War Department. *The War of the Rebellion: A Compilation of the Official Records of the Union and Confederate Armies.* Series 1, Vol. 38, Part 2-Reports. Washington, D.C.: U.S. Government Printing Office, 1891.

Vann, Samuel King. *"Most Lovely Lizzie": Love Letters of a Young Confederate Soldier.* Birmingham, Ala.: private printing, 1958.

Walton, Clyde C., ed. *Private Smith's Journal: Recollections of the Late War.* Chicago: Lakeside Press, 1963.

Watkins, Sam R. *"Co. Aytch": A Side Show of the Big Show.* New York: Collier Books, 1962.

Williams, Alpheus S. *From the Cannon's Mouth: The Civil War Letters of General Alpheus S. Williams.* Ed. by Milo M. Quaife. Detroit: Wayne State University Press and Detroit Historical Society, 1959.

Williams, Hiram Smith. *This War So Horrible.* Ed. by Lewis N. Wayne and Robert A. Taylor. Tuscaloosa: University of Alabama Press, 1993.

Wright, Mrs. D. Giraud (Louise W. Wright). *A Southern Girl in '61.* New York: Doubleday, Page, 1905.

Young, L. D. *Reminiscences of a Soldier of the Orphan Brigade.* [Louisville, Ky.: Courier Journal Job Print Co., 1918].

PERIODICALS

"Atlanta in the Civil War: The Personal Perspective." *Atlanta Historical Journal,* Summer 1979.

Cooper, James Litton. "The Civil War Diary of Captain James Litton Cooper, September 30, 1861 to January, 1865." Ed. by William T. Alderson. *Tennessee Historical Quarterly,* June 1956.

Gibbons, Robert. "Life at the Crossroads of the Confederacy: Atlanta, 1861-1865." *Atlanta Historical Journal,* Summer 1979.

"Governor Harris at the Close of the War." *Confederate Veteran,* August 1897, Vol. 5, no. 8.

Harvie, E. J. "Gen. Joseph E. Johnston." *Confederate Veteran,* November 1910.

Murphree, Joel. "Autobiography and Civil War Letters of Joel Murphree of Troy, Alabama, 1864-1865." *Alabama Historical Quarterly,* Spring 1957.

"Old Letters." *Georgia Review,* Summer 1961.

Peacock, Jane Bonner, ed. "A Wartime Story: The Davidson Letters, 1862-1865." *Atlanta Historical Bulletin,* 1975, Vol. 19, no. 1.

Sea, Andrew M. "An Incident of Rocky Face Ridge." *Confederate Veteran,* 1898, Vol. 6.

OTHER SOURCES

Belknap, William W. Letter. Durham, N.C.: Duke University, Special Collections.

Comer Family Papers, 1860-1864. Comp. by Elizabeth Pauk. Chapel Hill: University of North Carolina, Wilson Library, Southern Historical Collection.

Crane, Sarah C. Unpublished manuscript, MSS 518, Box 5, Folder 1. Atlanta: Atlanta History Center.

Deavenport, Thomas Hopkins. Diaries, n.d. Nashville: Tennessee State Archives.

Grant, L. P. Unpublished manuscript, MSS 100, Oversized Folder, Atlanta Defenses. Atlanta: Atlanta History Center.

Harper, George W. F. Diary, July 7, 1863-Dec. 31, 1865. Chapel Hill: University of North Carolina, Wilson Library, Southern Historical Collection.

Hayes, Edward. "My Last Battle." Unpublished manuscript from the William O. Bourne Papers. Washington, D.C.: Library of Congress, Manuscript Division.

Hunter, Joseph J. "A Sketch of the History of the Noxubee Troopers: 1st Mississippi Cavalry Company 'F'." Unpublished manuscript. Comp. by T. F. Jackson Sr. Jackson: Mississippi Department of Archives and History.

Kelly, William Milner. "A History of the Thirtieth Alabama Volunteers (Infantry) Confederate States Army." Unpublished manuscript, 1927. Montgomery: Alabama Department of Archives and History.

Moffatt, Thomas William, Sr., and Wallace Wilson Moffatt. "A Union Soldier's Civil War." Unpublished manuscript, 1962. Montgomery: Alabama Department of Archives and History.

Palmer Family Papers, 1812-1979. Columbia: University of South Carolina, South Caroliniana Library.

Rainey, Isaac Newton. "Experiences of I. N. Rainey in the Confederate Army." Memoirs, February 1925. Nashville: Tennessee State Library and Archives, Civil War Collection.

Rawson, Mary. Unpublished manuscript, MSS 36, Box 2, Folder 4. Atlanta: Atlanta History Center.

Richards, Samuel P. Unpublished manuscript, MSS 176, Box 1, Folder 3. Atlanta: Atlanta History Center.

"Williams' Atlanta Directory, City Guide and Business Mirror." Vol. 1, 1859-1860. Atlanta: M. Linch.

Wolcott, Laurens. Letters. GLC 653.11. New York: Pierpont Morgan Library, Gilder Lehrman Collection.

INDEX

VOICES OF THE CIVIL WAR

SERIES EDITOR: Henry Woodhead
Administrative Editor: Philip Brandt George
Picture Editor: Paula York-Soderlund

Editorial Staff for *Atlanta*
Deputy Editor: Kirk Denkler
Art Director: Barbara M. Sheppard
Associate Editors Research/Writing: Harris J. Andrews,
Gemma Slack
Senior Copyeditors: Donna D. Carey, Mary Beth
Oelkers-Keegan
Picture Coordinator: Paige Henke
Editorial Assistant: Christine Higgins

Initial Series Design: Studio A

Special Contributors: Brian C. Pohanka (text); Martha Lee
Beckington, Patricia Cassidy, Henry Mintz, Anne Whittle,
Barry Wolverton (research); Roy Nanovic (index).

Correspondent: Christina Lieberman (New York).

Consultants
Brian C. Pohanka, a Civil War historian and author, spent six
years as a researcher and writer for Time-Life Books' Civil
War series and Echoes of Glory. He is the author of *Distant
Thunder: A Photographic Essay on the American Civil War* and
has written, edited, and consulted on numerous works about
American military history.

Richard A. Baumgartner, a former newspaper and magazine
editor, has written, edited, or published several books dealing
with Civil War history. A longtime student of the Civil War's
western theater, he served as editor of *Blood & Sacrifice: The
Civil War Journal of a Confederate Soldier* and coedited *Yankee
Tigers* and *Echoes of Battle: The Atlanta Campaign,* recipient of
the 1994 Richard B. Harwell Award, given by the Atlanta Civil
War Round Table for best book on a Civil War subject.

William R. Scaife, an architect by profession and a direct
descendant of a Confederate surgeon, is one of the leading
historians of the Civil War in Georgia. He has published
extensively on the subject, and his book, *The Campaign for
Atlanta,* won the 1995 Richard B. Harwell Award. A tireless
defender of Civil War battlefields, Scaife is a consultant for
the Association for the Preservation of Civil War Sites.

Larry M. Strayer, an editor with Blue Acorn Press, has written
or contributed to more than a dozen titles on the war's western theater, including *Yankee Tigers* and the award-winning
Echoes of Battle volumes on the Atlanta and Chattanooga campaigns. Strayer presently serves as adviser for Accuracy Historical Productions. His next publication will photographically
chronicle Ohio's involvement in the Civil War.

Time-Life Books is a division of Time Life Inc.

PRESIDENT AND CEO: John M. Fahey Jr.

TIME-LIFE BOOKS

MANAGING EDITOR: Roberta Conlan

Director of Design: Michael Hentges
Editorial Production Manager: Ellen Robling
Director of Operations: Eileen Bradley
Director of Photography and Research: John Conrad Weiser
Senior Editors: Russell B. Adams Jr., Janet Cave, Lee Hassig,
Robert Somerville, Henry Woodhead
Library: Louise D. Forstall

PRESIDENT: John D. Hall

Vice President, Director of New Product Development: Neil Kagan
Associate Directors, New Product Development: Elizabeth D.
Ward, Curtis Kopf
Marketing Director: Pamela R. Farrell
Vice President, Book Production: Marjann Caldwell
Production Manager: Marlene Zack
Quality Assurance Manager: James King

First printing. Printed in U.S.A.
Published simultaneously in Canada.
School and library distribution by Time-Life Education,
P.O. Box 85026, Richmond, Virginia 23285-5026.

Time-Life is a trademark of Time Warner Inc. U.S.A.

Library of Congress Cataloging-in-Publication Data
Atlanta / by the editors of Time-Life Books.
    p.   cm.—(Voices of the Civil War)
    Includes bibliographical references and index.
    ISBN 0-7835-4702-1
    1. Atlanta Campaign, 1864—Personal narratives. I. Time-
Life Books. II. Series.
E476.7.A76 1996
973.7'37—dc20   95-42425
                                                       CIP

OTHER PUBLICATIONS

The Time-Life Complete Gardener
The New Home Repair and Improvement
Journey Through the Mind and Body
Weight Watchers® Smart Choice Recipe Collection
True Crime
The American Indians
The Art of Woodworking
Lost Civilizations
Echoes of Glory
The New Face of War
How Things Work
Wings of War
Creative Everyday Cooking
Collector's Library of the Unknown
Classics of World War II
Time-Life Library of Curious and Unusual Facts
American Country
Voyage Through the Universe
The Third Reich
Mysteries of the Unknown
Time Frame
Fix It Yourself
Fitness, Health & Nutrition
Successful Parenting
Healthy Home Cooking
Understanding Computers
Library of Nations
The Enchanted World
The Kodak Library of Creative Photography
Great Meals in Minutes
The Civil War
Planet Earth
Collector's Library of the Civil War
The Epic of Flight
The Good Cook
World War II
The Old West

For information on and a full description of any of the Time-
Life Books series listed, please call 1-800-621-7026 or write:

Reader Information
Time-Life Customer Service
P.O. Box C-32068
Richmond, Virginia 23261-2068